Japan as an Immigration Nation

Japan as an Immigration Nation

Demographic Change, Economic Necessity, and the Human Community Concept

Hidenori Sakanaka

Translated by Robert D. Eldridge and Graham B. Leonard

LEXINGTON BOOKS
Lanham • Boulder • New York • London

Published by Lexington Books
An imprint of The Rowman & Littlefield Publishing Group, Inc.
4501 Forbes Boulevard, Suite 200, Lanham, Maryland 20706
www.rowman.com

6 Tinworth Street, London SE11 5AL

British Library Cataloguing in Publication Information Available

Library of Congress Cataloging-in-Publication Data Available:

Library of Congress Control Number: 2020931313

ISBN: 978-1-7936-1493-3 (cloth : alk. paper)
ISBN: 978-1-7936-1495-7 (pbk. : alk. paper)
ISBN: 978-1-7936-1494-0 (electronic)

Contents

Translators' Preface

Robert D. Eldridge and Graham B. Leonard

I (Eldridge) have known Sakanaka Hidenori, the author of this book, only for the past year, but I have been familiar with his writings for more than a decade. He has been described by foreign journalists and academics as "Mr. Immigration" and "the Immigration Expert" for his calls for Japan to have a proactive policy on accepting immigrants. He has even been labelled the "Doomsday Doctor" for his predictions about Japan's declining population and superaging society.

Sakanaka, in other words, is a famous figure at home and abroad because of his warnings about the future of Japan population-wise, as well as economically and socially, if it does not proactively accept immigrants. While he has created his share of enemies, including among the right wing, for his outspokenness, he has consistently been the voice of foresight, reason, and compassion, and his views have not only shaped, but led the debate.

However, the pace of change has been far too slow for Sakanaka, and objectively speaking, for Japan, too, if it wants to remain viable and relevant in the future. As such, for a number of years, Sakanaka has been promoting a bold proposal for Japan to accept ten million immigrants over the next fifty years (some say Japan, the 11th largest country population-wise, can afford to take in more. That may be true, but Sakanaka's is by far the most dramatic, dynamic, and practical plan presented to date, as readers will find out). This book introduces that proposal, and the efforts of this one highly intellectual, highly energetic man over the past four decades to promote a more open and tolerant Japan.

Sakanaka was born on May 5, 1945, in Cheongju on the Korean Peninsula, which was then under Japanese control following its formal annexation in 1910. His father was a police officer, serving there for two years. His parents were from the same town in Kyoto Prefecture and they met when they were both working at the local post office.

After his father began his new assignment, he came back to Ine Town for the wedding ceremony and then returned to Cheongju. Sakanaka's mother subsequently joined her husband, six years her senior, there.

Sakanaka was the oldest of three children and the only boy. His mother told him in later years that his Korean neighbors treated him very kindly. Unconsciously or not, he reciprocated the kindness in his later work.

After the war, and the end of the occupation of the Korean Peninsula by Japan, Sakanaka and his family moved back to Japan, arriving via Hakata Port, Fukuoka City, Kyūshū Prefecture in October 1945. After that, they returned to Ine, which is on the Sea of Japan, literally across from the Korean Peninsula. His sisters were born during this time.

Sakanaka spent his elementary, middle, and high school years in near-by Maizuru City, a port city that hosted a base of the Imperial Japanese Navy and now the Japanese Maritime Self-Defense Force, where a lot of people continue to travel into and out of Japan by ship and ferry. His father held jobs related to the U.S. military stationed in the area and his mother managed a stationery store and a restaurant. He played baseball, a popular sport in Japan, in middle school but did not continue in high school. Instead, he did a lot of reading, as this book shows.

Sakanaka was accepted at Waseda University and Keiō University, two prominent private schools in Tokyo, and chose the latter. He entered Keiō in 1964, the year Japan hosted the Olympics. He stayed on for further research, attending graduate school. He particularly enjoyed reading about law, economics, cultural anthropology, and ethnic studies. He wrote his master's thesis on the rice riots (*kome sōdō*) that affected Japan during the summer and early fall of 1918, exactly fifty years before. The riots were some of the largest in Japanese history and had major direct and immediate economic, social, and political ramifications and indirect, more long-term diplomatic and military implications.

He was in graduate school at the time of the student protests that affected Tōkyō and other cities in the late 1960s but did not get involved, instead focusing on his studies. He seemed to have his eyes on the future even then.

After earning his master's degree in March 1970, he entered the Ministry of Justice's Immigration Bureau the following month. He served in that field for the next thirty-five years, rising to the position of Director General of the Tokyo Regional Immigration Bureau. He retired in March 2005, but not before giving a lot of interviews and publishing numerous op-eds.

During his time with the Ministry of Justice, he served in a number of positions requiring him to deal with foreign residents. As he explains in this book, one of his first assignments was in Osaka (beginning in 1971) addressing matters concerning the Korean-Japanese, or *Zainichi* Korean, population. This experience led him to submit in 1975 recommendations on reforming the system to allow this population to maintain their Korean names (i.e., not be forced to take Japanese names), among other suggestions. These recommendations (called here the "Sakanaka Essay") were later expanded upon and published in 1977 as the "Sakanaka Thesis," and became the basis for much of Japanese immigration policy over the past four decades.

When I asked him if his having been born on the Korean Peninsula may have made him sympathetic to the plight of Korean residents in Japan, he said he had not really thought about it before but thinks that it very well may have. In any case, he has a deep empathy for non-Japanese residing in Japan and is a strong believer in what he and others, such as Professor Duncan Williams, Professor of Religion and East Asian Languages and Cultures at the University of Southern California, call "Hybrid Japan" where people of different nationalities and ethnicities work and reside in Japan, learning from and adding to Japanese culture, and serving as bridges between Japan and world.

Other reforms he undertook while a civil servant in the Ministry of Justice, which are also described in this book, involved making it easier for Japanese-Brazilian residents to apply for permanent residency, based on his time as the head of the Nagoya Regional Immigration Bureau. His recommendations were not only truly humanitarian in nature, but also refreshingly practical. Not only did the residents benefit from the improved management, for example, but so did his co-workers and those that came after him by making their work more efficient.

I asked Sakanaka why no one else who had served before him in Nagoya had thought to do what he did. His answer was both concise and universal: "Most bureaucrats prefer to do routine work." This is certainly true in other areas as well. "Taking the initiative" and "shaking things up" are taboo phrases in the bureaucracy. The inability of Japan's bureaucracy to change its thinking and behavior continues to cost the country.

Shortly after retiring, Sakanaka established the Foreigners Policy Institute (*Gaikokujin Seisaku Kenkyūsho*) in August 2005, which became the Japan Immigration Policy Institute (*Imin Seisaku Kenkyūsho*) in April 2009. He serves as the director of it, as well as of a center within it dedicated to the issue of Japanese wives of North Koreans, who have had difficulty in returning to Japan, described in chapter 10 of this book.

He is a prolific writer, with a couple dozen books on immigration matters, including two English language booklets (*Towards a Japanese-style Immigration Nation* in 2009 and *Japan as a Nation for Immigrants* in 2015), both published by JIPI. He regularly updates his website, with some entries receiving 5-10,000 views a day.

His publishing began while he was still a bureaucrat, something highly unusual in that government officials anywhere, but especially in Japan, like to avoid the spotlight. In addition to the recommendations above that were originally submitted as part of an essay contest (in which approximately one hundred entries were submitted) and subsequently published in 1977 as the "Sakanaka Thesis" (officially titled *Kongo no Shutsunyūkoku Kanri Gyōsei no Arikata ni Tsuite* (On the Future Administrative Management of Immigration), (Tōkyō: Daieisha, 1977)), he published an updated version of the same recommendations through Nihon Kajo Shuppan in 1989, followed by *Kokusai Jinryū no Tenkai* (The Development of International Exchange), (Tōkyō: Nihon Kajo Shuppan, 1996); *Zainichi Kankoku-Chōsenjin Seisakuron no Tenkai* (The Development of Policy for *Zainichi* [South and North] Koreans), (Tōkyō: Nihon Kajo Shuppan, 1999); *Nihon no Gaikokujin Seisaku no Kōsō* (A Framework for Japanese Immigration Policy), (Tōkyō: Nihon Kajo Shuppan, 2001); *Nyūkan Senki* (Immigration Battle Diary), (Tōkyō: Kōdansha, 2005); *Dappoku Kikokusha Shien ha Watashi no Shimei* (My Mission Is to Assist Those Returnees Who Fled North Korea), (Tōkyō: Dappoku Kikokusha Shien Kikō, 2005); *Nihongata Imin Kokka no Rinen* (The Idea of a Japanese Style Immigration Nation), (Tōkyō: Tōshindō, 2011); *Nihongata Imin Kokka e no Michi* (The Road to a Japanese Style Immigration Nation), (Tōkyō: Tōshindō, 2011, expanded and revised in 2013); *Jinkō Hōkai to Imin Kakumei* (The Population Collapse and Immigration Revolution), (Tōkyō: Nihon Kajo Shuppan, 2012); *Shinpan Nihongata Imin Kokka e no Michi* (New Edition of The Road to a Japanese Style Immigration Nation), (Tōkyō: Tōshindō, 2014); *Nihongata Imin Kokka no Sōzō* (The Creation of a Japanese Style Immigration Nation), (Tōkyō: Tōshindō, 2016); *Nihongata Imin Kokka ga Sekai o Kaeru* (Japanese Style Immigration Nation Can Change the World), (Tōkyō: JIPI, 2016); *Tōkyō Gorin no Mae ni Imin Kokka Taisei o Kakuritsu Shitai* (I Want to Establish the Structure for an Immigrant Nation before the Tōkyō Olympics), (Tōkyō: JIPI, 2016); *Nihon no Imin Seisaku no Tenbō* (The Development of Japan's Immigration Policy), (Tōkyō: JIPI, 2017); *Sakanaka Imin Seisaku Ronshūsei* (Sakanaka's Immigration Policy Recommendations), (Tōkyō: JIPI, 2017); *Imin Kokka no Rekishi o Kiroku Suru no ha Watashi no Shimei* (My Mission Is to Record the History of an Immigration Nation), (Tōkyō: JIPI, 2017); *Nihongata Imin Kokka no Sekaiteki Tenkai* (The Global Development of a Japanese Style Immigration Nation), (Tōkyō: JIPI, 2018); *Nihon no Imin Kokka Bijion* (Vision for an Immigration Nation Japan), (Tōkyō: JIPI, 2018); *Shinpan Nihon no Imin Kokka Bijion* (New Edition of Vision for an Immigrant Nation Japan), (Tōkyō: JIPI, 2018); *Sakanaka Hidenori no Imin Seisaku Annai* (An Introduction of Sakanaka Hidenori's Immigration Policy), (Tōkyō: JIPI, 2019), and "Imin Kokka no Saikōhō o Mezashite," a recent, yet unpublished, manuscript upon which this English language book is based.

Furthermore, he has co-authored eight books: *Kaisei Nyūkanhō no Kaisetsu: Atarashii Shutsunyū koku Kanri Seido* (Commentary on the Revised Immigration Act: The New Immigration Management System), (Tōkyō: Nihon Kajo Shuppan, 1991); *Shutsunyū koku Kanri Nanmin Ninteih ō Chikujō Kaisetsu* (A Clause-by-Clause Explanation of the Immigration Control and Refugee Recognition Act), (Tōkyō: Nihon Kajo Shuppan, 1994, with new editions and revisions published in 1997, 2000, 2007, and 2012); *Imin Kokka Nippon: Issenmannin no Imin ga Nihon o Sukuu* (Tōkyō: Nihon Kajo Shuppan, 2007); and *Kitach ō sen Kikokusha Mondai no Rekishi to Kadai* (The History of the North Korean Returnees Issue), (Tōkyō: Shin-kansha, 2009).

This book, which is entitled *Japan as an Immigration Nation: Demographic Change, Economic Necessity, and the Human Community Concept*, is divided into eleven chapters, not including this Translators' Preface, the Foreword, and the Conclusion. Because it draws on the above exhaustive writings, the book may be somewhat long, but I encourage the reader to read it through in order to understand the evolution of his thinking and experiences, the views and recommendations he has promoted, and the challenges he has overcome. The detailed table of contents allows the reader to better pinpoint any specific topics he or she may be most interested in.

Sakanaka's call for a more open and understanding Japan has increasingly received national and international attention. He has been featured in major domestic and foreign newspapers, such as the *Wall Street Journal* (Asian Edition) and *The Guardian*, and magazines such as *The Economist*, and the Japanese language *AERA* and *Sekai* (The World). He has been asked to speak at numerous institutions for higher education, including Tsinghua University in November 2007, the University of Southern California in April 2015, and the University of Toronto in February 2019.

Moreover, Sakanaka has also attracted the attention of the international business community, speaking in Dubai at the World Economic Forum as a member of the Global Agenda Council on Immigration in the Fall of 2010 and before the American Chamber of Commerce in Japan, just five weeks after the devastating Great East Japan Earthquake and Tsunami of March 2011.

I feel fortunate to communicate and meet with him regularly and remain awed at his intellectual and physical energy. He is a rare visionary in a land famous for conformists.

My own story—residency in Japan for twenty-nine years and having a Japanese spouse and bicultural, bilingual children—is in many ways connected to Sakanaka's work, and my co-translator (Dr. Graham B. Leonard) and I seem to be the types of people that proponents of a multiethnic, multicultural, and multidisciplinary "Hybrid Japan" like Sakanaka seek to have come to or remain in Japan.

Interestingly, neither Graham nor I had planned to be in Japan long. Both of us participated in the Japan Exchange and Teaching Program(me)—I beginning in 1990 in Hyōgo Prefecture and he in 2003 in Wakayama Prefecture—but we both extended our contracts and came to greatly like and appreciate the country. I stayed on, attending language school, followed by graduate school, and then conducting a postdoctoral fellowship before being offered a tenured teaching position at Ōsaka University (that I continued until 2009) prior to joining the Department of Defense with assignments exclusively in Okinawa (until 2015), upon which I moved back to Kansai, and Graham eventually came back as a

Ministry of Education, Science, and Technology Ph.D. candidate initially under my care. Graham, who did the bulk of the translating and with whom I have done several other books, returns to Japan annually for several months and expects to move here again in the future. Japan has become infinitely more accommodating to non-Japanese residents in the three decades that I have been here, but I would agree with Sakanaka that there is still a great distance more to go.

We would like to thank Murakami Isaku who made the original introduction to Sakanaka and attended nearly every meeting I had with him regarding the project and was involved in almost all of the e-mail exchanges and conversations.

Graham would like to thank his many friends and mentors in Japan and his family, friends, and mentors back in the State of Washington and the Kansai for their help over the years, and I would like to thank my wife, Emiko, and children for their love and support as well as that of my friends and mentors. As I was completing the editing of this book, my daughter, Ami, turned twenty years old, the traditional age of adulthood in Japan, and my son, Kennan, turned eighteen years old, which since 2016 is the legal age to vote in Japan.[1] I am very excited for their futures, which I imagine will include working and living, at least a good part of their adult lives, in Japan as well.

On a final note, I wanted to draw the attention of the reader to Sakanaka's personal name, Hidenori, which means "hero (*hide*)" and "virtuous (*nori*)." This name was given to him by his father, and as the reader will see, he has lived up to this hope his family had for him. On December 9, 2018, as he was finishing the Japanese version of this book, his mother, ninety-six years old, passed away. The following day, a six-page story appeared in *AERA*, a well-known weekly published by the *Asahi Shimbun*, about Sakanaka in its "Modern Portrait (Gendai no Shōzō)" series. He had truly reached national fame. A copy of the magazine arrived prior to the burial. He placed it next to his mother's head in her coffin. We can assume that she and her husband are in heaven reading about their heroic and virtuous son now and must be very proud of him.

NOTES

1. For a recent article on youth voting trends in Japan, see Robert D. Eldridge, "Millennials and Japanese Politics: An Introduction," *Education About Asia*, Vol. 23, No. 1 (Spring 2018), pp. 22-26.

Author's Preface

This book—*Japan as an Immigration Nation: Demographic Change, Economic Necessity, and the Human Community Concept*—tells the story of the journey I, a former senior immigration official with the Ministry of Justice, Government of Japan, have travelled toward encouraging my country to become an immigration-friendly nation and the promotion of Japanese values globally. It also serves as my "graduation thesis" after nearly forty-five years of devoting my life to domestic and international immigration policy research.

Many sections of this book take on a heavily autobiographical flavor. This is in part because I have been called "Mr. Immigration" and am so closely identified with the above pursuits that the history of modern immigration policy in Japan is very much my story. I say this not to brag, however. Promoting a more open Japanese society has been my mission in life. Thus, this book hopes to answer questions I often receive from foreign intellectuals and media, such as "what kind of person is Sakanaka Hidenori and what is he promoting?"

Why am I publishing this book now? Because I feel an intense sense of danger about the current state of the world, where rampant rejection of immigrants and racial discrimination has led to a humanitarian crisis of epic proportions and I therefore wish to appeal to the Japanese government and the international community to be more accepting of immigrants, emotionally, physically, and legally. Human security is our security. As the Prime Minister of New Zealand Jacinda Adern tweeted immediately after the horrific shootings at the mosque in Christchurch on March 15, 2019, "Many of those affected [were] our migrant communities. New Zealand is their home. They are us." She said what many of us should feel, no matter what country we live in. She embodied humanity itself in her remarks.

I would summarize the sad state of affairs regarding immigrants and refugees globally as of the end of 2019 thusly: xenophobic thought toward those of different races and religions is intensifying in America, Britain, France, Germany, Australia, and New Zealand. This has renewed my conviction that we cannot permit an era when anti-immigrant xenophobes and racists are allowed to swagger around arrogantly, defying long established or recently won norms, and anti-humanitarian forces sweep across the world.

The time when Japan—alone among the developed countries—could close itself off to immigration and live comfortably in its safe, relatively isolated greenhouse has come to an end. We cannot ignore the issue of human security. The efforts to convince a hesitant public to open Japan to immigration must gain speed. Every second counts. Moreover, our own nation is entering dangerous waters economically and demographically with a declining population and super-aging society and may not survive. We thus have many reasons to become a nation friendly to immigrants, "an immigration nation" in other words.

The steep decline in childbirth and rapid increase in aging has made the collapse of the Japanese demographic order increasingly likely. As that day approaches, leaders of rural local governments are at the vanguard of the mad scramble to secure global human resources. Obtaining adequate personnel is also a life-or-death matter for the business community. In a scene reminiscent of the hiring practices of the era of high-speed economic growth in the 1950s, 1960s, and 1970s when companies went to the countryside to secure new hires, companies today are struggling to fill hiring requirements from the shrinking pool of fresh university and high school graduates, even having to go abroad in search of talent.

Continuing to close Japan off from immigration will make the disappearance of local communities due to population decline and the closure of smaller businesses due to a shortage of workers commonplace occurrences. Our politicians, who have been disappointingly slow to grasp these changes and needs, should heed the cries of the private and public sectors demanding the assistance of immigrants. The government should rapidly open Japan to immigration so that foreign human resources are abundantly available for nearly all sectors. And the general public should be prepared to create "a society where immigrants are warmly welcomed as members of the community."

The overall decline in childbirth has made Japan the country most in need of large-scale immigration. It is time for us to declare to the world that we will accept ten million immigrants (including refugees) over the next fifty years. I have no doubt that, should a humanitarian Japan emerge as an immigration power amidst the storm raging against immigrants and refugees worldwide, waving the banner of "an immigration nation where differences of race and religion are overcome and all of humanity can be as one" (which I call the "human community concept," or *jinrui kyōdōtairon*), it will be cheered on by people around the world.

The arrival of this "age of suffering" for immigrants has also brought about changes for me, personally. The "ten million-immigrant" and "human community" concepts that I have long advocated in my writings and policy proposals over the years are drawing the attention of international experts on immigration policy as having global, historical significance. I suspect that they may even fundamentally influence the immigration policies of existing immigration nations as well. I must prepare myself for the responsibility of propelling not just Japanese immigration policy but that of all the countries of the world.

As I looked back over a life spent in pursuit of the ideal immigration nation and realized that this might be my final book, I put my all into it, especially with regard to the release of my essays on the subject of the immigration revolution. While my thoughts on it have not changed, my theory for the creation of a Japanese-style immigration nation has gained life with the systematic, complete depiction of the human community concept.

At a press conference held on December 20, 2018, His Majesty the Emperor's birthday, Emperor Akihito provided a way forward for the future of our country when he spoke on admitting foreigners: "I hope that we can all welcome those who come from other countries to our country to work warmly as members of society." Upon hearing these heartfelt words, I, as a leader of Japanese immigration policy, strongly felt that the immigration society has a bright future ahead of it. Although he stepped down five months later on April 30 as previously planned, His Majesty's words carry great weight.

His Majesty's and my aspirations may not be realized at this time. My life may end before I see the immigration revolution I have long called for come to pass. But I hope that this book, an effort to create a nation and world based on my "human community" concept, will continue on as an immortal work, taken up whenever considering the nature of immigration policy domestically and internationally as, after all, they are inherently interlinked.

I pray for the arrival of a brilliant age in which the ideal of the human community—spawned from the mind of a Japanese expert on immigration policy—saves the world from its humanitarian crisis. The human community concept was cultivated within the spiritual climate of Japan, but I hope that constructive discussion of it spreads beyond that nation.

Sakanaka Hidenori
Director, Japan Immigration Policy Institute
June 30, 2019

ONE

The Need for an "Immigration Revolution" and a "Japanese Revolution"

IT ALL BEGAN WITH AN ENCOUNTER WITH A YOUNG *ZAINICHI* KOREAN

I spent the spring of 1970 (the year after I entered the Ministry of Justice) doing on-the-job training at the Ōsaka Regional Immigration Bureau. Every day, my job was to accept and inspect applications from foreign residents who were obtaining or renewing their residence status, or who were applying for a re-entry permit. At the time, virtually all of the foreigners coming into the immigration bureaus throughout much of the country were *Zainichi* Koreans (ethnic Koreans residing in Japan; former Japanese colonial subjects and their descendants).

One day, a young man who had just turned fourteen appeared before me to fill out the paperwork for his residency in Japan. He had only been informed by his parents the day before that he wasn't actually Japanese. Born and raised here, it had never even occurred to him that that might be the case. Prior to that day, he had lived a life no different from that of any ordinary Japanese.

Many parents placed in the situation that his were only broke the news to their children once their hands were forced by the need to appear at an immigration office. I remember feeling extremely angry at that moment at our system, as I realized that the discrimination against *Zainichi* Koreans was fierce enough that parents felt forced to raise their children as "Japanese," hiding their Korean identity and heritage. This experience became my "mental scenery" as an official working in immigration control.

1

A few years later, in 1973, I answered a call for essays by the Ministry of Justice Immigration Bureau on the topic of "The Future of Immigration Administration." My submission was written on the nuts-and-bolts of immigration policy such as the poor treatment of the *Zainichi* Koreans. It was chosen as the best entry and would eventually be published in 1977.

While my essay ironically received strong criticism from almost all *Zainichi* Korean academics and activists, most of the paper's suggestions (such as providing the *Zainichi* Koreans with firmer legal standing and joining the Convention Relating to the Status of Refugees) would ultimately come to pass in the early 1980s with the revision of the Immigration Control Law.

I write "ironically" because I worked toward stabilizing the legal status of Koreans in the country, abolishing discrimination in employment, and providing the benefits of social welfare to the Korean community. Previous policies were mistaken in their approach, forcing Koreans to use the Japanese language and Japanese names. Even though I was trying to change all that, as an official of the Ministry of Justice, I was sadly made out to be the embodiment of these bad policies and the discriminatory attitude of Japanese toward Koreans.

My thoughts have remained essentially unchanged from those I wrote down in that essay forty-four years ago. I am confident that it was a policy paper written taking into consideration what Japan and the world would likely look like a hundred years later. If not for the opportunity provided by that paper, it is likely that neither my vision of a Japanese-style immigration nation nor my idea of the human community would have ever come about. And with current international trends such as the disappearance of the spirit of tolerance toward those of other ethnicities and religions, I believe the task left to me now is bringing about the rebirth of Japanese society as a new immigration nation.

IS TAKING IN TEN MILLION IMMIGRANTS OVER THE NEXT FIFTY YEARS REALISTIC?

I believe that it is quite possible for Japan to admit ten million immigrants (when I use the term "immigrant," I mean "a foreigner who has received permanent residency in Japan in accordance with the Immigration Control Law." This is essentially the same meaning as a "green card holder" under American immigration law, in other words.)

The trend of Japan's declining birthrate will likely continue for the long term. And even if some sort of policy for effectively addressing the declining number of children born in Japan is devised and the birthrate begins to recover, it will still be many years before the effects of that change are felt. But I demonstrate here that Japan already has the social foundation necessary for admitting immigrants: an industrial base in which they can work and education institutions in which they can learn technical skills as well as the Japanese language and culture. And most importantly, the Japanese people are internationally known as courteous and considerate in nature. They will for the most part be able to sympathize with the situation the immigrants find themselves in and continue to welcome them.

At present, the number of foreigners with permanent residency in Japan (i.e., immigrants) is extremely small, making up roughly one percent of the population. Ten million immigrants would bring that number up to ten percent, a level still considerably lower than that of Britain, Germany, and France. I'm not suggesting that we take in ten million people immediately or even over a short period of time. The idea is that we would, for example, steadily increase the number of immigrants in Japan over the long term: 200,000 a year over the next fifty years. We would thereby ultimately approach the level of immigration found in the developed countries of Europe and North America. I believe that this is a realistic policy that can be reasonably achieved.

Population trends are determined by three factors: births, deaths, and migration. Barring an unexpected change, a hundred years from now the number of births in Japan will fall far short of the number of deaths. As Robert D. Eldridge, a former professor of international public policy at Ōsaka University and the translator of this book, argues in his recent book,[1] the statistics may be even worse if young people lose hope in the future and emigrate from Japan altogether, depleting the pool even further. In any case, there is no means by which this natural decline in the population can be reduced other than adopting pro-immigration policies. If the Japanese public and government properly recognize the economic and social effects that immigration policy will have on the country and work out such policy in a timely manner, we should be able to keep the economy on course.

THE POPULATION CRISIS CAN ONLY BE SOLVED THROUGH IMMIGRATION POLICY

I believe immigration policy to be an extremely effective method for solving the inter-related population problems of low birthrates and labor shortages. The decline in childbirth is a common social issue in developed countries and the competition over skilled foreign workers is becoming increasingly intense across the world. And yet, Japan remains virtually the only country whose government continues to assert that it will not implement an immigration policy.

How can the government continue to forecast economic growth when both the productive and consuming populations are expected to decrease at precipitous rates? This defies economic common sense. Japan is entering a period of sharp population decline. Immigration policy provides the only solution to the problems that will accompany this: maintaining the social welfare system (pensions, insurance, etc.) and changes to state finances (falling tax income, production, and consumption).

Logically, it's a matter of making a choice between a "small Japan" and "big Japan." The former, which keeps the doors closed to immigrants, can be described as the path to an inevitable decline. The latter, which proactively welcomes immigrants, is the path to maintaining a diverse, vigorous society. I believe that this second choice is the direction that Japan should follow. It is our only viable option.

Bringing foreigners in as temporary workers—the current policy—means that they will eventually return to their home countries unable to become full members of society with only limited ties to Japan. Attempting to deal with the increasingly serious labor shortage through work permits granted to exchange students and the problem-filled Technical Internship Program (TIP), discussed later, provides absolutely no benefits to Japan, only harming and tarnishing its image. The Japanese government seems to believe that it is encouraging talented foreigners to come to Japan. But think about it. If you're a foreigner who dreams of creating a new life for yourself in another country, would you choose a country where you'll be treated as nothing more than convenient, cheap labor and expected to leave at the end of your tenure? Or would you want to live in a country where you can obtain permanent residency and receive treatment equivalent to that accorded to citizens of that country?

Japan no longer has the ability to replenish its population, which makes the planning of immigration policy and its ability to increase the number of Japanese citizens a matter of extreme importance. Immigrants with permanent residency are, just like Japanese citizens, consumers and workers. They're also taxpayers. While there are those who speak of providing social welfare to immigrants as if it were somehow a "loss" for the Japanese people, in practice most of those who will come to Japan wanting to work will be young. Just think about how much economic and financial support they would provide for Japan if they came, worked, and paid taxes here for thirty years. Naturally, as they get older, they should receive a pension so that they can spend their old age in peace like any other Japanese. Where's the problem with according them such treatment?

THE TECHNICAL INTERNSHIP PROGRAM'S HUMANITARIAN PROBLEM

A firm conviction of mine, held ever since my time at the Ministry of Justice's Immigration Bureau, is that we must not accept labor under the guise of training. The Technical Internship Program (*Ginō Jisshū Seido*) should be abolished as quickly as possible. It is inhumane and exploitative and violates the spirit of the Immigration Control Law (*Nyūkoku Kanrihō*) by failing to make a clear distinction between "work" and "study." It's not simply a matter of reform. It doesn't matter how the law governing the program is amended or how much monitoring of the organizations involved is increased: it is a contradictory, warped system and its true nature as a system to provide cover for illegal labor will not change. Continued violations of the Immigration Control Law, such as visa overstays, and of the Labor Standards Law (*Rōdō Kijunhō*), such as non-payment of wages, are unavoidable as long as it continues.

Just as I had feared, the true nature of TIP and other foreign trainee programs has been apparent from the very beginning: to make them work at lower wages in exchange for residency in Japan and "training." These programs establish a framework under which the trainees are exploited by one and all: by the countries (or brokers or families) that dispatch them, by the foundations providing jobs to retired officials from the welfare and justice ministries, and by the farms, fisheries, and small companies that employ them. Very little of their wages remain in their hands. Deductions are made to their salaries, nominally for "rent," "food," "administrative expenses," and the like. Under this miserable state of affairs, they ultimately end up working for an hourly wage as low as 300 yen (US$2.70), or about one-third of the average. It should come as no surprise that an increasingly large number of these foreigners choose to flee the employers who bind them through tactics such as enforced loans and passport confiscation and instead remain in Japan illegally.

Because of this wretched Technical Internship Program, the business community gives no thought to employing and paying foreign workers and Japanese on an equal footing. But it should not be forgotten that should a business environment take shape where businesses are dependent on low-paid foreign workers, this will also have a negative impact on working conditions for Japanese workers as a whole and eventually on their own companies if labor wages rise. It is a temporary solution with disastrous consequences.

TIP has been subjected, correctly, to harsh international criticism. The United States, Japan's only military ally, has referred to it in its *Country Reports on Human Rights Practices* as imposing "conditions close to forced labor" and the United Nations has described its conditions as approaching "slavery or human trafficking." Even as just a temporary measure to relieve the severity of the increasing labor shortage, the price paid is too high. I believe that it will be a stain on the history of Japan's treatment of foreigners.

TIP has reached the level of a humanitarian crisis. Maintaining this "Japanese-style slavery system" harms the immigration policies that should have been adopted in the first place and could potentially prove fatal to Japan. The decline in childbirth rates means that Japan needs young foreign workers, but if the country becomes known as one in which foreign workers are treated like slaves, the talented young people of the world will avoid Japan. Naturally, the image of those industries that engaged in this embarrassing system and abused foreign workers will also be severely damaged.

Immigration, needless to say, is incompatible with slavery. Japan cannot develop as a healthy immigration nation without abolishing its slave-like system.

NOW IS THE TIME FOR DECISIVE ACTION TO OPEN JAPAN TO IMMIGRATION

In October 2018, the Japanese government released its framework for expanding the number of "foreign human resources (*gaikokujin jinzai*)," by, for example, revising the Immigration Control Law.

The media disagreed with the Abe Shinzō administration's shift to a more pro-immigration policy and responded by continually using the term "unskilled labor" in its coverage. The moves by the government, which hesitated to call it an outright immigration policy, were described instead as "an open-door policy for unskilled labor," for example. This had the effect of fanning the flames of anti-immigrant sentiment among the public.

I, however, believe that the government's new policies should be correctly viewed as a shift towards a *de facto* immigration policy because it allows those foreigners with recognized skills to settle permanently in Japan with their families. The government is exploring creating new residency categories for agriculture, nursing care, food manufacturing, construction, shipbuilding, lodging, restaurants, fishing, building cleaning, metal forging, industrial machinery, industries related to electrical machinery and appliances, automobile maintenance, and aviation. These are all industries requiring specialized knowledge, skills, and technology; they are not "unskilled labor." And as could be expected, the concept of "unskilled labor" does not appear in the Immigration Control Law. All activities with applicable statuses of residence require the applicant to possess certain knowledge or skills. The sectors open to the TIP program such as agriculture, fishing, and nursing care also all require expert knowledge.

My view, looking back through the history of industry, is that humanity has always, in every era, skillfully used the best industrial technology at their command to survive, making the most of their knowledge. There has never been either "unskilled labor" or "skilled labor," regardless of whether we're discussing hunter-gatherer society, the agricultural revolution, or the industrial revolution. Japanese newspaper reporters, commentators, and intellectuals who use the term "unskilled labor" may believe that their professions are special in requiring specialized knowledge. But I believe that when they use the term, they actually reveal the truth that they look down on those working in agriculture, industry, and commerce like in feudal times in Japan when there were five classes in society with samurai on top, farmers next, craftsmen, traders, and those that labored in what were considered particularly dirty areas. And it must be pointed out that these statements of vocational discrimination also deeply undermine the self-esteem of the Japanese people working in such fields today.

Currently the desirability of the further acceptance of immigrants is a matter of serious political debate within the world's major immigration nations, dividing popular opinion. Meanwhile, in Japan, the question of whether or not the country should welcome immigrants isn't even discussed in the Diet. That's a problem. Even now, as the nation is threatened with demographic collapse, the government holds fast to its stance that it will "not adopt an immigration policy." It is extraordinary how far politicians will go to avoid having to touch the issue of immigration out of fear of offending their "base."

Prior to the Second World War, Japan suffered from overpopulation and its rapid modernization had led to rural impoverishment and a labor surplus. In response, the government promoted the mass emigration of Japanese overseas and simultaneously heavily restricted the entry into Japan of any foreign workers who might permanently settle in the country. This is the historical background for Japanese immigration policy. After the war ended, the government again adopted a policy of, in principle, not allowing any immigrants or foreign workers into the country, although quite a few Korean, Taiwanese, and Chinese were allowed to continue to reside in Japan (for example, according to 1950 statistics of foreign residents gathered by the Ministry of Justice, there were 550,000 residents of Korean—both North and South—descent, 30,000 Taiwanese, and 10,000 Chinese). Recent shifts in popular opinion show, however, that the number of younger Japanese who believe we should allow immigrants into the country is dramatically increasing.

There should be exhaustive public discussion on the merits of making any historical changes to the country's basic policies before any such changes are made. If Japan gradually moves toward becoming an immigration nation without having gone through such discussion, the legitimacy of that change will be questioned. Friction and confusion will arise, and problems created for the nation's future. If the immigration nation is born out of constructive debate and the widespread approval of the public, however, then things will develop smoothly.

WHAT IS A "JAPANESE-STYLE IMMIGRATION SOCIETY"?

The "Japanese-style immigration society" that I advocate is a country in which policies are in place to firmly guarantee the social inclusion of immigrants and the Japanese cultural concept of harmony is emphasized. This is based on lessons learned from Western immigration nations that have struggled with the social integration of their immigrant populations. Immigrants will first receive education in the Japanese language and Japanese social customs before undergoing vocational training to provide them with specialized knowledge and skills. They will work diligently in their respective fields and, once they've achieved a stable life for themselves three or five years later, they will be granted permanent residency in Japan and the ability to naturalize if they desire to do so. As leaving this vocational training to the private sector would likely once again result in cases where the trainees were being used for labor under the guise of "on-the-job training," this should be conducted by public educational institutions, perhaps partnering with local universities, many of whom are facing a decline in student enrollment, due to the declining number of youth altogether. It will be important to establish a system under which immigrants who have mastered their skills enter into formal employment relationships and to have basic rights guaranteed with private companies.

The size of the workforce in primary industries such as agriculture, forestry, and fishing is rapidly declining due to an inability to secure successors. Construction, manufacturing, and distribution are also experiencing a serious labor shortage. The smaller enterprises that large companies rely upon are going out of business due to a lack of successors. Immigration policy is the only way of supporting industries like these.

By adopting an immigration policy, more areas will be able to escape the fate of watching their communities disappear. Ever since the 2011 Great East Japan Earthquake, the country has been faced with an unprecedented number of natural disasters such as earthquakes, volcanos, heavy rains, and floods in a short period. While these have occurred throughout Japan, the victims have been concentrated in areas with largely elderly populations. Rural society, already faced with communities on the verge of collapse, has lost the strength to withstand these disasters. The only remaining path forward for Japan's primary industries is for young foreign workers to be granted agriculture and fishing visas, welcomed as immigrants, and rapidly granted permanent residency so they can build a new life here.

THE ENACTMENT OF AN IMMIGRATION LAW IS URGENTLY NEEDED

An "Immigration Law" needs to be enacted, a basic law establishing the broad framework of Japan's system for accepting immigrants. The fundamental principles of Japan's immigration policy should be to justly and fairly accept a wide range of people of diverse nationalities, deepen Japan's bonds of friendship and goodwill with other countries of the world, and contribute to world peace.

Notably, if we use the text of this new immigration law to clearly lay out a national goal of creating a "society based on the human community" in which people of different nationalities, ethnicities, races, and religions can peacefully co-exist, it would, without question, serve as a "declaration of an immigration nation" that would become a model for the international community.

The first step in laying down the basic plan for admitting immigrants will be the creation of a council on basic immigration policy (headed by the prime minister) within the cabinet. This council will discuss and determine basic policies such as the number of immigrants to be accepted annually (including, if necessary, national origin quotas) and the industrial sectors and local governments that will be allowed to accept immigrants. Next, a ministerial position in charge of immigration policy will be established within the cabinet and an "Agency for Immigration Policy" created to serve as the administrative bureau for the aforementioned cabinet committee. This agency will assist in the formulation of plans for admitting immigrants. Immigration policy will then be enacted on the basis of these plans (as approved by the Diet) by the relevant agencies and ministries. The approval of the Diet will be sought so that immigration policy is pursued in an open and honest manner, with the agreement of both politicians and the public.

Having established in the new immigration law that the acceptance of immigrants in a well-balanced, fair manner is a basic tenant of Japanese immigration policy, it will then be necessary to lay down justifiable regulations for quantitative restrictions on the basis of nationality. And it will be particularly important to conclude "immigration agreements" with numerous friendly countries.

The government will, based on the regulations laid down in the immigration law, draw up annual immigration plans and ensure the smooth advancement of immigration policy. In doing so, it will comprehensively take into consideration factors such as the international environment encapsulating Japan and public opinion on immigration policy in addition to actual labor needs, the state of the system for admitting immigrants, the social response to immigrants, and the implementation of immigration agreements. It will also respect the opinions of the prefectural governors as they will be familiar with actual local conditions regarding demand for labor and other pressing needs.

I also want the government to seriously consider revising the Nationality Law (*Kokusekihō*) to follow the example of other developed countries and recognize dual citizenship. Establishing procedures to allow foreigners born in Japan as the children of permanent residents to gain Japanese citizenship at birth should also be considered to allow these second, and third-generation immigrants to be provided with the most stable legal status possible. It should be noted that France, which follows the principle of *jus sanguinis* (the principle that citizenship is not determined by place of birth but by having one or both parents who are citizens of the state) just as Japan does, recognizes those born as the children of immigrants as French citizens. Germany also makes an exception to *jus sanguinis* and grants citizenship to the children of the children of immigrants.

JAPAN WILL BE SAVED BY AN IMMIGRATION REVOLUTION

Xenophobia is becoming more visible in Japan, usually in the form of hate speech. What can be done to eliminate prejudice and discrimination against immigrants and some foreigners in Japan?

Once we enter an era of large-scale immigration, the number of immigrant children attending Japanese elementary and junior high schools (the years of compulsory education) will increase drastically. This will require a fundamental revision of the state of education at the preschool, elementary, and junior high school levels. The current education system, intended to produce "uniform Japanese," should be halted with the opening of the country to immigration. Moving to an educational model that values the individuality and diversity of children is essential to the stable development of an immigration society and Japan's success in a global economy.

And looking at the actual environment most of today's children find themselves in, it is gradually becoming normal for them to have non-Japanese friends among their classmates. By learning and playing together with the children of immigrants (and therefore experiencing close contact with other ethnic groups), Japanese children will develop an awareness of themselves as Japanese. But they will also learn first-hand through this close rapport, that human society is a gathering place for many diverse peoples, that we are all connected, and that we are all brothers. And that, while someone's race or religion might be different from ours, as fellow humans, our values—what is the right way to live? What is justice?—have much in common. These children and students will soon grow into Japanese who possess both a "spirit of tolerance" and a "spirit of identity." In other words, they will have become global citizens, in the true sense of the word.

Teaching the essence of traditional Japanese culture and how to coexist with those of other ethnicities should be undertaken as two parts of one whole. It is vital to the creation of citizens aware of themselves both as Japanese and as global citizens that we build a society of coexistence in which the hearts of Japanese and immigrants communicate with each other, not a rootless one in which cultural identity has been lost. The ideal immigration society that I imagine is one in which this kind of open-minded Japanese make up the majority.

I want parents and children to thoroughly discuss, not just at school but in the home as well, the fact that the world is made up of many different races, ethnicities, and religions, that none of these are superior to the others, and that the Japanese, with their spirit of global citizenship, are precious to world civilization.

The Japanese are a highly homogenous ethnic group to begin with, to which is added an education system intended to make them even more uniform. As I look at the elite of Japan—the politicians, the officials, the business leaders, and the intellectuals—I feel that the number of Japanese who have become conformist, who put all their energy into advancing themselves (usually at the expense of others) and making it in life, has become very high.

Japan needs to be reborn as a society that gathers the best from across the world, that avidly absorbs other cultures, that is pulsating with skilled people of multiple colors, that allows diverse ethnic cultures to flourish, and that produces talented individuals able to use multiple languages fluently. Opening Japan to immigration can serve as the trigger for this. I believe that ethnic diversity works to benefit every aspect of society, not just academia and the arts, but also in areas like sports, food, education, foreign tourism, innovative management of businesses and organizations, and political and administrative reform and local communities.

If we are unable to avoid the coming collapse of the demographic order caused by the rapid aging of society, there can be no doubt that it will become difficult to maintain the basic systems of the state. It will become hard, for example, to secure enough young workers for the Self-Defense Forces, police and fire departments, and customs and immigration.[2] The coming rapid decline in the population will have staggering effects on Japan's governmental, economic, financial, and social systems, as well as the livelihoods of the public and our ability to respond to natural disasters. Immigration is unavoidable but it will not be enough to preserve Japan by itself.

The Japanese population grew steadily from the late nineteenth century until recently. We need to fundamentally review the systems that came into being during this period of population increase from the position of the livelihood of the public. This includes our political, regional, and educational systems. This task will expand into a Japanese revolution the likes of which has never before been seen in our history.

There can be no doubt that a Japanese society that takes in diverse immigrants will become fascinating, vibrant, and tenacious. The youth of Japan feel trapped as they face the country's decline in population. Some have already left the country. Suicide is also very high in Japan and the largest killer of teens and those in their twenties and thirties. An immigration society rich in diversity will provide them with dreams and hope.

INTERNATIONAL POPULATION MOVEMENTS AND IMMIGRATION CONTROL

What developments can we see in global population movements in the twenty-first century and how are these connected to Japanese immigration policy? What immigration powers should be permitted to sovereign states under the current world order? I would like to discuss these two basic topics in general terms.

Looking back at human history, we can see that it is the story of people moving on a global scale, travelling and settling in new lands either for reasons of survival or in pursuit of a better life for themselves. Today, humanity lives across the planet divided into numerous ethnic groups and nationalities, but all of these people come from individuals who sought a new home for themselves and their descendants at one point.

And there can be no doubt that humans will continue to actively move in pursuit of a better or more comfortable life for themselves, both within and across national borders.

International population movements (immigration) can be generalized as follows: as long as global population distribution and economic development remain unbalanced, there will be population movements from countries with dense populations and surplus labor to those with small populations and labor shortages. Population movements from poorer countries to richer ones will never cease.

In other words, international population movements will continue as long as there are factors (poverty, war, conflict, inequality, and oppression) promoting emigration from developing nations (which make up the overwhelming majority of the world's population).

Meanwhile, most developed nations (Japan foremost among them) have entered a period of negative population growth and it is certain that they will soon have declining populations.

Viewing the twenty-first century world with these things in mind, it is inevitable that a "great migration" from developing countries to developed ones will spread across the planet. Other factors driving this will be the increasingly severe population and North-South problems and the global population's explosive growth toward ten billion people (the world's population grows by three persons every second as of late-2019, for a total of more than 7,755,000,000).

At the same time, the scramble by developed countries to secure human resources is intensifying as they approach population decline. The survival of their nations and economies depends on this effort and nowhere is this truer than Japan.

This situation does not, however, mean the arrival of an age where people can freely cross borders and live wherever they wish. The basic order of the twenty-first century world, the system of sovereign states, remains intact. And the barriers of "territory" and "citizenship" continue to be essential elements of that system and will not easily disappear. Borders will remain in place to restrict the global freedom of movement and the international legal order that allows sovereign states to classify people as either "citizens" or "foreigners" and give them different treatment accordingly will be maintained.

As long as the United Nations system continues and sovereign states exist alongside each other, they will exercise their authority to strictly control immigration to allow those foreigners they deem desirable in and keep those viewed as undesirable out. This is because protecting the livelihood of their own citizens and maintaining their national culture is the very reason that sovereign states exist.

States are the basic organizational framework that humanity belongs to today. These are communities formed at the national level over the course of history on the basis of such common characteristics as ethnicity, culture, language, historical experience, and customs. It is a fact that the modern world contains civilizations with histories stretching back thousands of years and national cultures that are derived from these civilizations, each with its own reason for existing. And it is also a fact of great importance that many in these nations are fiercely attached to their national cultures and their sense of belonging to that nation.

But that's not everything. The international order—this structure of sovereign states and nation-states—is still developing, as can be seen in the birth and reorganization of new states all across the world. While we do see associations of states such as the European Union make progress, it is also possible that we're headed for a golden age of states in which ethnic minorities within imperialist states like China, Russia, and France create new independent states.

It is realistic to believe that the nation-state system—in which humanity is organized into states which protect the interests of their members—will continue into at least the next century. It is believed unlikely that a new world order in which humanity belongs to a single human society (a unified global community, for example) will be established anytime soon. Or perhaps a hundred years from now the world will have reached the consensus that a decentralized style of nation-state systems in which each state has autonomy is preferable to a centralized world government as a global way to gather humanity's wisdom.

To summarize the above, there is a high probability that the global population will surpass ten billion during the next hundred years and that global population movements will occur on an unprecedented scale. The fate of humanity in the twenty-first century will rest upon whether or not the world's sovereign states will be able to appropriately control these population movements.

Countries commanding massive populations will be able to exert powerful "transmission pressure" on their neighbors via these population movements. And Japan finds itself in an international environment where such countries (most notably China) are present nearby just as it enters a period of rapid population decline expected to continue for at least a hundred years. Unless stronger border controls are put in place to act as a "dam," Japan will be unable to stop the population influx that descends upon the Japanese archipelago, particularly since the reciprocal visa-free program allows Chinese citizens to easily enter Japan.

Japanese immigration authorities should, in accordance with the principles of international law, make full use of the immigration control authority that Japan possesses as a sovereign state. They cannot permit the chaotic immigration of people into a Japanese society experiencing rapid population decline. I want the immigration authorities, of which I was one, to show no negligence in their duties.

But at the same time, I believe that working to accept ten million immigrants in an orderly fashion is the best plan for avoiding a situation where the "dam" (national border) breaks under the pressure of the population influx from overseas. Just as with a dam, a channel must be opened for the water to flow through to prevent the dam bursting or overflowing when too much pressure builds.

LET'S BEGIN THE NEW IMPERIAL ERA AS AN IMMIGRATION SOCIETY

In his 1960s novel *Ryōma ga Yuku* (Ryōma Goes His Way), Shiba Ryōtarō ascribes the following words to Sakamoto Ryōma, a *samurai* who helped bring about the Meiji Restoration 100 years before:

> You mustn't do everything yourself. Eighty percent . . . that's enough. Making it that far is the hard part; anyone can do the last twenty percent. Leave that to someone else and let them have the honor of completing it. If you don't, ambitious undertakings are impossible.

I absolutely feel the same way. When it comes to my life's work, the creation of an immigration nation, I honestly feel that I've managed to make it up the hard, steep road to eighty percent. I pointed out the necessity and urgency of resolving Japan's population problem and completed my theory of the immigration nation to serve as a fundamental solution to that problem. This was in my most recent book.[3] As I've done so, the number of people who approve of my immigration nation concept has constantly increased.

But I know that the final stretch of road leading from here to the summit is by no means a flat or easy one. We cannot reach it through my power alone, and possibly never could have. As I look up that steep, final stretch, it is necessary for me to ask for assistance from many others.

The remaining work—the last twenty percent—is securing complete popular support for a national commitment to immigration. Once we have a broad and unshakeable popular consensus, the often indecisive political world can be presented with an ultimatum. Overwhelming support for admitting immigrants will push the prime minister (who earlier appealed to the public on the necessity of discussing immigration policy) to make a decision. I have no doubt that if we manage to establish an immigration nation through the power of collective public support for immigration policy, future historians will regard it as an extraordinary accomplishment on the part of this generation of Japanese, achieved by our working together.

From here on, I will play a symbolic role as the pioneer of immigration policy. This doesn't mean that I will completely retire, but I am moving the focus of my work from devising immigration policy to promoting awareness. I will support my fellow people of Japan and foreign and immigrant supporters as they take on the creation of an immigration nation, but from the rear, as a symbolic figure of immigration policy.

Naturally, however, as the one who led the immigration revolution, I will be attacked by those who oppose immigration. I already have been, and am still now, prepared for whatever they throw at me, although there is really left nothing in their ammunition box.

I believe that by removing myself from my current position—rushing ahead, alone, on the path to an immigration nation and attempting to do everything myself—it will lead to a new energy arising to drive immigration policy forward. The completion of this century's grand undertaking will be hastened. New talents will appear, one after another, to shoulder the burden of the immigration nation.

In recent years, the winds have begun to favor a Japanese-style immigration policy. Phrases like "immigration," "immigration policy," and "the ten-million immigrant concept" have come to be commonly used online. I post short essays on the Japan Immigration Policy Institute (*Imin Seisaku Kenkyūsho*, JIPI) homepage from day to day. The number of people reading these has increased rapidly; recently the homepage has been accessed approximately five thousand times daily.

This surprisingly large number speaks eloquently of the great hopes being raised among the younger generation of Japanese. As we approach an era where immigration policy is enthusiastically debated in the Diet, young voices of approval are spreading explosively online. Like the current of a great river, this will grow until it becomes decisive and pushes the government to make a commitment to the immigration nation.

The times are moving toward Japan's once-a-millennium Big Bang. And as the immigration revolution stands at the vanguard, it is followed by social revolution. This too will gain momentum and develop into a genuine Japanese revolution.

As someone who stood at the head of the immigration revolution, I will be at its center. But the elderly can't do everything themselves. I wish to devote myself to the immigration revolution, my life's work. As for the social and administrative reforms that need to take place in Japan, my work will only be to point out potential issues and the path to their solutions. It will be the young people who carry Japan's future on their shoulders who will fire the second and third arrows and carry out the final reforms to ensure the eternal continuation of the nation.

Our ancestors overcame countless national crises through the indomitable Japanese spirit. And yet, this generation faces the gravest crisis in the nation's history; if mistakes are made in the response, it could lead to the total collapse of Japan. It is my hope that the youth of Japan band together, resist that fate stubbornly, and carry out the dual immigration and Japanese revolutions. I will support the efforts of the young from behind the scenes as their cheerleader-in-chief.

Global immigration policy fell into turmoil in 2016. I have been interviewed by international media outlets such as the *Economist, Washington Post, New York Times*, Reuters, and Agence France Presse. The recently emboldened anti-immigration movements in America, Britain, and France have caused foreign reporters to feel a sense of impending crisis. They have been seriously considering what exactly global immigration policy should look like and had hoped that, with Japan's population crisis only becoming more serious, the country would open itself up to immigration. They also regarded the vision of the human community proposed by a Japanese expert on immigration policy as the foremost vision for an immigration nation in the world.

Through my discussions with these journalists, I came to understand the universality and global significance of the Japanese immigration nation concept and that it could gain the approval of the world's intellectuals.

Let's bring the popular debate over a national commitment to immigration to a rapid conclusion so that we can meet the new imperial era in 2019, announced on April 1 as *Reiwa* ("Beautiful Harmony") and officially begun on May 1, as an immigration society. My sincere belief is that — should representatives of all parts of Japanese society adopt a global view and engage in exhaustive discussions taking everything into account —

the tolerant common sense of the Japanese people will win out. A historic national consensus will be reached to open the country to immigration.

Incidentally, in a February 2017 poll by NHK, the Japanese public broadcasting company, eighty percent of the public stated that they were "opposed" to the hardline stance toward immigration shown by U.S. President Donald J. Trump, who came into power the month before. I can say with confidence that the Japanese, the vast majority of whom are sensible when it comes to immigration, will come together and decide to open up the country.

I would like to make one additional remark, however. I believe that the human community concept that I advocate will receive a boost due to the blowback from President Trump's unqualified rejection of immigrants. I should also strongly emphasize that Japanese immigration policy should in no way mimic that of President Trump and its strong undertones of "white supremacy." To put it another way, we must learn from President Trump's negative example and strictly abstain from any "Japan-first" immigration policy.

FROM IMMIGRATION REFORM TO A JAPAN-WIDE REVOLUTION

The following should be considered a final testament left behind for the future generations to whom I, as the standard-bearer for immigration reform, entrust the eternal continuation of Japan. It is an "encouragement of revolution" written in the hopes that it may help the next generation of citizens as they work to restore Japan to a vibrant society.

Since 2007, shortly after I retired, I have publicly advocated for Japan to begin admitting immigrants on a scale unheard of in its long history. But I want everyone to face the unmistakable fact that, even if we do accept ten million immigrants over the next fifty years, the total population of Japan will still fall by thirty million. This decline will have an impact on Japan's governmental, economic, financial, social, and disaster relief systems and the livelihood of the Japanese people the likes of which have never been seen and never will be again.

Even if Japan becomes one of the world's foremost immigration powers, the collapse of the demographic order caused by the decline of the youthful population as the elderly population surges cannot be avoided. We will likely only barely be able to maintain the country's basic systems such as our security and public safety organizations. And even then, the Self-Defense Forces, police, and firefighters will have difficulty securing the personnel they need. Immigration reform that brings immigrants into Japan on the largest scale in its history will need to be followed by a Japan-wide revolution that reconsiders all of Japanese society from the ground up. This is the only way to create a society resilient enough to withstand a population decline on the order of thirty million people.

Or, to put it another way, Japan's continuation will only be secure once we have carried out both of these revolutions. It will only be after the popular consensus is reached that massive immigration reform (a revolution in reality) and a society revolution need to be resolutely carried out that there will be any chance of, for example, attempting to miraculously revive the rural societies on the brink of death due to the disappearance of their young people.

Even when struck by a once-a-millennium natural disaster, there's still the hope that the casualties can be minimized as much as possible.

We who live in the new imperial era must comprehensively reexamine the various systems that took shape during the lengthy period of population growth that continued from the late nineteenth century to the near present (Japan's population peaked in 2010 at 128,057,352). The values of the Japanese people, our political framework, the defense structure, other national systems such as those for higher education, justice, and transportation—all of these must be changed to create a nation suitable for a society whose population is shrinking. This will be the greatest revolution in Japanese history, a change to what I refer to as "small Japan."

The "Great Japanese Revolution" will be a massive historic undertaking that will determine whether Japan lives or dies. This will of course be far more difficult than the task of accepting ten million immigrants. The only way that the nation known as Japan will be pulled back from the brink of death is for Japan as a whole to give its all, overcoming the barriers of ethnicity, nationality, generation, and sector as it does so.

***

I would like to emphasize here that the nature of the current generation is the problem. To my eyes, the entire public appears consumed by laziness. I can see no sign of the bravery needed to cut away the lethargy of a society with a decreasing population. Surely there must be some limit to the Japanese people's lack of concern toward the collapse of the population pyramid! When did we devolve into a people so slow-witted as not to notice the population crisis creeping upon our peaceful world?

I'll give an example. I have seen no sign of anyone pointing out the need to reform the basic national and regional systems created during the era of population increase to make them more suitable to one of population decline. Many rural communities are in increasing danger of collapse; those involved aren't even making any efforts to investigate the root issues. And even though we've already entered an era of full-fledged population decline, the nature, customs, and systems of the old Japan are being preserved. Worse, unbelievable schemes that actively go against the needs of a society with a declining population are being pushed through the political sphere, such as counterintuitively increasing the number of seats of the House of Councillors.

I am ringing the warning bell. The only way to create a society capable of being maintained is for "fat" Japan—bound hand and foot by vested interests—to be reborn as a "slim" Japan in which all vested interests have been wiped clean. For the government and public to undertake fundamental systemic reform, in other words. I've continually spoken out on the necessity of Japan, with its declining population and worsening financial situation, carrying out both an immigration and Japanese revolution ever since I retired as a national public official in 2005. Thankfully, the first glimpses of the immigration revolution can now be seen.

The theory of a Japanese revolution that I, the "last samurai" of the *Heisei* era (1989-2019), have put effort into writing has been met with silence from the nation's intellectuals and politicians, however. It seems to have an even worse reputation among the public than my theory of an immigration revolution. As this issue will determine whether the nation survives, I'm painfully aware of the need to develop a more persuasive theory in order to broadly capture the public's interest by expanding its research to include more on the livelihoods of the people.

Fourteen years ago, I launched my theory of the Japanese revolution, writing in 2005 that "the arrival of an era of population decline must be taken as an opportunity to fundamentally review the Japanese lifestyle, the ethnic make-up of the Japanese state, and the economic system. It is an opportunity for the country to be reborn as a 'new Japan'."[4] I called it the problem of the century. However, not a single step of progress has been made on this issue in that time. And this is absolutely my fault. Had the issue of the ethnic make-up of the Japanese state, the immigration issue, in other words, been more quickly resolved, other issues of the Japanese revolution—massive reforms to livelihood, the political system, and industry, for example—could have been started on earlier. I regret this.

I believe that some experts have noticed the existence of this problem, although it's possible they had no idea where to start, given its massive size. Or perhaps Japan's intellectuals just adopted the same approach that they took toward the immigration issue and are pretending not to see that population collapse is directly tied to national collapse. Government authorities such as political leaders and high administrative officials make no reference to this serious issue, either. No doubt they're convinced, as always, that it's better to let sleeping dogs lie. I'm outraged that the Japanese elite has adopted the extremely irresponsible attitude of just sitting around and waiting to die, which some call a "beautiful death," because it accepts the inevitable calmly, without the resistance that often gets ugly or messy.

For example, I don't see any signs that the high officials of Kasumigaseki—the district of Tokyo where most of the main government ministries are located—feel any sense of impending danger concerning the continuation of our national systems and are at all prepared to tackle this issue. This should come as no surprise. The bureaucratic apparatus, concerned only with protecting its territory, would never undertake the kind of administrative reform that would shed its own blood. The issues involved affect the core of the country's governing systems, so our only choice is to wait for our politicians to experience an awakening.

But given that our politicians are passive or oblivious even toward the less painful immigration revolution, it is absolutely unthinkable that they would make revolutionary changes to the political system to make the government more suitable to a society with a declining population; those changes would negatively impact them. Examples of the kind of systematic reform to be undertaken include 1) reducing the number of Diet members by one-third and making this number proportional to the size of the electorate; 2) fundamentally reconsidering the bicameral legislature; and 3) comprehensively reforming the centralized nature of the government by increasing regional autonomy.

There can be no hope that our politicians, who have no intention of giving up their vested interests, will make comprehensive changes to our national, political, and regional systems. The sovereign voter can thus only apply pressure on them to engage in the necessary social revolution and reform of the political system. If these *are* carried out, it will also be necessary for the public to have the backbone to carry out a lifestyle revolution that fundamentally changes the way we've been living.

To be more specific, we will need to 1) thoroughly cut down on luxury and waste and adjust to a civilized lifestyle of honest poverty in order to live peacefully in a society with extremely few children and long lifespans, the likes of which humanity has never before seen; 2) prioritize having a healthy lifestyle, as those who are healthy will work their entire lives; 3) withstand increased burdens such as higher taxes and reductions in social welfare services.

The lifestyle revolution will lead to the public being faced with bitter choices. Even so, there is something I must say to the people and government: the people will find new value in Japan's traditional manner of lifestyle, such as living modestly. The country will create an equal society in which the people all equally share a sense of belonging to the middle class. These two things are the minimum requirements for Japan to be able to survive the era of population decline.

It breaks my heart that I can only raise these problems related to what I call the "Great Japanese Revolution." But providing a plan for rebuilding the Japanese state to make it suitable for an era of population decline is beyond my abilities right now. My hands are full with the national commitment to an immigration nation and all I can do is make clear where there are problems related to the immigration revolution and provide a path toward their solutions. Despite all this, I'm not worried about our country's future. I have no doubt that large numbers of ambitious people will appear to inherit my aspirations, as will great political leaders willing to wager their political lives on the Japanese revolution. But will these actions be too late?

In the near future, young people will appear one after another, willing to wager their own futures and the fate of Japan on the immigration revolution. I have no doubt that they will deeply understand that the immigration and Japanese revolutions will need to be seen as necessary parts of one integrated whole if a new Japan capable of continuing is to be created. I shall participate in the beginning of the immigration and Japanese revolutions and leave the future of Japan to the younger generation who will rise up to engage in the social revolution and reform of the political system. The young (including the ten million newly added immigrants), free from the vested interests, will tirelessly take on the fundamental reform of their nation and society. I predict that within fifty years the Great Japanese Revolution will be considered to have been a brilliant success.

***

I will add one thing, in connection with the Great Japanese Revolution. The issues of overpopulation, climate change, natural disasters, environmental damage, and the food and energy security are worsening on a global scale. Taking that into account, I believe that a society with a population of seventy million or so is desirable. We shouldn't fixate on the number one hundred million. It is important, however, that the population is spread across the country and not concentrated in a few cities, as is increasingly tending to be the case. Doing so makes them vulnerable all at one time to natural disasters or other calamities.

This chapter has emphasized the domestic component. The next chapter introduces the international, humanitarian aspects.

NOTES

1. Robert D. Eldridge, *Jinkō Genshō to Jieitai* (Population Decline and Its Impact on the Self-Defense Forces), (Tōkyō: Fusōsha, 2019).

2. On this issue, see Eldridge, *Jink ō Gensh ō to Jieitai.*

3. *Nihon no Imin Kokka Bijion, Shinpan* (Vision of a Japanese Immigration Nation, New Edition) (Tōkyō: JIPI, 2018).

4. Sakanaka Hidenori, *Nyūkan Senki*(Immigration Battle Diary), (Tōkyō: Kōdansha, 2005), p. 235.

TWO

The Development of the "Human Community" Concept

TAKING UP THE CHALLENGE OF CREATING A GLOBAL HUMAN COMMUNITY

With the inauguration of President Donald J. Trump and his seemingly placatory stance toward white supremacy, the belief in America as a racial melting pot that has existed from the nation's founding has taken a strong hit. The America that was seen as welcoming to immigrants ("Give me your tired, your poor, your huddled masses yearning to breathe free, the wretched refuse of your teeming shore.") is now being viewed as hostile to foreigners. As some people have said, Lady Liberty is crying now as her torch is being extinguished.

At the same time—or perhaps because of this situation—my immigration policy, based on what I call the "human community" concept, has drawn the attention of discerning people of the world. I am trying to push Japan, traditionally closed (but not necessarily "anti-"), to become more open to immigrants.

Driven originally by a sincere desire to save Japan from demographic collapse, I laid down the blueprint for a Japanese-style immigration nation that provided a just way for the country to accept ten million immigrants over the course of fifty years. Such an ambitious vision and clear course to become an immigration nation has rarely been seen in world history.

And yet, from about the year 2016, the world's great immigration nations suddenly changed direction with regard to immigration. The spirit of tolerance toward those of different ethnic groups and religions that had existed in America, France, Britain, and Germany—all leading nations of global civilization—has been abandoned in favor of xenopho-

23

bia. Trump, for example, as candidate and now president, makes no effort to hide his aberrant hardline stance toward immigration, and Trump-like politicians in other countries, such as multi-cultural Brazil, where many Japanese had previously emigrated to, are adopting nationalistic policies. Britain chose the Trump-like Boris Johnson, too, in 2019.

As Japan's standard-bearer for immigration policy, I have set forth to try to prevent the ideology of xenophobia from spreading across the world. Born and raised in the spiritual ground of Japan and waving the banner of a tolerant, Japanese-style immigration policy, I have pushed for Western Europe's immigration policies to return to normal.

But the Japanese government has been in no position to counter President Trump's recklessness, having itself continued to bar its doors against immigration. In fact, when an angry Trump criticized Japan, saying that "it's extremely irresponsible of Japan to not fulfill any of its international responsibilities on the immigration problem," it could potentially be seen as an attempt to press the Japanese prime minister on Japan's failure to admit immigrants. And on that, President Trump would have a point. Perhaps it should have been expected. The AFP and Jiji Press reported on June 16, 2018, that at the summit held in Canada on June 8 and 9, President Trump told Prime Minister Abe that "I can send you twenty-five million Mexicans and you'll be out of office very soon." While it was an abusive statement that violated international courtesy, the American president's warning, aimed right at the Achilles heel of the Japanese society, should be taken seriously.

I have a request for the Japanese government. I would like it to preempt the American president by announcing to the people of the world that "as a great economic power, Japan is certainly capable of accepting immigrants. We are prepared to welcome large numbers of immigrants, including refugees, fairly via our innovative immigration policy."

With the fear of immigrants spreading across the globe, Japan's immigration policy can do more than just save the country from its population crisis. It can also help save the world from its ongoing humanitarian crisis. Those across the world who wish to leave their countries are in the depths of despair; if Japan seizes the opportunity and takes up the banner of an immigration nation, the warm-hearted people of Japan will surely shine in the annals of world history for relieving the global immigration and refugee crisis.

I have solemnly interpreted it as divine providence that the Japanese people have been entrusted with the global mission of resolving the immigration issue. And I will continue to appeal to the world's conscience with the human community concept that the rich spiritual climate of Japan produced.

In April 2015, I gave the keynote speech at a symposium on Japanese immigration policy hosted by the University of Southern California's

Center for Japanese Religions and Culture. The title of my speech was "Japan as a Nation for Immigrants: A Proposal for a Global Community of Humankind." My speech was received enthusiastically by the scholars in attendance and I received many questions from the audience. I believe that these world intellectuals understood my passionate beliefs about taking on the challenge of creating a global human community.

The organizer, USC Professor Duncan Williams, an authority on Japanese Buddhism, had described the event to me as "a 'small project' through which to introduce your immigration policies to the world." Having been born and raised in Japan, Duncan is a humble person. In my eyes, it was actually a grand project, the best possible setting through which to unveil my philosophy of the global human community to the world's intellectuals. I am grateful to him for the opportunity. And more than anything else, he also translated the Japanese draft of my speech into dignified English.

As this concept for a global human community ("the ideal of an immigration nation in which humanity can be as one, overcoming all differences of race, ethnicity, and religion") was released into the world, translated into wonderful English, I foresaw that it would have a serious impact on international immigration policy. I continue to receive feedback from foreign friends who have read the paper. One told me that they were "very moved by it. I agree with it wholeheartedly." I believe that many were surprised by the concept, as it is uniquely Japanese and may not have occurred to a Westerner.

But, as is well known, the global atmosphere for immigration policy changed dramatically in 2016. Led by Trump's America, or parts of it, the countries of the West have experienced a surge by far-right groups calling for the expulsion of illegal immigrants. The immigration issue has evolved into a task for all humanity, one that the world is pressed to solve urgently. I believed that the time had come to appeal to the world with my human community concept.

Then came January 2017. The first act by President Trump, who had won his presidential election in part through an anti-immigration campaign, was to issue an executive order temporarily banning the entry into America by people from seven Muslim countries. As a result, the torch of the Statue of Liberty, that symbol of the immigration nation, was reduced to a candle flickering in the wind, if not yet extinguished outright. The world has been greatly shaken by the immigration issue, nowhere more than America. And yet the Japanese government is completely out of the loop on global immigration matters, holding fast to its policy of closing itself off from immigration. It is not an anti-immigration policy per se, but a non-immigration one. Although historically it has sent many immigrants abroad, Japan has almost never contributed anything to the world through its immigration policy. I can only say how disappointed I am at this.

Even so, we absolutely must avoid the international community drawing the conclusion from this that the Japanese prime minister and American president are in agreement when it comes to excluding immigrants. I say this because there is no country in the world more in need of immigrants than Japan with its ever-increasing risk of demographic collapse. We need to actively appeal to the world and convince them that the immigration policy that Japan is considering is diametrically opposed to that of President Trump and those of his ilk. Japan should immediately lift its ban on immigration and promise the international community that it will contribute to the world through a rational and humane immigration policy.

Ten years ago, a Western intellectual critiqued my immigration policy by asking, "is modern Japanese society really capable of accepting ten million immigrants over fifty years? Can we expect the Japanese people to take in that many? They have very little experience with immigrants and coexisting with foreigners."

I responded by saying that the latent strength of the Japanese civilization will be brought to the surface, that "Japan is well equipped to do so as it possesses both the necessary industrial base and higher educational institutions needed to absorb ten million immigrants as well as a national spirit able to accept those of other ethnicities with a spirit of compassion."

I particularly emphasized that Japanese society has a tradition of emphasizing "harmony between people" and "tolerance," and that the polytheistic Japanese people have passed down a "gene of tolerance" from generation to generation that allows them to willingly accept diverse peoples and values.

The type of "human resource-cultivating immigration policy" that I advocate is one where immigrants receive a thorough education in the Japanese language and are introduced to stable employment. If immigrants are provided with the opportunity to adapt to society—living stable lives, receiving a good education, and working in their chosen fields—then there is little chance of the kind of social problems that the Japanese public is concerned about. In fact, isn't it likely that these immigrants, well-versed in the language and culture of both Japan and their home countries, could prove to be "golden eggs" for a nation thirsty for global human resources?

***

As mentioned earlier, the situation in which my immigration nation concept finds itself has undergone a sea change from that of ten years ago. Recently I have increased my criticism of the anti-immigrant and anti-Muslim movements that have arisen in countries like America and France. I have also pressed the Japanese government to open the country to immigration, intellectually armed with the human community concept that the tolerant intellectual climate of Japan has produced.

I have the self-confidence to outright state that, having spent the past nearly fifteen years on the theoretical groundwork for the ideal immigration nation, my vision for a Japanese immigration nation has attained a higher level of theoretical development than those of the West.

THE ESSENCE OF THE "HUMAN COMMUNITY" CONCEPT

Where did the human community concept, the fundamental idea behind the vision of a Japanese immigration nation, come from? From the standpoints of biology and cultural anthropology, I have focused on the ultimate Japanese theory of immigration policy.

The world's immigration policy specialists emphasize the diversity of humanity and set multicultural existence as their objective. In contrast, I emphasize the unity of humanity as a single species and extol the ideal of human community where mankind can be as one, overcoming differences of race, ethnicity, and religion.

My vision of an immigration nation is comprised of three pillars: (1) the formation of a society based on the human community on the Japanese archipelago; (2) the creation of a global human community; and (3) the establishment of permanent world peace. It is a grand global framework anticipating a golden age of immigration—an era in the near future when immigration power is at its height—and the formation of a new world order in the twenty-second century built upon the increasingly reciprocal relationships between the peoples of each nation. The starting point for my theory of immigration policy can be found in the Japanese spirit of harmony.

This spirit arises from the animistic view of nature and religious piety of the Japanese. These originated in the *Jōmon* period (a Neolithic, hunter-gatherer era), a time of peace that lasted for fifteen thousand years. The belief that "all of creation is one" that can even now be found in the hearts of the Japanese people has its roots in that era. It is believed that the *Jōmon* people and their descendants knew intuitively that all living beings on the face of the Earth were the providence of nature, born from the same material. This is the same perception of nature that can be found in modern natural sciences such as biology, chemistry, and physics.

And ever since this ancient time, this belief emphasizing harmony between people and feelings of reverence toward nature has been passed down as the spiritual heritage of the Japanese people.

Behind the Japanese spirit lies a religious piety unique in civilized society, an animistic view of the world that venerates all that exists in nature. This is the people that so cherish the work of the Edo period artist Itō Jakuchū who portrayed the compassion of animals. This is the country that gave birth to the leader (Tokugawa Tsunayoshi) who issued the Laws for Mercy to Animals (*Shōrui Awaremi no Rei*) in 1687. The Japanese are the ones able to deeply understand the meaning of the cicada *haiku* by the famous poet Bashō.

Humanity may be divided into a diverse number of races, ethnicities, and nationalities, but at heart we are all one. All of humanity is biologically classified as a single species, *Homo sapiens*. Our core values and culture are largely shared, the biggest being that we can feel compassion for other living things. Even if differences of race, ethnicity, and religion exist, being human means that we all have our own individual identities and can communicate with, emphasize with, understand, and help, if needed, each other.

Having inherited the beliefs of the *Jōmon* people who managed to peacefully coexist with all of nature, I have set as my goal the creation of a human community in which all of humanity can peacefully coexist. I base this on a universal view of humanity that holds that "all of humanity is one. Even if there are differences of race or ethnicity, we are all human. Even if there are differences of culture or values, they are few."

Now, it could possibly be said that, when viewed with non-Japanese eyes, this concept is fantastical. But it is absolutely not just mere theory. It is in agreement with the fundamental spirit of humanity. It is the deep-felt desire that humanity has for eternal world peace. And given that humanity is all biologically the same species, it is not at all an unrealistic pipe dream for the Japanese to make the creation of a global human community a national goal.

It may take centuries, but I dream that someday in the near future, this vision of an immigration nation will stir up the sense of human camaraderie of those living in a global age and lead to the creation of a utopian immigration society on the Japanese archipelago. If we, the descendants of the *Jōmon* people and their rich spirit of harmony, sincerely take on this challenge, it can happen.

THE JAPANESE SPIRIT OF HARMONY AND HUMANITY'S FUTURE

Where will Japan be headed fifty years from now if even admitting an unprecedented number of immigrants fails to prevent the population from falling rapidly? What new national goals do we Japanese need to set in order to survive this period of population decline?

The goals clearly can't be those of recent years, seeking to become one of the world's preeminent economic powers and playing a global role militarily. I would like to propose new national ideals suitable for a twenty-first century immigration power as a replacement for those outdated national goals.

Japan should aim to become the world's foremost immigration nation through our love of humanity. With the world's immigration policies increasingly in turmoil, we should seize the initiative and make our national goal the creation of a society based on the human community: a place where ninety million Japanese (the expected population in about fifty years) and ten million immigrants cooperate with one another, where the hearts of one hundred million citizens living and working together have become as one.

In other words, as the threat of nuclear war draws near, Japan—the only country to ever be attacked with an atomic weapon (twice, actually) in wartime—should assume leadership of the world peace movement.

The ultimate goal of the vision for a Japanese immigration nation is to bring about a global society based on the human community, one in which the peoples of the world share the same belief of peace through the spirit of harmony. However, just as I was taking on the challenge of deploying this vision of the immigration nation filled with the Japanese spirit of harmony worldwide, we saw the arrival of President Trump and his open advocacy of ethnic nationalism. This was accompanied by anti-immigrant factions and xenophobes expanding their power in America, Britain, France, and Germany.

I would like to give my opinion on the relationship between the arrival of an ice age for immigration and my theory of immigration policy below:

> With the world facing a once-a-century humanitarian crisis, the idea of the human community that came to life in the head of the director of the Japan Immigration Policy Institute has suddenly taken on global historic significance and could affect the fate of humanity. If a thoroughly prepared Japan changes gears and becomes an immigration nation, it will recover the honor it has lost for maintaining a closed-door policy towards immigrants for more than a thousand years. And that's not all. It will also give the immigrants dealing with this global humanitarian crisis the courage and hope to live by providing them with a new world and guaranteeing their right to pursue happiness. My dream is that the Japanese with their rich spirit of harmony seize the initiative and lead the people of the world to a "golden age of immigration" and a "society based on the human community."

***

My friends inside and outside of Japan who have watched over me as I worked on my theory for immigration policy consider my new theory for an immigration nation—the idea that the creation of an ideal immigration nation and the establishment of a human community and a system for world peace need to be viewed as parts of one indivisible whole—to be the culmination of that work.

I continue to dream that the ideal of the immigration nation—the fruits of Japanese culture and its respect for harmony—opens up a new frontier for world civilization. By no later than the twenty-second century, the concept of the human community—born in the rich spiritual soil of Japan and its spirit of peace—and its philosophy of world peace will spawn a new era in human history and capture the hearts of the world. The age will come where it shines as bright as a star guiding the peoples of the world to reconciliation.

I can imagine how this profound vision that drew its first breaths on an island nation in the East will be received by most of the world's intellectuals: they will treat it as an unrealistic utopian tale and pay it no heed. But the origins of my theory can be found in my spirit of harmony, something that was cultivated by the Japanese linguistic environment (which is highly distinctive among the world's languages), and in the cultural anthropological knowledge I've gained through close contact with foreigners of differing languages, cultures, and religions who lived in Japan over the previous half-century. The Japanese, with their spirit of tolerance second to none in the world, will not be shaken in the slightest by my conviction that we should stand at the forefront of the world and create a global human community.

The Japanese possess a great spiritual tolerance toward those of other ethnicities and religions. And they have the wisdom needed to use that spirit of harmony to guide the world toward the resolution of the ethnic and religious conflicts deeply rooted in human society. The Japanese, with our belief that a *kami* (god or spirit) dwells within everything on the planet, are a rare presence and one that can deal with all ethnicities and religions in a fair and disinterested manner. The latent power to calm the ethnic and religious tensions that flare up around the world through the spirit of peace and thereby peacefully resolve these ethnic and religious issues is written into the Japanese DNA.

This is a philosophy of world peace that can lead all races to reconciliation. The Japanese believe that all races, ethnicities, and religions on the planet are equal, even pursuing a racial equality clause, unsuccessfully, in the discussions leading up to the establishment of the League of Nations (the predecessor of the United Nations). As a sense of unity is fostered among humanity on a global scale in the near future, they will reach a mental state far beyond that of other ethnicities and take on the historic mission of creating a world without nuclear war.

WE MUST NOT RETURN TO AN AGE OF RACIAL DISCRIMINATION

I foresee no future for Western civilization and its increasingly hostile relationship with Islam and its 1.7 billion adherents. But can Japanese civilization, with its ability to approach different religions with a spirit of tolerance, take the West's place? Can its ability to accept all faiths with a spirit of tolerance bring an end to the religious war between Christianity and Islam, the greatest crisis facing the world of today as outlined a quarter century ago by Samuel Huntington in *The Clash of Civilizations and the Remaking of the World Order*?

Looking over the present-day world from the perspective of the comparative study of civilizations, my perception is that the world is about to enter an age of tectonic shifts; a pall has fallen over the universality of Western civilization and its last days are approaching. After that happens, there will be intellectual efforts to gather the world's wisdom and find new values, a new global spirit, a new world order. When that happens, I believe that Japanese civilization, with its spiritual culture and worldview so different from that of the West, will need to take on much of the responsibility for the creation of a new world civilization.

Right now, racial bigotry, religious discrimination, and xenophobia are rapidly spreading throughout Western society. The peculiar spectacle of xenophobes shouting, "No immigrants!" can be seen, with President Trump standing at the forefront. Racial and religious conflict is intensifying, and it seems like the gears of history have gone out of sync. I fear that this conflict could potentially spark a Third World War in which nuclear or other weapons of mass destruction are used.

I plead to the world's leaders: we cannot let history repeat itself. We cannot return to an era when the ideologies of ethnic nationalism ruled the world as it did before the Second World War (epitomized by Adolf Hitler's genocide of the Jews). Japan cannot pretend to not have a stake in this.

I make this appeal to the Japanese government: the immigration and refugee issues have taken a dangerous turn in Western society. Now is the time to issue a promise to the people of the world that "the Japanese people will welcome ten million immigrants over the next fifty years in accordance with the ideals of the human community."

If Japan discards the armor that closes it off from the rest of the world and transforms itself into an immigration nation that welcomes immigrants and refugees amidst a humanitarian crisis, it can become their savior. Japan's image as a humanitarian power will spread like wildfire across the globe. The Japanese people's courageous act in the dawn of the first half of twenty-first century will surely go down in the annals of world history as having resolved a major crisis.

The human community concept is attracting the attention of the world's major media outlets. In November 2016 I was interviewed by reporters from the *Washington Post* and *New York Times* who were greatly concerned that Trump's immigration policies reversed American's founding spirit. They immediately grasped the global significance of my call for a Japanese-style immigration policy based on the human community concept. It was at that point that I foresaw that I might have to take on a portion of the responsibility for leading world immigration policy.

There is a high probability that the polytheistic Japanese with their rich spirit of tolerance could grow into a people aware of the camaraderie of humanity and establish a human community by the end of this century. Conversely, wouldn't it be extremely difficult for Westerners with their innate feelings of racial and religious superiority to do so? To do so would require first wiping away the exclusionary sense of ethnicity that is embedded in their hearts.

As I earnestly discussed the nature of world immigration policy with these reporters from the two most influential American newspapers, it truly struck me that my original immigration policy must become a model for the world.

***

Let's move this discussion to the future. As previously mentioned, I continue to dream that the Japanese of a hundred years from now will have taken the initiative among the peoples of the world and established a human community on the Japanese archipelago. But that dream has since become even bigger, to imagine countries across the world following Japan's lead and creating human communities, one after another. Ultimately these will lead to the creation of a human community across the globe as these surpass the national level and merge.

Among my close friends is a Pakistani Muslim who is an advocate for permanent world peace. Syed Tahir first came to Japan as a refugee thirty years ago. Even now, eight years after the disaster, he is passionately engaged in activities to assist the areas affected by the 2011 Great East Japan Earthquake, for example.

He is a believer in my revolutionary ideas on immigration, especially that of the human community. When I visited him at one of the earthquake-affected areas in February 2013 to give him encouragement, he gave me a surprising appraisal of my vision for an immigration nation: he lauded me as an apostle of world peace. A pious Muslim, he began to speak about the ideal human society with an urgent look on his face: "Your thoughts on the human community will contribute to permanent world peace. Allah will protect you so that in the near future the human community, the ideal society, will come into being within global society. You'll become the savior of the world." Not being particularly pious myself, I was surprised to have been named a servant of God

War and terrorism are widespread across the modern world, often for reasons based ironically in religion, which should be about people and their relationship to their god, others around them, and their surroundings. And the world's powers, America foremost among them, have been unable to exercise leadership in religious conflicts such as the Palestine issue. I therefore expect Japanese political leaders, being in a position of neutrality on foreign religious issues, to play a proactive role toward world peace by striving to reconcile Islam and Christianity.

A WORLD PEACE BUILT ON A GLOBAL HUMAN COMMUNITY

After carefully deliberating what the ideal immigration nation would look like, I presented the world's experts with a vision that had never before been considered: the creation of a global human community. But just as I did so, the situation for immigrants and refugees changed dramatically for the worse around the world. I was not to be granted the time to leisurely go about my work. This is because the possibility has arisen that my vision of a Japanese immigration nation—and its ultimate goal of the creation of a human community—could develop into a global ideal that leads to the resolution of the immigration and refugee issues facing the world.

The concept of the global human community has, as always, received very little attention from the Japanese intellectual community. But among the larger international intellectual world, there has been a steady increase in the number of experts who echo my vision of "the creation of a global human community" (i.e., a world community where humanity is as one and differences of race, ethnicity, and religion are overcome). I have felt a definite, positive response.

Some fifteen years ago, I told myself that Japan could not follow the path taken by the Western immigration nations and became determined to devise an immigration policy unique to Japan. That decision has brought unforeseen good fortune. With xenophobic and anti-immigrant forces on the rise in the West, Western immigration policy has ground to a halt. And the concept of the human community and vision of the immigration nation originating in Japan have come to be highly regarded by some of the world's intellectuals.

***

Reviewing the history of the treatment of foreigners in the first countries to accept immigrants, we can see that it has not always made sense. Little progress seems to have been made in achieving coexistence between citizens and immigrants in the countries of the West, where the populations have deep-seated racial discrimination and Islamophobia. In fact, one cannot help but be surprised by the extent of the spreading anti-immigration movement in the West despite the pride it takes in its high level of civilization.

Using the existing immigration nations as useful examples of what not to do, I devised an ideal immigration nation that reflected the world view universally held by the Japanese. Taking the Japanese beliefs that "all humans are equal to one another" and "humanity is as one" as the basis for my ideal immigration nation, I have been advocating for the establishment of a global human community in which those of all races are linked by the spirit of harmony as a national goal.

This point is where the definitive difference from the immigration policies of Western countries lies. The profound Japanese immigration nation concept has the potential to develop into the world's highest-level theory of the immigration nation.

I believe that the Japanese, with their lower level of prejudice toward other races, ethnicities, and religions, have the potential to create a human community faster than anyone else in the world. Reflecting on the history of minority ethnic issues in Japan being resolved through innovative immigration policies (most notably the postwar policies toward the *Zainichi* Korean community), I can picture the children and grandchildren of immigrants spontaneously assimilating into Japanese society if they are educated within a Japanese language environment full of the spirit of harmony. A distinctive characteristic of Japanese society is its great ability to assimilate other ethnic groups, to make their hearts one. Given this, I have confidence that this age is coming where Japanese immigration policy breathes fresh air into that of the world and immigration nation Japan rises high as a global model for the world's immigration nations.

***

Let's change the topic. Should Japan choose the path of becoming an "immigration power"—orderly taking in ten million immigrants over the next fifty years as it joins the Japanese-led reconfigured Trans-Pacific Partnership (TPP), then an "immigration nation alliance"—major powers sharing the ideal of a national commitment to immigration—will be formed along the Pacific Rim. And things won't stop there. Population transfers among the members will be easy and vigorous, and a sense of solidarity will be fostered among the peoples of these nations. There is the possibility that a path toward a "Pacific community," a dream of the peoples of this region, will be opened.

I have a request for the Japanese government. Don't allow the opportunity provided by the beginning of the TPP pass by. I want you to appeal to the world. Issue a declaration saying that Japan is becoming an immigration nation and that it will be coordinating with representative immigration powers like Canada, Australia, and New Zealand to expand the movement of people within the Pacific region and contribute to world peace.

As you do so, I want you to emphasize the significance that the existence of a distinctive immigration nation born outside of Western society has. Immigration nation Japan will obtain an immovable status in the world as it pushes on to the creation of a global human community.

FROM AN ERA OF WESTERN IDEAS TO ONE OF JAPANESE VALUES

The year 2016 will go down in the annals of history as the year the world entered a period of upheaval. It saw the election of President Trump and increasing global upheaval over immigration issues. And I expect that we will now see the emergence of various moves toward the formation of a new world order. When that happens, I believe it will be necessary for Japan as one of the leaders of civilization to take some of that grave responsibility upon itself.

Prior to this point, America had literally led the world in immigration policy and established for itself the reputation of a racial melting pot. But far from becoming a place of racial harmony, the struggle between white and black in the country is only growing more intense. President Trump's numerous racist statements and condoning of violence by right-ists and domestic terrorism by white supremacists reflect the deep-seated racial discrimination that still incredulously exists in American society, and more and more people are becoming aware of the systemic problems and institutionalized injustices that exist there.

Western civilization is sometimes criticized as a prejudiced civiliza-tion, created and maintained by white supremacists and believers in the monotheistic religion of Christianity. The belief that "the religion we be-lieve in is absolute and correct and other religions are all heretical" lies at its root. Previously it had been relatively tolerant toward accepting immi-grants due to its overwhelming advantage in economic and military power. But now, with its economics slumping and absolute military pow-er fading, the true nature of Westerners—"Whites First"—has reared its head. Trump, who has departed from existing practice on immigration policy, is a politician that embodies the discriminatory nature of Western society.

As racial and religious conflict intensifies around the world, what can Japanese civilization do for those subject to persecution?

The Japanese people do not consider racial and religious differences to be of significance. We believe in the infinite *kami* (spirits) and Buddhism and *Shintō* are all able to co-exist in Japan. We feel as one with nature and believe that even animals have potential Buddhahood.

I suspect that the Japanese, with our animistic world view, have the ability to withstand the propagation of monotheistic (and sometimes ex-clusionary) religions like Christianity and Islam. The majority of Japa-nese, for example, believe that the different races, whites and blacks, for example, are equal, none superior to any other.

The following is just my supposition, but it seems to me that for young Japanese, it doesn't matter what country someone comes from or what race or religion they are. Their hearts are open to accepting immi-grants and the only questions they ask are: "what has this person done?" and "what do they want to do in Japan?" That is my inference regarding how the youth of modern Japan view non-Japanese.

If Japan, backed by its young people and their tolerant spirits, advo-cates worldwide for its Japanese-style immigration policy based on the philosophy of the human community, it seems likely that it would become a powerful focus for resistance against Western immigration policies rooted in the spirit of wWhite supremacy.

***

Looking back over their respective histories, it becomes immediately clear that the West and Japan have taken utterly different stances toward immigration.

Immigration in the West bears the original sin of the forcible transport of black Africans to the New World as slaves, a dark stain in the history of human rights. Additionally, the Western countries of the present day find themselves trapped in a situation where their societies and economies have become dependent upon the power of immigrants.

How could this be the European and American civilizations that Japan took as models to learn from, from the late nineteenth century on? Restricting the discussion to just immigration, they were remarkably unethical and unjust—banning or restricting others through quotas based on race and ethnicity. Meanwhile, under the immigration policy that I, a typical Japanese, advocate for, immigrants are warmly welcomed as fellow humans in the spirit of equality.

The idea that "harmony is to be valued" (quoted from the "Seventeen-Article Constitution" of 604) has been a fundamental part of the national character of Japan since ancient times.

It is believed that the Japan of the Asuka period (592–710 CE) was what would be referred to today as a "multiethnic state." A diverse assortment of peoples lived on the Japanese archipelago including the indigenous population remaining from the earlier *Jōmon* and *Yayoi* (the latter, 300 BCE to 300 CE) periods, the peoples newly arrived from the Korean Peninsula and Chinese mainland, and those who had followed the Kuroshio Current north from the South Pacific. Since that time, the peoples living in Japan have been fortunate enough to have had a history without either large-scale infusions of outside ethnic groups or foreign invasions. The "spirit of harmony"—ethnic integration—has thus been allowed to progress uninterrupted. The Japanese of today, having inherited this spirit of harmony from their ancestors, don't perceive those of other ethnicities as "barbarians." There is little xenophobic sentiment toward them.

The Japanese government should make the following promise to the world: "All of humanity is equal and we accept all the peoples of the world in this spirit; differences of religion, culture, or skin color are irrelevant. We will welcome immigrants with the spirit of understanding found in the hearts of the Japanese."

If Japan steps out into the world as a new immigration nation based on the universal ideal of the human community, it will drive away Western immigration policy with its deep-seated white supremacist thought and discrimination toward other religions.

And it might even trigger a change in the trends of world civilization away from the age of Western civilization to a Japanese-led one.

THE FORMATION OF A NEW WORLD CIVILIZATION AND THE "HUMAN COMMUNITY" CONCEPT

I, the outlaw of immigration policy research, can peer a hundred years into the future. I am hopeful that this ambition that humanity unites and creates a human community will be realized by or in the twenty-second century.

It goes without saying that the amount that any one person can achieve within their single lifespan is severely limited. I started this journey in the mid-1970s, if not before, and want to spend my remaining days pursuing the ideal immigration nation and refining my human community concept. I believe that there will be those in every country of the world who appear and share my philosophy.

This might be the heaviest responsibility that a private citizen can assume. I will work alongside those who share these ideals, train the younger ones, and try to open the eyes of my fellow citizens in order to come closer to realizing the dream of creating an ideal immigration nation, even if by just one step at a time.

Dreams are infinite. Once one dream is achieved, it merely becomes a point along the path to a new dream. Recently I have been actively working (with the cooperation of the international media) to spread the concept of the global human community to the people of the world so as to block the spread of xenophobic thought and give hope to people for the future. While I predict it will take more than a century for this to become a realistic global undertaking, it's possible that the era where the human community concept pulls at the world's heartstrings will arrive surprisingly quickly.

Unfortunately for human society, I increasingly fear the possibility that the human community concept will become the basic ideal supporting a new world order in the first half of the twenty-first century due to a sudden collapse of the Western-led world order, or because of the outbreak of a Third World War in which nuclear weapons are used on a large scale.

***

Let's examine the relationship between the risk of nuclear war and the human community concept in further detail.

Can humanity, all members of one species (*Homo sapiens*), overcome our ethnic and religious differences and establish a system for permanent peace? Or are we destined to repeatedly engage in nuclear war in the struggle for ethnic or religious hegemony until we ultimately disappear from the face of the Earth?

If we look over the long history of humanity, it is very much the repetition of wars fought between different ethnic groups. And in the modern twenty-first century world—a mature industrial society—there is no shortage of wars and terrorist acts caused by individuals espousing, in particular, ethnic or religious identity issues and/or political statements. And the number of states armed with nuclear weapons only seems to increase. My perception of the current global situation is that the survival of humanity is at risk. Nuclear war could break out at any time; there is North Korea's nuclear problem and the Trump administration's development of tactical nuclear weapons and creation of a "Space Force," China's actions in the South China Seas, and Russia's Crimean grab. And if such a conflict should occur on a global scale (or even expand out into space), it will not just be the guilty that are destroyed. Everything living on the face of the Earth could be consumed by the militaristic acts of monstrous humans.

But while all that is true, it is also true that humans are programmed on a genetic level to seek peace. I make this appeal to humanity's better nature: as the self-acknowledged leader of all life on Earth, do not permit human egotism to bring about the slaughter of all life on our planet. As just one of our world's inhabitants, we humans should consider the ultimate fate of non-human life as well.

I sincerely pray that the intelligence of humanity will bring about the fruition of my dream for the establishment of an impregnable world peace framework in the twenty-second century. I call for the creation of a global community in which all of our fates are linked and earnestly entrust my hopes to the common sense of the citizens of the Earth. We cannot allow humanity's madness to wipe out all living creatures, including ourselves.

The fundamental reason that war does not disappear from our world can be found in the human tendency for ethnic pride and religious piety to change and take on an exclusionary character. Each ethnic group and religion struggles against the others in an attempt to achieve cultural or religious hegemony. I continue to appeal to the intelligence of the world: a world without war will never be realized unless humanity respects ethnic, cultural, and religious diversity. Bonds between these diverse groups must be strengthened until coexistence and co-prosperity is achieved based on the universal ideal that "humanity is one" and the spirit of the human community.

There are times when I am tempted to give up, when I think that things have gone too far, that this is all wasted effort on my part. I am attacked by the fear that the competition between America, Russia, and China to develop and deploy nuclear weapons—now expanding even into space—has already gone past the point that the wisdom of humanity could reign it in, that foolish humanity has already embarked on the road of self-destruction and humans will kill each other with civilization-destroying nuclear weapons.

But I have an idealist streak in me, and when I awaken from that nightmare, I am stirred to action. Embracing my dream of striving for an ultimate world peace in which the Japanese have a central role, I think that now is the time to rise up and take on this historic task! And at times like that, my thoughts rush to a new age, one with a new world civilization and global thinking formed through a union of Japanese civilization with its tolerance and peace and Western civilization with its liberty and charity. But I am also a realist and the frightening thought occurs to me that even if a world free of nuclear war is achieved, it might only be after a nuclear-centric Third World War in which hundreds of millions of human lives have been lost.

I would like to say one more thing on this point. The other higher animals have mechanisms that prevent them from wiping themselves out through intra-species conflict. Humanity could learn many things from the way that animals prioritize coexistence and self-sacrifice for the sake of leaving descendants.

As someone second to none in being proud to have been born a Japanese, I would like to make the following appeal to the world's conscience:

> The Japanese believe that all humans are equal and have the same right to life. That belief enables us to engage well with those of other ethnic groups and religions. We are a rare people that can calmly and peacefully resolve the ethnic and religious problems that flare up across the world. The Japanese have believed since ancient times that humanity is emotionally connected to everything that exists in the natural world, that we exist in harmony with nature, and that *kami* (spirits) dwell within everything in nature. We hold the animistic view that nature and humanity are one. This is a natural philosophy that ties into the coexistence of everything in creation, including humanity. It is this wisdom of the Japanese people that cautions us against thinking that we are the lords of creation.

THE GLOBAL SPREAD OF THE "HUMAN COMMUNITY" CONCEPT

This rare revolutionary who seeks the creation of a new world order is expanding beyond small Japan into the wider world in pursuit of his dream of opening a new future for human society. I am proposing to the world's intellectuals that the globally dominant ideology of prioritizing your own country's interests over those of other countries be replaced by the concept of the human community (which prioritizes the benefit of human society as a whole). This doctrine shall eventually become the communal intellectual property of global citizens who live in the Immigration Age of the twenty-second century.

The ultimate goal is to make the Japanese-led concept of the human community into a global universal ideal and lead humanity to eternal world peace. This is, in the truest sense, a philosophy of world peace.

But if I—the old Japanese man who voices this grand, unique philosophy of peace—lacks the strong will and ability to bring it to fruition, this will all just be a pipe dream. I will become the object of global scorn for speaking the wild dream of an earthly paradise. And I know it well. But what is one to do who has made the creation of a Japanese-style immigration policy his life's work?

Before worrying about achieving world peace, I first need to guide Japan along the path to becoming an immigration nation, one filled with the desire for world peace held by the Japanese as the only people to have been attacked with nuclear weapons in wartime. But I do not have the power to bring my ideas to fruition. All I can do is hole myself up in my study, wrack my brains, and continue to frantically write my words of warning, hoping to stir the conscience of the Japanese and the intelligence of the world through the power of the pen.

Fortunately, leading members of the global media like *The Washington Post* and the *Economist* have expressed approval of the immigration nation vision that I have been calling for. Now is truly the opportune time. If Japan steps forward as an immigration nation, it will breathe new life into global immigration policy and serve as a turning point that fundamentally changes the nature of that policy. And that is something that I may, perhaps, be able to make happen.

The work of establishing a framework for permanent world peace is beyond my abilities as the director of an immigration policy institute on an island nation in the East. All I can do is continue to carry the torch of the human community concept until the day I die. I am betting on the chance that in the first half of the twenty-second century, global citizens with immigrant origins will become a great force. And these people of different races, ethnicities, religions, and nationalities throughout the world will stand up as one and aim to create a human community on a global scale. It is in my nature to believe in the power of this philosophy.

It is likely that the curtain will close on my life while I am still voicing my dream of a global human community. It is a task of historic proportions. But even if this unprecedented work breaks down just as it is getting underway, I believe that I can take pride in having had a life in which I devoted much time to considering the future of human society, brought up these issues, and did all in my power to solve them.

THREE

Politician, Bureaucrat, Revolutionary

AN UNPRECEDENTED REVOLUTION FOR AN UNPRECEDENTED NATIONAL CRISIS

Japan is currently in a national crisis as we experience both a falling birthrate and a superaging population. At the time of my retirement as a government official in 2005, I intuitively knew that our country faced an unprecedented demographic crisis that would see our people disappear at this pace from the face of the Earth and that no matter how many half-baked reforms were implemented, the chances for the continuation of the Japanese people were slight. It immediately occurred to me that an unprecedented national crisis calls for an unprecedented revolution. And having made the formulation of immigration policy my life's work, I swore to myself that I would take the initiative in having the Japanese survive this crisis through a once-a-millennium immigration revolution.

I announced the idea of a Japanese revolution in chapter 9 ("A Utopia in 2050") of my book published in Japanese on the occasion of my retirement from the Ministry of Justice's Immigration Bureau entitled *Immigration Battle Diary*. This fantasy portrayed what Japan would be like in 2050 if it greatly changed course, accepted twenty million immigrants, and strove to reach the ideal of a society based on multiethnic coexistence.

But the idea I put forth in the book of admitting twenty million immigrants attracted little attention when it was published. (A *Japan Times* reporter did do a book review, however.[1]) Even though projections by various institutes and agencies made clear to all that the Japanese population would sharply decline from 2005 on, the slow-to-act Japanese intellectual world ignored the vision of an immigration nation as unlikely to be discussed.

Now that discussions over the ten-million immigrant concept have reached their final phase, I will make my true intentions clear. While I portrayed the creation of an ideal immigration nation as a Utopian tale when I first announced it, I did not believe that it was something that should be allowed to remain just a dream. I saw that it would become an urgent national task as Japan entered its period of population decline.

And when I decided in 2005 to take on the challenge of creating a new nation, an immigration nation, I believed that I needed to unveil all the concepts and ideas in my head and stimulate public discussion of them. I knew that it would be necessary to gain as much popular acceptance of them as possible. But at the same time, I knew that it would not be easy to resolve the uneasiness and wariness that the public had toward admitting large numbers of people of other ethnicities into Japan.

Now seventy years old, I recently have given increasing thought to the question of how I should live out my final years. There have been times when I have felt like I was being crushed by the heavy responsibilities I bear. And above all, I have frequently worried about how to cultivate the human resources that will be needed to support the newborn immigration nation.

It goes without saying that a once-in-a-century great undertaking like the creation of an immigration nation will fail if young people of great talent do not rise up as Yoshida Shōin and Sakamoto Ryōma did during the end of the Tokugawa Shogunate in the mid-nineteenth century. Now is the time for the samurai of this generation to appear and carry out a Japanese revolution as the revolutionaries of the Meiji Restoration of 1867 did.

In every era, it is the young who open the doors to new history. The rational way to have the revolution would be for the capable young elite with innovative ideas to play the primary role in the creation of an immigration nation; the elderly man familiar with immigration policy will stay in the back and provide them with support.

My final mission as director the Japan Immigration Policy Institute will be cultivating the human talent that will take on central roles in securing the future of Japan. But this isn't something that I'm overly worried about. Whenever the fate of Japan has been on the line, giants have appeared as if dispatched by Heaven to save it from its crisis.

Despite having said that, there is the possibility that no one will appear in the realm of immigration policy to take over for me once I'm gone. But even if no successor arrives, I leave behind more than thirty volumes of immigration policy theory to serve as a reference for future generations. I am sure that the politicians and administrators who use these works as references shall create the ideal immigration nation, perhaps even better than my vision. Great numbers of people will emerge from the public for whom my ideas resonate. Popular leaders will rise from among them to drive forward the immigration revolution and the Japanese revolution that follows.

DISCOVERING PROBLEMS—PROPOSING POLICY—ENACTING POLICY

Most of the papers and other writings I released while at the Ministry of Justice's Immigration Bureau involved discussing "policy." I found problems related to foreigners in Japan, proposed policies to solve them, and then played a leading role in the revision of the Immigration Control and Refugee Recognition Act (Immigration Control Law) to put those policies into practice. Through the natural course of things, I found myself in the position of being one person tasked with these three heavy responsibilities. How did I end up walking such a difficult path? I was always more fixated on drawing up and enacting policy than most, so at some point I became an expert on policy.

If I were to summarize my career, I would say that it was a fulfilling life for an official largely devoted to the aforementioned three tasks: "finding problems," "proposing policy," and "enacting policy."

There is nothing more dangerous for an immigration control official than discussing immigration policy. Immigration policy is a classic example of something that is at the discretion of the state; deciding it is something that should, by nature, be done by elected officials and not bureaucrats. In the Japan of the 1970s (the time when I became an official), however, immigration issues—particularly that of the *Zainichi* Koreans— were regarded as an absolutely untouchable area of politics and virtually no politicians expressed an interest in immigration policy. That meant that I didn't need to worry about any politicians complaining if I, an administrative official, strayed into the realm of politics and gave my opinion on *Zainichi* Korean policy.

Furthermore, as part of the political culture of Japan at the time, the bureaucrats tended to have more knowledge of policy, and basically politicians deferred to them in practically all fields.

But there was another problem. I needed to be considerate of potential criticism or pushback from within the bureaucracy. When I made policy proposals that went against the established policy of the ministry, I did so knowing that it might mean my being demoted or dismissed. Fortunately, the problems I raised and the policies I proposed were recognized as being correct by my superiors. Most of my immigration policy proposals were enacted through legislation and I had the good fortune of being able to play a central role in the revision of the Immigration Control Law.

While at the ministry, a head of the bureau I was working in once commented to me that "You were able to get a policy you proposed enacted. Your life here must be a happy one." And when I retired in 2005, the Public Prosecutor General gave me the excessive praise that "Your history is the history of immigration control."

How should I interpret these assessments of my work? In order to realize the policies that I had proposed in the Sakanaka Essay (of 1975) I had taken on things that no one wanted to touch, like providing the *Zainichi* Koreans with stable legal status. I felt that those efforts had been recognized. I felt that I had been truly blessed as an official. I had good superiors, worked there at a good time, and have been able to remain faithful to my word in my life.

After retirement, I moved my base of operations to the JIPI and threw myself into researching the best immigration policy for a society with a declining population. I also put a lot of my effort into writing on immigration policy and released a number of books such as *Nihongata Imin Kokka e no Michi*.[2]

But even so, these books have achieved no real popularity in Japan. In fact, I am still subjected to fierce criticism from some of those usually on the far right opposed to immigration. But my theory of immigration policy is held in high regard among intellectuals and journalists overseas.

Recently, I've frequently been asked "how did a closed society like Japan produce an enlightened person like you?" by foreign intellectuals. The following is my answer for the time being:

> I think that if I, someone born with only an average level of talent, have accomplished any great deeds, it has been due to the blessings of Providence. The only gifts I have been blessed with are the ability to find problems, the insight to find solutions, and the sixth sense that plays a deciding role in critical moments. I have been given the ability to formulate a philosophy of world peace like the human community concept.

I am now growing old and enjoying a life filled with dreams. My routine work has become spreading the inspirations that come to me through the JIPI website and then gathering them into books. And the project of publishing a compilation of my writings on immigration policy in English is making progress. This book may be well received overseas.

Through my efforts, I want to unify the public on my longed-for national commitment to immigration. I do not want to wait for luck; I am determined to complete my life's work by exerting my abilities to the fullest.

I don't want the completion of my theory for an immigration nation to be where I quit. I still have many things to do, like the establishment of legal institutions for immigration. Nothing would make me happier than being able to conclude my life's work through legislation on immigration.

If I could ask for more, it would be to tour the country after the immigration nation has been born, speaking about its founding spirit so that the ideals behind the Japanese-style immigration society are widely understood by the public.

Having reached my final years, I've drawn the conclusion that relying upon divine assistance is not the way to accomplish great matters of state. I also feel, strongly, that I've already received enough good fortune. I used up all of my good luck during the forty-nine years of my working life. I don't care about myself as I don't have that much time left, but I hope that large amounts of heavenly fortune descend upon the newly born immigration nation.

MARKING THE END OF THE *HEISEI* ERA WITH THE DECLARATION OF AN IMMIGRATION NATION

The questions of how to achieve a sustainable social welfare system and revitalize dying rural areas have become urgent issues of political discussion. And yet that has oddly not happened for immigration policy, the most effective way of addressing the issue of demographic collapse that lies at the root of these problems. Even though the population crisis is becoming more serious and the time has come for an active discussion of immigration policy, the various and constantly re-morphing political parties make no campaign pledges about it. Opening the country to immigrants will determine the future of Japan, but the government will not take it to the people. Instead, politicians make token gestures such as calling loudly for more foreign workers to be admitted as an emergency countermeasure to the labor shortage in rural areas, but this is not a practical nor sustainable solution.

The desirability of future immigration is a matter of serious debate in the world's major immigration nations such as America, Britain, France, and Germany, where the question divides popular opinion. But here, there isn't even any discussion in the Diet of whether Japan should admit immigrants or not. The government takes advantage of this fact and adheres to the "closed-off policy of a dying nation," refusing to adopt pro-immigration policies. The current state of national politics and this irresponsible failure to discuss immigration fill me with a sense of crisis and I have begun to think like a radical revolutionary. I now believe that the only possible course of action is for those people concerned about the nation's future to join together and push for the replacement of all politicians who are uninterested in carrying out their responsibilities to the nation.

The fate of Japan depends on it opening to immigration, yet Japan's politicians—regardless of party—are avoiding the issue. They remain bystanders unwilling to even discuss the topic with their head in the sand. I wonder if they have reached some sort of tacit understanding to avoid discussion of immigration policy because it won't win them votes. Speaking as an expert who has been watching the state of immigration policy for the last fourteen years (and forty years as a government bureaucrat), it seems that not taking up the issue of opening the country to immigration is the one point that the entire political class is in agreement on.

Isn't actively working to save the country from its demographic crisis a fundamental responsibility of our politicians? If they're not going to do it, then who will? There were times in the past when the question of whether or not to open the country to immigration could be expected to lead to fierce debate in the Diet. But not now. I've completely given up on waiting for our politicians to act. I've lost hope in the current generation who only show concern in immediate party interests and take for granted their lack of interest in immigration policy (despite it being something that will determine the future of our country).

It goes without saying that rebuilding Japan into an immigration nation is a task entrusted to the ruling authority of the prime minister. And should we manage to secure a popular majority in favor of accepting immigrants and the prime minister foolishly pushes off the decision to do so, it will go down in Japanese political history as an archetypical example of bad governance. And fifty years from now, the public will point their fingers at the politicians of today and say, "they abandoned their responsibilities to the future public and plunged the nation into despair." This is the ultimate dishonor for officials charged with the governance of a nation.

But an opportunity has come for Japan's politicians to regain their honor. Namely, the abdication of the Emperor, who is revered by not only the Japanese people but by the people of the world as well.

I, Sakanaka Hidenori, director of the JIPI, would like to make a humble request of our politicians from the bottom of my heart: please let the end of the reign of Emperor Akihito, a man interested in the happiness of all the people of the world without regard to their race, religion, ethnicity, or nationality, be marked by a declaration that Japan will become an immigration nation.

When President of Vietnam Tran Dai Quang and his wife visited Japan as state guests on May 30, 2018, His Majesty reportedly asked him, "do the Vietnamese people in Japan live in happiness here?"[3] And then at the press conference held for his birthday on December 20 of that same year, His Majesty made the statement on accepting foreigners that will shine brightly within Japanese history: "I hope that we can all welcome those who come from other countries to work warmly as members of society."

I await the arrival of a prime minister with the wisdom to take the lead in immigration policy of Japan and of the world and through which he/she simultaneously resolves Japan's demographic crisis and the world's humanitarian crisis. Having received the calling of devising an immigration nation, I will accept the responsibility for Japan's future. I want both the public and our politicians to stand on the starting line of an immigration revolution that will clearly surpass the Meiji Restoration in terms of opening the nation up to talented people.

I have a deep attachment to the *Heisei* era, the time during which I continually wrote on immigration policy in order to open a breakthrough leading to the immigration nation. I strongly hope that the phrase "the *Heisei* declaration of an immigration nation" finds its place in the annals of Japanese history. As Japan moves into the *Reiwa* era, perhaps there will be an even bigger *Reiwa* declaration too.

POLITICIANS AND THE REVOLUTIONARY

Isn't it generally acknowledged that—no matter the time or place—politicians and revolutionaries hold irreconcilable positions? But in that case, what kind of relationship exists between me—champion of the immigration revolution—and the politicians entrusted with governing Japan?

In late 2014, an esteemed friend who happens to be a British journalist posed a question to me: "Given your advocacy for a revolutionary immigration nation, don't you receive any negative pressure from the Prime Minister's Office?" I answered that "while it doesn't change the fact that I'm operating all on my own, I've received absolutely no criticism of the Sakanaka Plan from them, nor have they applied any pressure." Sometimes, being ignored is worse than being criticized. At least with the latter, you know that you're having an effect.

I don't know whether it's because they want to maintain a respectful distance from the revolutionary preaching radical immigration policy or are keeping an eye on public opinion trends as they allow a private citizen to do work that is meant for politicians, or if it's out of consideration for my past accomplishments as a public servant. But despite sticking my neck into the middle of politics, I'm left to do as I please. I took advantage of the political vacuum caused by politicians wanting to keep their distance from immigration policy and developed the theory for an immigration policy that is both fair and just. That proved fortunate. While subjected to global scrutiny, I was able to work out a vision for the immigration nation that is of the highest standard in the world.

The formulation of immigration policy was my area of expertise and I worked completely unrestricted to create a vision of the ideal immigration society. Over the years, I have published my work on my theory of the immigration nation on an almost yearly basis as I incorporated new knowledge.

Every time I release a new book, I send complimentary copies to the political leadership. I believe that the logic holding my idea of a Japanese-style immigration society together grows stronger and my argument more persuasive every year. And I have recently had reason to believe that the Prime Minister's Office has been watching the development of my theory and the public's response.

In June 2015, I was invited by central government figures to give a lecture for the principal leaders of the Cabinet Secretariat, both bureaucrats and politicians. Twenty elite officials listed to my talk, "The Path to a Japanese-style Immigration Nation." I was told that my concept was a "good idea" and the younger officials applauded when I finished. As I departed, I told them that they would be the ones to create a new Japan if they followed my path.

Given the importance of speaking on immigration policy for high government officials, I attended the lecture with a well-polished draft. I later heard that the essay I distributed at the lecture had a major impact in political and bureaucratic circles.

Incidentally, when I asked the audience if they had questions, the politician (then Deputy Chief Cabinet Secretary and now Minister of State for Economic and Fiscal Policy Nishimura Yasutoshi) who had invited me to speak, asked, "What does the public think about your ideas on immigration policy?" I answered that "judging from recent circumstances, such as the *Asahi Shimbun* public opinion poll from April of this year which showed support for immigration significantly overtaking opposition and the rapidly increasing number of people accessing my opinion pieces on the JIPI homepage, my perception is that public opinion shows an increasing tendency toward approval of immigration, especially among younger Japanese."

As I answered, it occurred to me that both the Prime Minister's Office and the revolutionary had anticipated each other's moves. While we have differing views on whether or not to adopt pro-immigration policies, we're in agreement on the national objective of saving Japan from its demographic crisis by opening the country and having a target of maintaining one hundred million people as Japan's population in the middle of the century (of which ten million would be immigrants).

And if that perception is correct, then I am not a "destructive revolutionary" calling for the tearing down of state systems but rather a "peaceful revolutionary" promoting the preservation of law and order. I have been following my grand dream and devising my concept of the immigration nation in the hopes of preserving the continuation of Japan with the tacit approval of the government leadership.

I received big news in October 2018 that rewarded my many years of effort. The Cabinet Secretariat has decided to elevate the Ministry of Justice Immigration Bureau (my former employer) and reorganize it as the Immigration and Residency Management Agency (*Shutsunyūkoku Zairyū Kanrichō*). The ministry's duties have been greatly expanded and now include creating a society that coexists with foreigners. I hope that my successors at the bureau are enthusiastic about this and devote themselves to their new duties. I'll be supporting them from the shadows.

I see this as a first step toward a future "Ministry of Immigration." Or perhaps this should be understood as a *de facto* acceptance of the Sakanaka Plan by the government leadership. Either way, there can be no question that the government has made a historic first step toward a national commitment to immigration.

The following is the monologue of a revolutionary. As it is the sole prerogative of the prime minister to dissolve the House of Representatives, readers should feel free to pay this no heed. I write the following so that it will remain behind as historical testimony. For many years, I have appealed for the necessity of a national discussion of whether to open Japan up to immigration. The proper nature of a democratic state is for the government to make decisions on great matters of state after securing the approval of a majority of the public, repeatedly discussing it with them until their acceptance is received.

> When carrying out a revolution that rivals the Meiji Restoration in its scope, it is necessary to determine the views of the people and whether they agree or disagree with it. If Japan transforms into an immigration nation solely through decisions made by the government rather than through democratic procedures, the legitimacy of this change will be questioned. And it will cause lasting problems for the nation. But if it is done with the people's blessing—if the government holds exhaustive public discussions and the people decide that they are prepared to sincerely become a society open to immigration—then the future of the Japanese immigration nation will be a bright one.

THE DIET MEMBERS' LEAGUE FOR PROMOTING EXCHANGES OF FOREIGN HUMAN RESOURCES

In February 2008, I was asked to be a lecturer at the first study session held by the Diet Members' League for Promoting Exchanges of Foreign Human Resources, a group of about eighty LDP Diet members (*Gaikoku Jinzai Koryū Suishin Giin Renmei*, chaired by Nakagawa Hidenao) who believed that with Japan's population declining, its future relied upon the admission of talented foreigners into the country. I prepared a speech designed to communicate my thoughts on immigration policy to these politicians and titled it, "The Time Has Come for a Long-Term National Plan: On the Founding of the Diet Members' League for Promoting Exchanges of Foreign Human Resources." At the conclusion of this speech I made the following appeal: "I cannot help but hope that this new caucus of Diet members—formed by politicians giving serious consideration to the nation's future—shall play the role of a locomotive for the 'Japan as an immigration nation' project as we approach the time for creating a long-term national plan."

I also gave a lecture at the group's second meeting in March that year. I wrote a speech entitled "Time to Change Course and Accept Immigrants" in which I proposed a "human resource-cultivating system for accepting immigrants," that would be unique to Japan. In my speech, I emphasized that the reason I spoke of "immigrants" rather than "foreign workers" was because I believed that "the only proper foreigners' policy for a state whose citizens are disappearing is an immigration policy that admits foreigners as a way of securing future citizens."

The Diet members in attendance raised many questions regarding my immigration proposal, but no one voiced opposition to a policy for immigration. In fact, there was a conspicuous number who wanted even more foreign human resources to be admitted. I felt that my pet theory of a Japanese-style immigration society had received a decidedly positive response.

The group held seven study sessions in total and collected and published the findings of this earnest discussion in June that year (2008) under the title "A Proposal for a Japanese-style Immigration Policy" with the goal of revitalizing Japan through a national commitment to immigration. This report was then incorporated into the LDP National Strategy Headquarters' "Path to a Japanese-style Immigration Nation" project team. Ultimately another report entitled "A Country Open to Human Resources! The Path to a Japanese-style Immigration Nation" was submitted to Prime Minister Fukuda Yasuo. I heard that Prime Minister Fukuda told the leaders of the Diet members' group that he wanted to study it when he received it. And thus, comprehensive immigration policy leapt onto the stage of government for the first time in the history of Japanese policy toward foreigners. (Unfortunately, Fukuda stepped down as prime minister in September that year.)

Immigration policy is one of the highest-level national policies that determine what Japan as a country looks like. Formulating immigration policy is a classic example of the exercise of national sovereignty and therefore something that politicians should take the initiative on. By a trick of fate, however, it was I—the former director of the Tokyo Regional Immigration Bureau who has devoted himself to immigration policy— who wrote the initial draft of "A Proposal for a Japanese-style Immigration Policy." I did so in a last-ditch attempt to save my homeland from the threat of demographic collapse. Feeling elated at having been chosen for the task by these politicians with foresight and wisdom, I threw myself into the task, providing an outline of the Japanese-style immigration nation. I specified the number of immigrants that should be accepted, writing that "it would be appropriate for ten percent of the Japanese population to be made up of immigrants fifty years from now."

Of course, it is up to the politicians how this paper is to be used. Fortunately, through a courageous decision by the aforementioned Nakagawa and Nakamura Hirohiko—both Diet members who understood radical immigration policy—the report that I wrote was placed on the LDP's agenda. Eleven years ago, the world of Japanese politics included politicians who possessed great foresight and determination. I have no doubt that the historians of the future will feature this Diet members' group's report in any history of Japanese immigration policy. It will be seen as a historic achievement that helped lead the way to Japan becoming an immigration nation.

The June 19, 2008, issue of the *Japan Times* included an article on the "proposal for a Japanese-style immigration policy" by the aforementioned group of LDP Diet members which featured the views of intellectuals both in support and opposed to it.[4] Toward the conclusion of the article, the reporter introduced me—the writer of this radical immigration policy's initial draft—in the following way: "Sakanaka is ready to face such criticism just as all revolutionaries have in the past. His proposals would shake up Japan from the inside and it would be a historical moment if they all became law, he said. 'The Meiji Restoration was the first stage in opening up the country to foreigners,' he said. 'Now we are entering the second stage.'"

Since then I have diligently pursued the ideal form of the immigration nation and written many books directly connected to the idea of building a new Japan. These have included *The Road to a Japanese-style Immigration Nation* and *Vision of a Japanese Immigration Nation*, both previously mentioned.

As seen above, the coordination between the LDP Diet members' group and me resulted in an historic result that will remain as our joint intellectual property. And now in the present (late-2019), we have entered the final stage of this historical undertaking that will determine the fate of Japan. It may well be that this relationship of trust between us will play a decisive role when it comes to politicians making their decision on a national commitment to immigration.

THE UNCOMPROMISING BUREAUCRAT BECOMES A REVOLUTIONARY

In October 2012, I, the former director general of the Tokyo Regional Immigration Bureau and a man considered by both himself and others to be a typical conservative, became a revolutionary.

In a *Japan Times* article, an American journalist living in Japan introduced me as the "face of change" and described me as a revolutionary.[5] Having such a heavy burden suddenly thrust upon me made me want to curl up. I knew that once I had been labeled a revolutionary, there was no going back.

So, what was it that had caused a former national public official, especially one who had previously been called an "uncompromising bureaucrat," to be called a revolutionary? Perhaps it was the hands of fate that—by aligning my life's work of immigration policy with an era of population crisis that demands the world's best human resources regardless of ethnicity and nationality—made me the theoretical leader of the creation of the immigration nation.

***

I am not, by nature, a professional revolutionary. I am nothing more than a radical thinker who advances an innovative vision of an immigration nation as a private citizen belonging to the JIPI.

The following is a broad outline of my life, the life of a Japanese man branded later as a revolutionary. In my final years as a senior official, I devoted myself to the development of my basic theory for the immigration nation. In 2005—my last year as a bureaucrat—the ambition to create a theory for the immigration nation that would be the best in the world sparked inside me. Since leaving the civil service, I have released several books on immigration policy as the director of a private immigration policy think tank. I have written more than eighteen volumes over the past fourteen years.

It was only after writing "On the Future Nature of Immigration Administration," the essay that caused a major sensation in 1975, that I became a pioneer of immigration policy research. Since then, I have striven to uncover the ideal immigration nation.

Let's return to 2012, when *The Japan Times'* Michael Hoffman called me a revolutionary. At the time, I felt as if I had received a divine command. Having been named the "standard-bearer of the immigration revolution," I became determined to carry out the greatest revolution in Japanese history.

As becomes immediately evident when perusing the pages of history, those called "revolutionaries" generally come to untimely ends and are regarded as heretics in their own time. I, too, literally risk death (from "rightists") by taking on the untouchable issue of a national commitment to immigration. While I would never have dreamed that my revolutionary immigration nation concept would make it into the limelight during my lifetime, immigration policy was placed on the political agenda of the Diet in October 2018 to discuss the bill to boost the number of foreign workers, which was eventually passed in December that year and went into effect on April 1, 2019.

Perhaps, in the peaceful world of the twenty-first century, a revolutionary can achieve a great objective and still die peacefully at home. I'm a fortunate revolutionary in that my accomplishments have largely been attributed to destiny and are only partly due to efforts on my part.

***

I'm surprised to have received so many nicknames over the forty-nine years of my professional life. First, my 1975 essay, "On the Future Nature of Immigration Administration," became known as the "Sakanaka Essay." I have been called the "savior of Japan" and the "demon, Sakana-ka," introduced to readers as "Mr. Immigration," been described on the jacket of my 2005 book *Immigration Battle Diary* as an "uncompromising bureaucrat," and was recently introduced as a "portrait of modernity" in a recent issue of a weekly magazine, *AERA* (December 17, 2018), published by the left-leaning Asahi Shimbun Company.

I've also received numerous nicknames from foreign journalists. I was introduced as "an expert on immigration policy" in a January 2009 *Washington Post* article in which I advocated a human resources-cultivating immigration policy. When I gave the speech "Vision of Immigration Nation Japan" at the Foreign Correspondents' Club of Japan in May 2014, the club described me as "Japan's 'Mr. Immigration'." And in 2016 *The Economist* (August 20, 2016) introduced my concept of an immigration revolution to the world's intellectuals, saying that "Hidenori Sakanaka, a former immigration chief who now heads the Japan Immigration Policy Institute, a think tank, reckons Japan needs ten million migrants in the next fifty years."[6]

My vision for an immigration nation has attracted the following "brief reactions" from a diverse group:

- "An historic change away from a millennium-long closing of the country to immigration" (Noda Kazuo, a historian of Japanese civilization)
- "A more difficult task than constitutional revision" (Tateishi Haruyasu, a member of the Tokyo Metropolitan Assembly)
- "A grand Utopian plan" (Kiyotake Hideyoshi, a reporter for a national newspaper, the *Yomiuri Shimbun*)
- "Thoughts born from the traditional spiritual culture of Japan and its respect for harmony" (an authority on Japanese Buddhism, the Reverend Wakaomi Takashi)
- "An emissary of peace leading to an eternal stable order for human society" (a Pakistani in Japan, introduced earlier—Mr. Syed Tahir)
- "The idea of the human community marks a new epoch in human history" (a *Zainichi* Korean, Seo Won Chul, of the Korean Residents Union in Japan)

With that kind of assessment of my theory circulating among intellectuals within Japan and overseas, I am destined to finish my life as a revolutionary who fundamentally changes the nature of Japanese and human society.

I have been labeled with various adjectives. This was initially due to stories from my time as an uncompromising bureaucrat, but they later came from my accomplishment of repeatedly producing ground-breaking works on immigration policy. This multi-faceted image is my sole weapon as I attempt to shift popular opinion both within and outside of

Japan all by myself. And I believe that it does serve me well as I try to guide Japan toward becoming an immigration nation.

To give one example, I believe that it is because the ten-million immigrant concept is an immigration policy devised by the man that was once known as the "heretic of Kasumigaseki," the center of the bureaucracy in Tokyo, that high officials there have voiced their support for it. The names given to me serve as blunt evaluations of my character. During my time at the Ministry of Justice, I was known as "an official who was as good as his word." And I am now referred to as a "legendary bureaucrat" among official circles and former colleagues.

STEPPING FORWARD WITH A GRAND UNDERTAKING TO CHANGE THE REALM ALL BY MYSELF

In the aforementioned novel, *Ryōma ga Yuku*, Shiba has Sakamoto Ryōma says the following words to his comrades following the Kinmon Incident of 1864 (an attempted rebellion against the Tokugawa shogunate): "The coming times will be ones where daring, reckless bravery will not be enough. You will need the intelligence and grit to change the realm all by yourself."

As a national debate raged from the end of the Edo period to the beginning of the *Meiji* era (1868-1912) over whether or not to open Japan to the world, great heroes appeared who concerned themselves with the state of the nation and the world. Ryōma was not alone: there was Katsu Kaishū, who was knowledgeable about foreign affairs; Ii Naosuke, who made the decision to open the country; Yoshida Shōin, who attempted to smuggle himself to America aboard the "black ships" of Commodore Mathew C. Perry; and Saigō Takamori, who decided to capture Edo Castle without bloodshed.

As eloquently told in the history books of all ages and nations, exceptional people appear during times of national crisis. And yet, even though we face the looming threat of the collapse of our social systems, our politicians are fighting no rhetorical battle over whether or not to open the country to immigration. Why have no people of great talent and foresight appeared? Will no one be willing to step up and risk their life to bring down this ridiculous system closing off our country? Have the 126 million Japanese facing an unprecedented national crisis decided to just wave the white flag and give up? Well, here stands one person willing to say that "we cannot give up. There has to be something we can do if we think hard enough."

As the majority of our current politicians, officials, and intellectuals are determined to remain silent in the face of our nation's life-or-death crisis, I call upon the people to rise up and demand that we "embark upon an immigration revolution to deal with the population crisis." As I am forced to take on this fight initially on my own, I will need "the intelligence and grit to change the realm."

I am well aware of that fact. But I am also painfully conscious of the fact that I have neither the power nor the talent to change the country. Right now, I am a private researcher who thinks of nothing but creating immigration policy. But can a former public servant well-versed in all aspects of the Immigration Control Law and immigration policy use his experience to create a popular consensus on a national commitment to immigration? How far will my title and my renown in the field of immigration policy research get me in the real world? And yet, I have the self-confidence to think, "If I don't do it, then who will?"

The worries are endless. But I can't fixate on my personal feelings as the footsteps of demographic collapse can be heard approaching. The irreplaceable Japanese people will disappear from the face of the Earth unless this generation produces a sage with a brilliant plan to enable us to survive this crisis. I do not speak like a "commercial" intellectual whose statements change to fit popular trends. During my time as a public servant, I was known for being absolutely true to my word and I took stands on difficult immigration issues.

There's something I realized during my time working in immigration amidst all the criticism and abuse—taking on issues that everyone else is afraid to touch actual gives you a high chance of success. I never lost a battle during my career. Bringing my plan to create the world's premier immigration nation to fruition might seem impossible, but I believe that I do have some chance of success.

The time is ripe. Heaven's will has become known. My back is against the wall, but I am setting forth on a great undertaking that will change the realm. I'm taking the chance that this reckless bravery will resonate with those among the 126 million Japanese who will rise and join me in great numbers.

THE BEGINNING OF A YOUTH-LED HISTORICAL SAGA

I have a goal that will cheer up the younger generation of Japanese for whom the time of demographic collapse is steadily approaching. It's a rebuilding of the nation that is perfect for those awaiting a cruel fate, one in which the youth of Japan and the world, joined by their love of Japanese culture, work together to build a Japanese-style immigration nation.

The young generation upon whom the future of Japan rests will join with immigrants and take on the challenge of creating the world's foremost society based on the human community. Could any other objective galvanize youthful ambition more?

It is also a path along which the youth of Japan and the world will search for a new way to live. If these two groups address each other seriously—the Japanese with their great spirit of tolerance and the immigrants with their love of Japan and the Japanese—then they will join together and establish a relationship of peace, friendship, and coexistence.

Recently the number of junior high school, high school, and university students who visit me has noticeably increased. Young journalists and national civil servants in their twenties also visit to study immigration policy with me. They've already read my opinion pieces and books available on the JIPI homepage and understand the essence of the Japanese-style immigration nation concept. "We will have no tomorrow unless we gather the strength of Japan's youth and create a society based on the human community." "That it is a difficult task is what makes it worth taking on." "I agree with the proposal for a Japanese-style immigration policy. I will carry on your aspirations."

I believe that we will soon be able to fulfill the dream of Japan's youth. According to an *Asahi Shimbun* poll in April 2015, fifty-one percent of respondents support immigration. Politicians concerned about the disappearance of rural communities have made clear that they too support an immigration policy. Debate over whether to adopt immigration policy finally began in the Diet in October 2018. The thousand-year-old taboo on opening the country to immigration has been broken.

I have spent my life working toward the creation of an immigration nation. The last task left to me is encouraging the government to make a national commitment to immigration.

I want the completion of this work to be accomplished with the cooperation of the public. In particular, I would like to tap the strength of the youth who will carry Japan into the future. With public opinion having reached the point that a majority of the public (especially younger people) approve of accepting immigrants, I, this pioneer of the immigration revolution, am optimistic that we can establish an immigration nation without the frictions and tragedies that have affected other nations in recent years.

If Japan makes the transition to becoming a new state without the active participation of the public in the rebuilding—simply bowing to foreign pressure or other concerns, for example—it will leave behind regrets for both the current and future generations of Japanese. It would mean that the public never experiences the spiritual thrill, nor receives the honor of taking part in this historical undertaking. The energy necessary for creating a new nation will not arise.

It is the public who should have the principal role in this once-a-millennium grand work of creating an immigration nation, especially those in their teens and twenties who will have to live in the era of population decline. I want there to be exhaustive discussion of whether or not to adopt the immigration policy necessary for correcting our demographic order. I want all of the young people to participate in the creation of an ideal immigration society. I want us to march forward toward an ultimate objective of forming a society based on the human community. The youth of Japan who take on this task of historic significance for all of humanity shall develop into global citizens with a love of humanity and a spirit of compassion toward the immigrants who they live alongside.

Their passion will break through the political world's passivity on immigration policy and reshape the country into an ideal immigration nation. We will accept immigrants with an open mind toward all of humanity, correcting the inclination to face inward that developed as the country was closed off. And from there the grand youth-led historical drama will begin.

It is no overstatement to say that a spirit of tolerance is spreading among the youth of Japan that is equal to that of any other country in the world. This can be seen in the August 26, 2015, *Yomiuri Shimbun* poll in which fifty percent of people in their twenties agreed with the idea of adopting a pro-immigration policy.[7] While in recent times there has been some reporting of racist and anti-immigrant sentiment rising among the youth of the West, there's no question that those in Japan will treat immigrants without discrimination as fellow human beings due to their healthy view of foreigners.

POLITICIANS AND BUREAUCRATS

While discussion of the immigration nation is becoming more vibrant, most politicians resist immigration policy being placed on the political agenda. Whether a member of the government or the opposition, they avoid any discussion in the Diet over the desirability of opening the country to immigration, even though it is the most important political matter facing Japan. Popular opinion is increasingly supportive of opening the country to immigration (especially among those in their twenties), yet you won't find a political party that attempts to capture the youth vote by including "making Japan a nation open to global human resources" in their platform.

Not a single politician is willing to stake their political future on immigration policy even though it is an inherent aspect of national sovereignty. I've never met one with their own ideas for a long-term national plan for immigration. There's no sign of any politicians with the backbone to take up the challenge of remaking Japan into an immigration nation, despite it being a task that will shine in the annals of our history.

It is the single greatest issue determining the future of our nation. So why is it that now that the time has come to debate immigration policy — an issue that our national survival depends upon — the politicians of Japan are loathe to touch it?

Having discussed this with those few politicians with an understanding of immigration policy, my impression is that most are extremely frightened of being targeted by the far right's xenophobia. It seems that they are suffering from the delusion that these groups have the ability to mobilize voters or exert some kind of covert influence. But even if this idea—that sticking their necks out on policies detested by the far right is a bad idea—is widespread among Japanese politicians, the future of Japan can only be described as desperate. And proper governance cannot be expected of politicians who cower before the far-right threat.

With popular opinion strongly shifting toward support of immigration, it is now time for the Japanese political sphere to recover its honor. I want all politicians, regardless of party or faction, to rise up, make a national commitment to immigration, and sever the far right's influence—no matter how real or imagined—over politics. That will correct the distorted state of Japanese politics.

The following is the story of something that happened during the formulation of the long-term plan for the immigration nation, something that could be called a silver lining. It is the mysterious tale of how a happy ending was reached for our people and nation despite extremely half-hearted and irresponsible governance on immigration (contrary to its great national importance) and the absence of even a single politician with a backbone and how the professional on immigration policy research—a man who had dealt directly with politicians in the past and been widely known as an "uncompromising bureaucrat"—wrote steadily, taking the place of the politicians who had forsaken the performance of their duties, and established a monumental theory of immigration policy while they looked on blankly.

How was I able to draw up my grand design for an immigration nation that would rewrite the history of Japan and the world? I believe it was because I obeyed the words of a wise man from long ago—"If you see what is right but fail to act on it, you lack courage"—and chose to devote myself to the work that I had left undone as a national public official from my position of freedom as a private citizen.

Research on immigration proceeded at a snail's pace but perseverance is power. Allow me to give an example. The effect of posting approximately two thousand policy pieces online has been massive: the public's views on immigration have changed drastically from zero support for immigration fourteen years ago to a majority supporting it today.

The strait-laced national public official who applied the law impartially has undergone an unforeseen transformation into a "revolutionary" (according to the *Japan Times*). But thinking about things calmly, it is likely that due to my knowledge of immigration law and policy, I was the only Japanese who could be entrusted with the great mission of saving this country from the demographic crisis it finds itself in.

Looking back on my time as a public servant, while I worked stead-fastly to find the ideal immigration society, I wasn't aided by any special talent and didn't exert any unusual amount of effort as I did so. At most, I was like a wolf that had caught a scent. I sank my teeth into a problem that no one else would approach out of fear and charged ahead at full speed toward my objective like a wild boar, known for its straight charge.

My animal instincts kicked in. Having encountered the historic mo-ment that would determine the future of Japan, I decided to entrust my-self to fate. Looking back now, I believe that there are mysterious encoun-ters in life that are beyond human understanding, turning points where streams change into mighty rivers. For me, that encounter came in the spring of 2005 when I retired as a civil servant. I realize now that I stood at a crossroads when I decided to wager the rest of my life on the creation of an immigration nation. In August of that year I founded the Foreigners Policy Institute (*Gaikokujin Seisaku Kenkyūsho*), a private immigration poli-cy think tank (and the predecessor of JIPI). But establishing this base of operations and devoting myself to writing on immigration policy would, before I knew it, make me a revolutionary who would not be constrained by bureaucratic norms.

Having had the honor of serving in government, I knew well that if the bureaucracy became a center of resistance against the immigration revolution, then my concept of the immigration nation would never see the light of day. In the summer of 2015 when I spoke at the Cabinet Office, I met with leading figures of Kasumigaseki and spoke frankly with them about the future of immigration policy. They told me that they agreed with my "concept of a Japanese-style immigration nation" and that "it's the way that leads to the revitalization of Japan."

I realized that my immigration policy had won the hearts of high officials in Kasumigaseki. It seems likely that my accomplishments while working on immigration issues as an official in the Ministry of Justice played a role in their appraisal of the Sakanaka immigration nation con-cept.

The economic officials of the Cabinet Office have also made their sup-port for the concept clear. During my time as an official, I was known as "the heretic of Kasumigaseki" and other officials worried about the coun-try's future gathered around me. I believe that patriots who share my sense of crisis about Japan's future—that it will only continue to deteri-orate due to population decline—will emerge from the bureaucracy and carry on my dream. And with the support of the patriotic officials of Kasumigaseki behind it, I believe there is no need to be concerned about the future of an immigration nation Japan.

What is my state of mind now, in the spring of 2019? I believe that there's a chance that my passion as the leader of the immigration revolu-tion will move the hearts of the public and our politicians and that my dream of creating an immigration nation in the first year of the new imperial era will be realized.

THE GOVERNMENT'S APPROVAL OF THE SAKANAKA PLAN

At the Ministry of Justice, I took the lead in the dangerous job of plucking chestnuts out of the fire. At the time I was appointed to the Immigration Bureau in 1970, I would never in my wildest dreams have imagined that I would ultimately end up engaged in a desperate struggle with that most difficult of issues: immigration.

But in the essay that I wrote in 1975, five years after joining the justice ministry, I brought up problems that existed in areas that were being left untouched such as issues related to the *Zainichi* Koreans, the North Korean returnees, refugees, and immigrants. Looking back now, that was quite the starting point. And ever since then, devising immigration policy has remained a field of one. I have steadily walked alone through the world of immigration policy, one step at a time, usually more, remaining focused on my goal.

After retiring from the ministry, I founded the JIPI and committed myself to my desire to create the world's leading theory of the immigration nation. That brings us to 2019, a time when the global situation over immigration policy is in turmoil. As the forces of anti-immigrant sentiment have surfaced in the developed immigration nations of the world—most notably America, that symbol of tolerance for immigration—I am proposing the philosophy of the human community as a new model for the immigration nation. That idea has been spreading among the intellectuals of the world thanks to *Japan as a Nation for Immigrants: A Proposal for a Global Community of Humankind* (Tōkyō: JIPI, 2015), an English-language booklet. I hope to apply the brakes through this and stop the world's immigration policies from making their reckless turn in an anti-humanitarian direction.

Let's move to a different topic. I'd like to now provide a bit of an introduction to the ecology of the bureaucrats of Kasumigaseki, a group to which I used to belong. You might find it enjoyable for the "heretic of Kasumigaseki" to reveal the true faces of these bureaucrats who rarely speak their true thoughts.

My perception is that ministries like the justice ministry are generally not fertile ground for active support of the ten-million immigrant concept as the sentiment that "it is dangerous for the bureaucracy to enter the domain of politic" pervades when it comes to immigration. And yet, there aren't many officials passionate enough about the issue to voice opposition or argue against it, either. It was an immigration policy that breached all conventions and would never have come from the world of the bureaucracy (which generally does not permit free-thinking). But there was no criticism of it from the ministries. Possibly this was because my fame as "Mr. Immigration" and an "uncompromising bureaucrat" from my time as an official was working in my favor. Or perhaps this grand theoretical framework easily entered the minds of the high government officials because it was proposed by a man who shared the same bureaucratic culture as they and was the leading authority on immigration law, having written a clause-by-clause explanation of the Immigration Control Law.

Since leaving the justice ministry, I continue to be proud to have been a public servant. It is possible that my "samurai spirit" has aroused the sympathy of the bureaucrats as I have worked hard to clarify my proposition to enable the nation of Japan to endure. Or it may be that the government's high-level officials were put at ease once it became clear that my grand concept had aroused no active opposition from the world of politics. Japan's bureaucrats are skilled at "reading the room" when it comes to politics and waiting for the right opportunity to surface with new ideas or approaches.

There are times when major national projects mysteriously manage to reach the level of basic government policy through their own momentum even though the high officials at the center of the government who shape the country had no desire to actively deal with them. That is to say, my idea of a revolutionary immigration nation has been accepted within the government as a new national vision that meets the needs of this time of increasing demographic crisis.

There's evidence that this has happened: high officials in the Cabinet Office called me to give a lecture in June 2015. I was working all alone without any support at that time and was thrilled by the good news of their invitation and gave the lecture of my life under the title "The Path to a Japanese-style Immigration Nation." The high officials listened earnestly as I spoke and then praised my immigration nation concept—built around two pillars, the enactment of an Immigration Law and the conclusion of immigration agreements with other countries—as "a good idea." I realized then that I had successfully driven a wedge into the central government leadership on immigration policy.

The following is my assessment of the status quo as of January 2019. In the "Big-Boned Policy" approved by the Cabinet in June 2018, the government laid out a policy for promoting the acceptance of foreign human resources. While not so named, this was a *de facto* shift to a pro-immigration policy, recognizing permanent residency in Japan for those fulfilling certain criteria and allowing them to be accompanied by their families. My colleagues in Kasumigaseki who had watched me work from the shadows had taken a clear stance in favor of promoting immigration policy. The strongest think tank in Japan, one able to shape politics, had taken my side. The prospect had come to life that a framework supporting an immigration nation would be established through the efforts of all of Japan—including the Ministry of Justice, the Ministry of Finance, and the Ministry of Economy, Trade, and Industry.

SAKANAKA HIDENORI: THE MOST DANGEROUS MAN OF HIS GENERATION?

Japan has not experienced a large-scale influx of people from other countries for more than a thousand years. It is therefore obvious that an immigration revolutionary in Japan would attract criticism. It is also obvious that a flurry of personal attacks would be targeted at me for advocating the ten-million immigrant concept. All the responsibility lies with me for standing at the forefront of the effort for a national commitment to immigration. And if my playing the part of the villain helps move the gears of history, I am happy to do so.

I am an immigration policy professional who has released more than thirty volumes on immigration policy theory and a scholar of the Immigration Control Law (having written a full commentary on the Law). And with my rich administrative experience as "Mr. Immigration," I am prepared to take on any criticism. I am confident that I can stand against anyone in the debate over my calls for an immigration nation.

But even so, why did a wave of criticism sweep toward me? I have done nothing immoral to feel ashamed of. Why do I stand alone without any support? Why must I fight on single-handedly?

Is it not because the Japanese intellectual climate loves to maintain the *status quo*? Heretics who defy the common sense and authority of society are hated, as are revolutionaries who desire to fundamentally change society. Viewed through the eyes of the public, it might be that my unending drive to overturn the anti-immigration system that has existed in Japan for more than a thousand years would make me the most dangerous man of my generation.

Sometimes I think that I must possess an unusually tough spirit. There have been many times when I have escaped critical moments by the skin of my teeth. No matter how powerful the forces of opposition were, no matter what threats were made, I told myself that the path to an immigration society was a necessity of history and continued to wait for the day when most of the public understood.

And my deep commitment to the immigration revolution may have paid off. In any case, the winds of popular opinion have changed direction and Japanese immigration policy made dramatic progress in 2015. The time when I was viewed as a dangerous figure has passed. Public sentiment has rapidly shifted in favor of immigration policy; an aforementioned public opinion poll conducted by the *Asahi Shimbun* in April of 2015 showed that those supporting immigration (fifty-one percent) greatly outnumbered those opposing it (thirty-four percent).[8]

The times have certainly moved in favor of opening the country to immigration. All of the following happened in 2015:

1. The fear of demographic collapse widely permeated the public.
2. The rapid increase in the number of foreign tourists increased the number of Japanese who have had close contact with foreigners.
3. High officials in the Cabinet Secretariat expressed support for the immigration policy created by JIPI Director Sakanaka Hidenori.
4. Japan Business Federation (*Keidanren*) President Sakakibara Sadayuki pressed the government to accept immigrants.
5. Minister of State for Regional Revitalization (and repeated candidate for head of the ruling party, the Liberal Democratic Party) Ishiba Shigeru clearly stated his support of immigration policy.

And in October 2018, debate over immigration policy began in the Diet. My time as a lone wolf has come to an end. From here on I will stand with those who share my hopes and march together with them onward to our goal.

THE RIGHTISTS ARRIVE WITH THEIR TRUCKS

Looking at the current global state of affairs regarding immigration and refugees as of January 2019, xenophobic thinking toward those of different races and religions has grown in strength in Western societies such as America, Britain, France, and Germany, and far right political parties calling for anti-immigrant measures have gained a certain amount of support among the public. However, as the driving force behind Japanese immigration policy, my determination to take on the rightists and ultranationalist groups who rant about immigrants head-on is as firm as a rock. There has been no change in my conviction to stand at the front and prevent the calls for racial purity—the idea that lies at the root of ultranationalist ideology—from infecting society. Even if people cannot always move to and live in the place they most want to, they should be able to marry whomever they want (as long, of course, as the feeling is mutual).

By declaring that I will overthrow the systems that have closed our country off from immigrants (and which have been maintained unchanged for over a thousand years), I have naturally become a mortal enemy of the ultranationalists and those who believe in racial purity. Having experienced personal attacks and jeers aimed at me from all sides over the past forty-four years, I am a resilient man. I am someone who can persevere until the storm of criticism dies down.

In June 2008, the LDP's Diet Members' League for Promoting Exchanges of Foreign Human Resources released its "Proposal for a Japanese-style Immigration Policy" in which I was involved in the writing of its draft. This was a revolutionary concept of an immigration nation built around the idea of "accepting ten million immigrants over fifty years." It was not something that anti-immigration activists and ultranationalists could stand still for. As the theoretical leader of the pro-immigration faction, I was targeted by personal attacks and called "anti-Japanese" and "a traitor."

On July 29 of that year, several dozen members of an anti-immigration group crashed a symposium I was hosting, arriving in the infamous ultranationalist loudspeaker vans. I yielded absolutely no ground to this protest and argued against them head-on. After I finished the farewell address for the symposium, the five hundred attendants who had been listening intently rose up and unanimously gave me thunderous applause. I was deeply moved by the show of support.

And since then as well, whenever there was a gathering related to immigration policy, ten or so ultranationalists would come and chant loudly and try to disrupt the proceedings. Then police officers would come and prevent them from entering, allowing me to finish without further incident.

The degree of abuse leveled at me by xenophobes and hate speech groups and within right-wing internet circles increased after Prime Minister Abe Shinzō stated at a meeting of the House of Representatives' Budget Committee in February 2014 that "it is necessary for the issue of accepting immigrants to be explored from various angles, taking into account public discussions."

Receiving these attacks from anti-immigration forces is my responsibility as someone exercising leadership in the promotion of immigration policy. You cannot carry out the great work of the nation if you fear the ridiculous attacks of the ultranationalists. While I've found that I've lost the will to read pieces full of criticism and abuse toward me this year, my commitment to stand and fight against the ultranationalists with an indomitable spirit is still firm. There has been absolutely no change in my plan to confront the taboo against immigration—one of the strongest in our culture—through the ten-million immigrant concept.

Fortunately, there has been no sign that xenophobia or the ideology of racial purity advocated for by the ultranationalists is spreading among the public. This is only to be expected. That kind of thought is unscientific and contrary to the common sense of the Japanese. Most of the public have a reasonable view of foreigners. While far right political parties holding anti-immigrant positions have gained a certain amount of support in countries like France or Germany, they are viewed as having no place in Japan. I see nothing that indicates that the very small, but vocal, anti-immigrant and racist xenophobic movements here are following in the footsteps of what is happening in the countries of the West. In fact, as mentioned previously, the great majority of the Japanese people are opposed to President Trump's hardline stance on immigration (according to a February 2017 NHK opinion poll). But, unfortunately, it does not mean they have proactively moved to make my concept a reality yet.

***

From my 1975 essay to my immigration nation concept of today, I have experienced countless battles and learned many things. The stronger the far right's criticism of me becomes, the more it proves the validity of my theory. I take it as a positive. I consider challenging the taboo on immigration a path to glory to be walked with my head high.

I got here by steadfastly maintaining a proud independence, facing concentrated attacks alone. My minority views—from my beginnings with the *Zainichi* Korean issue in 1975 to my pursuit of the acceptance of immigrants today—have been hated and targeted by both the far left and the far right. How should I interpret this harsh life of being subjected to a one-two punch from both the far left (on the *Zainichi* Korean issue) and the far right (on the immigration issue)?

Unafraid of the criticism, I did not adopt a moderate and neutral path. I did the opposite. I understand that making only radical arguments and seeking the culmination of my ideals led me to such a fate. For a long time, no Japanese appeared to support my ideas because there was almost no one who wanted to take on both the far left and the far right. But times—and the social climate—have changed. I have gained the active support of the silent majority. And the day is in sight when many of my immigration policies such as improved treatment of the *Zainichi* Koreans will be realized.

Looking back on the forty-nine years of my professional life, I became almost entirely involved in issues where I knew speaking up would draw a backlash. But I said what I thought was best for Japan's future and put those ideas into practice.

There are apparently no patriots among the anti-immigration camp. None of them are concerned about the Japanese people disappearing from the face of the Earth. I remember the "progressive intellectuals" of the past. They were a group of academics and intellectuals who, for about the first forty years after the war, criticized Japan and sang the praises of communist states like the USSR, China, and North Korea.

The theory I proposed for *Zainichi* Korean policy from the late 1970s to the early 1980s was savaged by these "progressive intellectuals" (who commanded a degree of influence in the intellectual world of the time). The North Korean sympathizer Oda Makoto is a representative example. He stood at the front of demonstrations carrying placards reading "Down with Sakanaka" and "Close the Ōmura Internment Camp."[9] I remember it vividly. I was also persistently criticized in the far left's newspapers, which dedicated significant coverage to attacking me, dubbing me a "colonialist" and "assimilationist." Around that time, there was an incident in which far-left activists attacked two high-level immigration officials with bombs. While that didn't happen to me, there's no question that I was the biggest target of the far left.

Forty years later, history repeats itself. It is now elements of the anti-immigrant camp (such as hate speech organizations) that abuse me, saying that "Sakanaka Hidenori is selling out his country by calling for ten million immigrants."

The progressive intellectuals of the *Shōwa* era (1926-1989) were far-left intellectuals sympathetic to communism and immersed in anti-Japanese ideologies. The reactionary intellectuals of the current *Heisei* era are far-right intellectuals focused on racial purity and ultranationalism. Both share the trait of being unconcerned about the fate of their homeland. They are being irresponsible, content to merely criticize without offering any counterproposal.

Among those opposed to immigration, there are apparently no true patriots concerned about Japan's future and the economic, social, and cultural downturn that will accompany rapid population decline. They are merely passionate xenophobes who wish to inflame anti-immigration sentiment among the public. But I will state firmly that the young people of Japan—with their tolerant spirit toward those of other ethnicities—will not succumb to the far-right ideologies of racism and racial purity.

Incidentally, according to a public opinion poll conducted by the *Nihon Keizai Shimbun*, sixty percent of those between eighteen and twenty-nine said they agreed when asked "Do you agree or disagree with expanding the number of foreigners admitted into Japan for permanent residence as a countermeasure to population decline?"[10]

THE 2020 TOKYO OLYMPICS AND PARALYMPICS—THE BEGINNING OF THE IMMIGRATION ERA—A YEAR OF HOPE

The government is attempting to greatly increase the number of foreign tourists that visit Japan. Notably, it is promoting a "national commitment to tourism" with a goal of welcoming forty million foreign tourists in 2020. (In 2011, the number was six million, and in 2018, it reached thirty-one million.) I believe that this dramatic increase in the number of foreign tourists will have a major effect on the effort to advance immigration policy.

Increasing the number of foreign tourists will also increase the number of foreigners who come to love Japan, who wish to visit again, and who desire to live permanently in Japan. It will also increase opportunities for Japanese and foreigners to become familiar with each other and weaken the Japanese allergy toward accepting immigrants. Increasing the number of Japanese having contact with foreigners will provide a boost for immigration efforts. I've called for a "national commitment to immigration": welcoming ten million immigrants over the next fifty years. It goes without saying that there will be many among these foreign tourists who fall in love with the Japanese lifestyle and culture and desire to emigrate here.

If prior to the opening of the 2020 Tokyo Olympics and Paralympics, the government makes a declaration that Japan will become an immigration nation, it will be an act in line with the Olympic spirit of international peace, friendship, and unity. It will be fitting for a festival of peace that gathers the youth of the world, overcoming differences of race, ethnicity, religion, and nationality.

And if the government carefully selects immigrant candidates from among the forty million foreign tourists projected to come to Japan to see the Olympics, it should find many talented individuals who wish to immigrate. It will be able to secure global human resources who love Japan. And given that our society and economy are breaking down due to the lack of human resources caused by the decline in childbirth, nothing could be more welcome for Japan.

We can't allow this once-a-century opportunity to pass us by. I hope that the government makes 2020 the year that Japan opens up to immigration. With the Ministry of Justice's Immigration and Residency Management Agency beginning operations in April 2019, its first job should be laying the groundwork for the acceptance of immigrants, such as establishing immigration screening counters in Japan's major cities.

I have a request for the government. I want it to make the year of the Tokyo Olympics not just the first year of the immigration era but also a "year of hope" for the youth of Japan. Our rapidly declining population makes them despair for our country's future.

During the Tokyo Olympics, events will be held throughout Japan in which the youth of Japan and the world will be able to socialize. Multicultural exchange will flourish between youths of different nationalities, ethnicities, races, and religions. Friendship and love will be fostered between the youth of Japan and the world. And the world's media will provide an unvarnished look at Japan and show that it is a country where multiethnic coexistence is making rapid progress.

But should Japan, the host of this festival for the youth of the world, instead foolishly refuse to allow immigrants into the country, they will do harm to the hearts of young people both inside and outside of Japan. The reporting of the global media will spread an image of Japan as a country obstinately closed off to immigration. Those in government should be aware that the damage done to Japan in such a situation would be incalculable.

THE PRIME MINISTER'S 2014 DIET TESTIMONY

On February 13, 2014, Prime Minister Abe was asked at a meeting of the House of Representatives' Budget Committee about "the acceptance of immigrants as a countermeasure for the declining population" by Furukawa Motohisa, a committee member from the opposition Democratic Party of Japan (now with the Democratic Party for Japan, or *Kokumin Minshutō*, following the former's disbanding). He answered that "it is necessary for this to be explored from various angles, taking into account public discussion." This was a groundbreaking statement, one that marked a change in posture by a government that had previously opposed immigration policy. I regarded this as a momentous statement relevant to a declaration of an immigration nation by the Japanese government. I intuitively knew that a political taboo had been broken and that we had entered an era of moving toward a national commitment to becoming an immigration nation.

The following were the main points of Prime Minister Abe's testimony:

- Noted the necessity of examining the question of accepting immigrants from multiple angles as an issue that concerned the future of Japan and the livelihood of the public.
- Noted that if population decline continued that it would have a negative effect on economic growth as the size of Japan's working population and the number of Japanese consumers would also decline.
- Noted the importance of incorporating growing markets in the Indo-Pacific region.

Following Abe's remarks in the Diet, the Cabinet Office, always sensitive to opportunities, announced that month a long-term national policy of "aiming to admit 200,000 immigrants annually from 2015 and quickly achieving a target birthrate of 2.07 so that a century from now Japan will have a population of 100 million."

Having called for public discussions on immigration policy since 2005, I was overwhelmed with happiness at seeing my efforts rewarded. But at the same time, I was restrained by my knowledge that gaining popular acceptance for the "ten-million immigrants in fifty years" concept would be extremely difficult as it would be a historic change for Japan. That was an unnecessary worry, however. Abe's Diet testimony marked the beginning of rapid progress toward opening the country to immigration. Politicians should know what the outcome of the "popular discussion" will be.

The following is the status as of mid-2019, a year before the Tokyo Olympics and Paralympics begin, as well as my urgent proposals for that period:

1. A majority of respondents (particularly younger ones) approved of immigration in a 2015 opinion poll conducted by a national newspaper.
2. The rapid decline in the birthrate is having serious effects on all areas of society.
3. Industry is suffering from an unprecedented labor shortage.
4. The necessity and urgency of adopting pro-immigration policies has become obvious to everyone.
5. The Immigration and Residency Management Agency begins operations in April 2019.

Put the above together, and the environment has been prepared for the prime minister to make a historic decision.

As an opinion leader on immigration policy, I will increase my efforts to promote public awareness of this issue to secure even greater popular approval for it. I want the prime minister to declare this year that Japan will become an immigration nation. That way, the year of the Tokyo Olympics and Paralympics can serve as the grand opening of Japan's true face as an immigration nation to the people of the world.

CLOSING JAPAN TO IMMIGRATION LEADS DIRECTLY TO NATIONAL DECLINE

While the discussion of Japan being an immigration nation is gaining steam, this is being resisted by politicians who want to prevent immigration from becoming a political issue. They advocate raising productivity through the increased employment of women, the elderly, and foreign workers, as well as the use of technology such as robotics, all the while proclaiming a target Japanese population of 100 million fifty years from now.

However, these policies are fundamentally economic ones intended to increase productivity and the size of the productive population. They are not what are needed to maintain Japan's national systems: countermeasures to the declining birthrate. These kinds of policies are a digression. Even if implemented, they will not contribute to the resolution of the fundamental population problems facing the country, such as by increasing the number of births.

Do the politicians and bureaucrats implementing these kinds of makeshift policies really believe that they will be able to maintain a population of one hundred million even as the population declines by forty million over the next fifty years? Where do they plan to come up with the ten million people that demographic statistics tell us they will absolutely be short? Without immigrants, the math doesn't add up. And the female and elderly populations will dramatically decrease over this time. With the continued rapid decline in the population and no sign of an increase in the birthrate, I will state it frankly: any countermeasure to population decline that lacks immigration policy to directly increase the size of the population will end in failure.

I have a question for our government officials: have the population decline countermeasures enacted by the government over the past ten years shown any effect? No, there are no results to be seen, only time that has been frittered away. Hasn't the problem of Japan's population already reached the point where there's nothing to be done? I want these politicians and bureaucrats who focus solely on these counterfeit population decline countermeasures lacking an immigration component to change their thinking.

And by continuing to choose political leaders who steadfastly refuse to adopt pro-immigration policies and recognize permanent residency for foreigners, Japan has become a global laughingstock, a country committing suicide. There can be no question that we are tumbling down a road that ultimately leads to the total collapse of our state systems. Are our government officials prepared to take responsibility for that result? When I think about the fact that none of the politicians of today will follow the example of the samurai of the Edo period and commit *seppuku* in acknowledgment of their failure, I can't help but be incensed.

With demographic collapse becoming increasingly likely, it is clear to all that Japan is headed on a course that leads straight to the grave. If there's actually some kind of special reason why, despite this fact, we must not open the country to immigration, it is the government's responsibility to explain what it is to the public until their acceptance is gained. And if there actually is a national policy other than immigration that can save Japan from its life-or-death crisis, I would like to be told what it is. I should caution that the people of Japan—who know firsthand the fear of rapid population decline and the necessity of immigration policy—will not forgive this, no matter what kind of sophistry politicians employ in an attempt to evade responsibility.

Or perhaps there is a tacit understanding in place among Japan's powerful political figures to keep immigration policy in reserve as a "final trump card in case nothing else works." But even if that sort of thinking is present within the world of politics, Japan is coming closer to demographic collapse with each passing moment. There's no time for such a foolish approach. If we wait until the last minute, it will be too late for immigration to be effective. And then Japan will truly be placed in a grave situation.

Japan's population is falling and becoming increasingly elderly in a way unrivalled in the world; if the prime minister does not immediately decide to open our country to immigration now that the outcome of the immigration debate has become clear, our future is a society where more and more of the Japanese archipelago becomes uninhabited. Our economy will immediately stall. And financial failure means a countdown to the collapse of our social security systems.

WE CAN'T JUST LIE DOWN AND WAIT FOR DEATH

At the February 13, 2014, meeting of the House of Representatives' Budget Committee, Abe stated that "it is necessary for [immigration as a countermeasure for population decline] to be explored from various angles, taking into account public discussion" in response to Furukawa's question. This landmark Diet testimony revealed a complete change in position by a government that had previously been negative toward immigration policy. Particularly significant is that it was the prime minister himself who called for public discussion of accepting immigration.

And yet, I'm not aware of any intellectuals discussing national affairs along lines comparable to my calls for an immigration nation. The majority of Japanese scholars and intellectuals make no reference to immigration policy even though it is the most important topic for our country. There are some who will occasionally touch upon the issue of whether or not to admit immigrants. But they are outnumbered by those who haughtily spout baseless nonsense at length in an attempt to prevent Japan from opening to immigration. "Immigration policy will ruin the nation," "Letting in immigrants will destroy law and order," "Japan's pure culture will be harmed," "Japanese people just don't like immigrants." I feel that the decline in the intellectual level of Japan's intellectuals is even worse than the decline in the political acumen of the country's politicians.

I have a request for these uninspiring university professors who do nothing but criticize: if there's an effective policy comparable to immigration policy out there that can be used as a national strategy for avoiding demographic collapse and societal disintegration, please let me know what it is. I'll take that class.

It should be noted that there is no exception to the rule that a country's total population is determined by three factors: births, deaths, and net immigration.

In light of Prime Minister Abe's aforementioned Diet testimony, what should these intellectuals—who hold a certain degree of influence over national policy or at least the natural debate—do? First, I want them to become more interested in immigration policy given its importance to the national strategy for addressing the danger of demographic collapse. Second, I want them to take the issue of immigrants seriously and not just superficially.

The prime minister's historic statement has created an environment in which immigration policy can be freely discussed. I look forward to white-hot debates on the immigrant issue to be held in every field. Intellectuals are in the position to objectively perceive the relationship between national population and national strength. Thus, I want intellectuals to take the lead in and encourage these public debates while holding to the position that the introduction of immigration policy is unavoidable if we are to avoid a total collapse of demographic order. And I want them to assemble a popular consensus in favor of immigration on this basis.

Japan's scholars, journalists, and business leaders should settle on the policy of a national commitment to immigration and then work to alleviate public ignorance on the issue and apply pressure to the government to make the political decision to implement it. Now, with the debate over immigration policy beginning to gain momentum, is the time to act.

It would be the height of foolishness to just lay back and wait for Japan's death. If our government continues to refuse to implement immigration policy, our national strength will dissipate at a breathtaking pace. I have a request for the patriotic among the Japanese people. Let us rise up and raise the banner of opening the country to immigration as a result of the new imperial reign which began on May 1, 2019. Let's show off the true worth of the Japanese people—who tend to be more tolerant than others in the world—and establish a "new world for immigrants" that the youth of the world would love to move to or be a part of.

With the threat of imminent demographic collapse, Japan has reached a critical moment where it must decide whether it will be a society in decline or one that is vibrant. This is not the time for the government to hesitate over whether to introduce pro-immigration policies. It is the time to rally national opinion around a national commitment to immigration. Across the country, people are crying out for the country to be opened to immigration. And hearing those cries, I am pressing the government to make a national commitment to immigration.

With national polls finding support for immigration surpassing fifty percent (largely due to the views of young people in their twenties) and resolving the low rate of childbirth becoming the most important issue on the political agenda, I earnestly hope that the prime minister will consider the current situation on immigration policy and make the decision to open the country to immigration.

FROM A COUNTRY CLOSED TO IMMIGRANTS TO ONE THAT IS OPEN AND WELCOMING

In the world's leading nations, immigration has become a political issue of the greatest importance. The Trump administration in America and its call for the expulsion of immigrants is a notable example. It defies all reason that the question of whether or not to admit immigrants isn't on the political agenda of Japan, the country that most needs their help. Does the current generation of politicians really believe they can stand aloof from the reshaping of Japan into an immigration nation? This is an undertaking of national and historical significance and should be carried out through the leadership of politicians. It must be said that any politician who approaches it without reflecting on its importance is unqualified to take on the burden of running a state.

At the end of the Tokugawa shogunate, the question of whether or not to continue to close off Japan was a debate that nearly split the nation in two before Japan ultimately opened in the Meiji period. But even now, 160 years later in 2019, the ideological belief that "we must keep the nation closed to immigration" is still resolutely maintained. I will point out that failing to urgently correct our anachronistic governmental policy of refusing immigration is not only risking the collapse of our national systems, but it's only a matter of time before we are inundated with criticism of this policy from around the world ("Japan doesn't want immigrants!").

I advocate a "Japanese-style immigration policy" of accepting ten million immigrants over the next fifty years. What I'm suggesting is that we conclude immigration agreements with friendly and like-minded countries so that these immigrants can be welcomed in a planned, orderly manner. At the same time, we will enact an immigration law and create an agency with jurisdiction over immigration policy so that we will be prepared to accept immigrants in accordance with the national consensus.

These immigrants will pay taxes and contribute to the social security system currently in danger of not having enough funds for the future. If we accept them as "permanent residents" and "consumers" rather than as temporary foreign labor, they will form a market. Our financial and social security systems will recover and there will be economic growth at least at a level commensurate with the immigrant population. A second generation will be born as marriages between immigrants and with Japanese increase, thereby applying the brakes to the declining birthrate. Immigration policy is both the most effective countermeasure for the declining birthrate and the best economic policy for the era of population decline.

The number of international students also working in Japan is increasing rapidly, but we cannot allow a system in which migrant workers enter our country in the guise of international students. International students being allowed to work up to twenty-eight hours a week has resulted in various distortions and problems, including illness and death among these students as well as illegally overstaying their visas. Under the Immigration Control Law, the "student" status of residency is meant for foreigners engaged in full-time study. It is not for foreigners who are equally engaged in study and work. The misuse of this status has caused a host of problems: crimes committed by those remaining in the country illegally; a flood of refugee applications from foreigners with absolutely no chance of being accepted; a host of malicious Japanese language "schools" which are actually businesses engaged in near-human-trafficking. The Ministry of Justice should return the "student" status of residency to its original, purely scholarly purpose and greatly restrict part-time jobs by international students. The Ministry of Education, Culture, Sports, Science and Technology should direct universities and other educational institutions that they should be properly training international students in the Japanese language and/or specialized skills.

Japan is facing the dual crises of population decline and the collapse of rural society. It should greet capable foreign workers with the status of permanent residents (immigrants) so that they can make contributions to the Japanese economy and society as full members of society rather than just as a supplementary labor force making up for personnel shortages. In addition to the new statuses of residency currently under consideration by the government, others need to be created with a focus on areas deeply affecting the lives of the public: for example, "shipping (delivery services)," "convenience stores," and "dry cleaning." It goes without saying that atypical employment is out of the question for these immigrants. As a general principle, they should be given the same work and pay that Japanese employees receive.

The younger generation holds the key to a national commitment toward immigration. In multiple opinion polls, nearly sixty percent of those in their twenties have responded positively to the idea of accepting immigrants. This is an extremely reassuring result. The hearts of young Japanese are remarkably more open to accepting immigrants than those of young people elsewhere in the world. I have no doubt that if the government decides to open the country to immigration, the young people of Japan will become broad-minded global citizens and create an immigration society that those elsewhere in the world would love to live in. They have remarkably little prejudice toward other races, ethnicities, and religions.

THE NATIONAL COMMITMENT TO IMMIGRATION IS A POLITICAL ISSUE THAT SUPERSEDES PARTY

I have been vigorously writing papers on immigration policy for many years. One of the results of this effort was my book *Nihongata Imin Kokka no Sōzō*.[11] On August 3, 2016, a party was held where my friends gathered to commemorate the book's publication, sponsored by Noda Kazuo, chairman of the Japan Research Institute (*Nihon Sōgō Kenkyūsho*), whom I greatly respect.

Five Diet members knowledgeable about immigration policy were in attendance and I received undeserved praise from politicians of various parties including the Liberal Democratic Party and Kōmeitō, both ruling parties, and the Democratic Party. After they expressed their appreciation for my many years of toil, we all gave the cheer, "Let's work together to build a new country (*Issho ni kyōryoku shite atarashii kuni o tsukurō*)." I realized that the Japanese-style immigration nation concept had captured the hearts of those politicians who were concerned about Japan's future. The Sakanaka Plan would be carried on by conscientious politicians.

I was also showered with enthusiastic words of encouragement from public servants and the hall, filled with sixty or so of my comrades, became filled with an atmosphere of excitement about immigration policy. Noda, one of the most sharp-eyed figures of this generation, told me that it felt "like a rally of patriots seeking the creation of an immigration nation." Hearing everyone's heartfelt speeches, I couldn't stop my tears. I will never forget that day, one where the creation of an immigration nation was recognized as the most important political task facing Japan.

Since that day, I have known that the immigration nation concept has become a political issue that supersedes party. It has become clear to me that there will be no far-right political party demanding the expulsion of immigrants as has been seen in countries like France and Germany, and that an agreement on immigration policy will be reached unanimously among Diet members.

I will also predict that there will be no rise of politicians openly declaring that they "hate immigrants" or that Japan should "refuse all immigrants." There are many people with moderate views within Japanese society, and any politician who becomes labeled a "xenophobe" or "ultranationalist" will meet an ignoble end.

***

Contrary to popular perception, my understanding is that those in rural areas desperately want Japan to accept immigrants. Their hearts are more open to warmly welcome immigrants than those living in cities. Picture the underpopulated villages where only the elderly remain, the young people having left. Imagine the extremely worried feelings of those in the agricultural and mountain villages that are being deserted. Any politicians unable to believe that those in rural areas want to accept immigrants can't read people.

Well, long-awaited good news has arrived: the appearance of a politician who feels the same way I do and supports "regional revitalization through immigration promotion." I'm speaking of Diet Member Ishiba Shigeru (former minister for the Promotion of Overcoming Population Decline and Vitalizing Local Economy in Japan), a man who truly perceives the threat of a society that has experienced demographic collapse. In November 2015, as Ishiba was serving as minister, he declared that he was determined to "further promote the policy of accepting immigrants as the population continues to decline." One of the leading polemicists of the political world had risen up and begun promoting immigration as a way to save the rural areas of Japan from their plight.

This was the long-awaited arrival of a comrade after I had stood alone for so long. This proactive statement on immigration by an influential member of the political world boosted the prospects for immigration policy.

Ishiba Shigeru, who hails from the rural Tottori Prefecture in western Japan and has run for the presidency of the ruling party on several occasions, broke the political taboo against touching immigration policy. And yet, there came no voices of protest from the cabinet, the government party, or the opposition. To what can we attribute this welcome political situation? First, the perception that immigration policy is the only viable option available for saving Japan from its demographic crisis has gained currency with some politicians. And second, it has become clear that no proactive opposition to immigration is forthcoming from the public. Given these factors, it seems to be that no politicians have been able to oppose the policy that properly answers the yearning of the rural communities increasingly in danger of the social collapse that accompanies demographic collapse.

My understanding of the contemporary political situation is that the threat of the disappearance of rural communities has united Japan's politicians and made them accept Diet Member Ishiba's historic statement.

***

The truth is, I have been quite concerned about my relationship with politics over the past fourteen years of my post-retirement life. I, a private citizen, have played the leading role in the immigration nation project, something that seeks to greatly change the shape of the country. The thought that I should probably wait for politics to catch up has sometimes reared its head. But I grew impatient with politicians and their treatment of the immigration issue as taboo even though the fate of the country rests upon it. And so, while it was a difficult decision, I boldly stepped into the realm of politics. The turning point was writing the draft for "A Proposal for a Japanese-style Immigration Policy" for the LDP's Diet Members' League for Promoting Exchanges of Foreign Human Resources in June 2008.

This could be considered to have been my "lucky break" as it brought me an unforeseen positive result. I was able to formulate immigration policy without it becoming a pawn in political fighting. Because I was working with broad-minded politicians who placed no restrictive demands on me, I was able to write up my complete vision for a Japanese-style immigration nation without interference. The result of this was that the building of an immigration nation—the great work of this century— took form not under the leadership of politicians but rather through the initiative of a private citizen.

Now, that might be considered fine when looking at things from the broader perspective of the public coming together to overcome an unprecedented national crisis. But from a view that emphasizes proper procedure, there could be criticism that as a private citizen I was overstepping my place. There could also be the criticism that by leaving the formulation of immigration policy to me, a prime opportunity for cultivating politicians with a mastery of immigration policy was allowed to escape. But while I do pay these types of criticism some heed, I still believe that I should contribute to the theoretical aspects of policy as a private citizen, mainly with regard to minority issues.

As we've reached a critical stage for the road to an immigration nation in early 2019, I'm very careful when involving myself in politics to make sure that politicians are given ways to save face. The need to remain behind the scenes is carved into my memory. I have discarded my former title of director of the Tokyo Regional Immigration Office and retreated to the position of the director of the JIPI, a private role. I tackle our national crisis solely through my words and activities. Naturally, there has been no change in my determination to fulfill my duty as an opinion leader on immigration policy, and I will continue writing pieces on immigration policy in the future as well.

As the debate over the immigration nation concept becomes more serious, I am prepared for my role to become more important. In particular, it is necessary for the political situation to be arranged so that Diet members who approve of immigration policy command a majority.

I have something I'd like to say to all members of the Diet. I want the successful conclusion to Japan's grand historic undertaking—creating an immigration nation—to be accomplished through the authority of politicians. I want you to devote yourselves to passing laws related to immigration policy in 2019, the first year of the new imperial era, so that immigration nation Japan is in full swing during the 2020 Tokyo Olympics and Paralympics. Japan will take off into the world as a budding immigration nation during its new imperial era.

THE STAGE IS SET FOR THE PRIME MINISTER TO MAKE A HEROIC DECISION

I imagine that not a few citizens feel some discomfort toward the immigration nation vision that I have proposed. However, it has been met with only sporadic emotional backlash and theoretical counterarguments. It feels like even the ultranationalists' attacks on me are quieting down. And there could be no greater proof. There were almost no protests by the anti-immigration camp against the large-scale expansion of the number of statuses of residence (the range of foreigners that can enter Japan) that the government proposed in the Diet in October 2018. I was surprised by this unlikely development. And I'm afraid that I haven't heard any counterarguments that upset the Sakanaka theory or other policies that effectively counter population decline.

I was prepared to be flooded with criticism and jeers from all sides. But it seems that's not going to happen.

While a rapidly increasing number of people in the Western immigration nations are fearful of a large-scale influx of immigrants, I believe that no anti-immigration movement will rise on a national scale in Japan (where the threat of demographic collapse is imminent).

Judging from recent shifts in public opinion on immigration policy, the time has come for the government to make the decision to open the country to immigrants. I will raise the following points as evidence of this:

1. The aforementioned *Yomiuri Shimbun* poll showing that fifty percent of those in their twenties approve accepting immigrants.
2. I gave a lecture at the Cabinet Office entitled "The Path to a Japanese-style Immigration Nation."
3. New movements in the political world; Diet members are dealing with immigration policy regardless of party.
4. The special feature in the *Economist* introducing the essence of a Japanese-style immigration policy to the world. [12]
5. Younger Japanese increasingly believe that bold immigration policy is the only way to preserve Japan in the face of the increasing risk of demographic collapse.

I'm trembling with anticipation that the time has finally come for the showdown over the immigration nation concept. I am firmly determined to do all in my power to take on the greatest work of my life. At the same time, there are moments when I feel like I'm being driven into a corner. The remaining time in which I'll be able to work healthily (both physically and mentally) is steadily slipping away. Why can't I enter a state of mind where I'm able to relax and wait for the time to be ripe? It's likely because I've come this far doing everything by myself that I'm driven by such a feeling of impatience. It's a little late at this point, but it's possible that a lone wolf incapable of leading an organization might be ill-suited for taking on large-scale tasks.

In October 2018, the dominant theme in Diet discussions was what Japan's immigration policy should look like. It was the historic moment that I'd been waiting for. The main role of the immigration policy drama has been passed to the politicians. My job is almost finished. I can give a sigh of relief at having been released from some of the heavy burden of being responsible for Japanese immigration policy.

***

The following happened in November 2015. Influential cabinet officials in the Abe administration made their position in support of immigration policy clear. Minister of State for Government Revitalization Kōno Tarō (recently foreign minister and now defense minister, and a future candidate for the party presidency and possible premiership) and then Minister of State for the Promotion of Overcoming Population Decline and Vitalizing Local Economy in Japan Ishiba both made references in close succession to accepting immigrants. These were timely remarks by politicians well-informed on immigration policy.

These statements by cabinet officers were not criticized for causing discord within the cabinet even though they went against the government's basic policy of stressing that it will not adopt immigration policy. There was no criticism by either the LDP or the opposition. In other words, these important statements had no negative effect on the political situation. Even though influential polemicists of the political world openly spoke of the importance of immigration policy, the political mood just let time pass as if nothing had happened. How should we understand this unusual political spectacle?

It's natural to think that a tacit agreement has been reached among powerful political figures on how to proceed on immigration policy, the most important task facing Japan. It's likely that we will not see the arrival of politicians who argue against immigration.

I had been waiting for the day when tumultuous debate over whether or not to open the country to immigration began in the Diet. But it doesn't look to me like Japanese politics is going to go in that direction. The cabinet leadership has decided to open the country to immigration without having any serious debate among politicians on this important state matter. In other words, they will work zealously behind the scenes to obtain consensus in advance (the specialty of Japanese politicians) and then, when the time is ripe, pass it through the Diet unanimously.

This goes back to June 2008, the honeymoon period between myself and LDP politicians when I was putting together "A Proposal for a Japanese-style Immigration Policy." I believe that there are many LDP politicians who have inherited the beliefs of the Diet Members' League for Promoting Exchanges of Foreign Human Resources. And for that reason, my understanding is that there will be no high-profile anti-immigration moves within the LDP. With the government wrapping up the debate on an immigration nation, I believe that the comradely relationship between myself (who was involved in the above-mentioned policy suggestions) and the LDP leadership will be restored. I am prepared to, if the LDP calls on me, help prepare the legal system for immigration.

I would like to touch upon the current state of the vision of Japan as an immigration nation as of February 2019, eleven years since the historic policy suggestions were made by that league of LDP diet members.

1. The concept of a Japanese-style immigration nation was initially nothing more than the personal idea of Sakanaka Hidenori. But as a result of theoretical refinement in the pursuit of the ideal immigration nation, it has progressed into becoming the foremost theo-

ry of the immigration nation not just in Japanese immigration policy but in the world.

2. The Sakanaka Plan has, through increasing international and domestic support, become a national issue that should be urgently
   taken up by the government.

3. It is necessary for countermeasures to be rapidly implemented to
   prevent areas with primary industries from being potentially devastated by the collapse of the demographic order.

4. Many smaller companies are facing an ongoing crisis due to the
   increasing labor shortages caused by low childbirth.

5. It is likely that if Japan does not adopt a policy of advocating
   immigration, negative economic growth will become the new normal.

6. Popular support for opening the country is rapidly increasing, especially among the younger generation who feel despair concerning Japan's future.

7. Debate has begun in the Diet over whether to adopt immigration
   policy.

8. The government, having decided to establish the Immigration and
   Residency Management Agency, has prepared the environment for
   accepting immigrants.

Based on the above points, the humble opinion I offer the government is
that it should listen to the voices of the public. The people long for the
resuscitation of Japan through a national commitment to immigration.
The time has come for the decision to be made to open the country to
immigration as soon as possible.

NOTES

1. Eric Johnston, "Immigration Battle Diary," published on May 24, 2005 at http://
www.debito.org/ericjohnstonsakanakareview.html, was originally written for the *Japan Times* but was not published because of the latter's policy to review only English
language books.

2. Sakanaka Hidenori, *Nihongata Imin Kokka e no Michi* (The Road to a Japanese-
style Immigration Nation), (Tōkyō: Tōshindō, 2011).

3. *Yomiuri Shimbun*, May 30, evening edition.

4. Masutani Minoru, "Radical Immigration Plan under Discussion," *Japan Times*,
June 19, 2008.

5. Michael Hoffman, "Only immigrants Can Save Japan," *Japan Times*, October 21,
2012.

6. "Immigration to Japan: A Narrow Passage," *The Economist*, No. 420, No. 9003
(August 20-26, 2016), pp. 19-20.

7. "Jinkōgen Shakai ni Kansuru Zenkoku Yoron Chōsa (National Opinion Poll on
Society with Declining Population)," *Yomiuri Shimbun*, August 26, 2015.

8. "Sengo, Imin: Nichidoku Yoron Chōsa (Postwar Immigration—Japan-Germany
Public Opinion Poll)," *Asahi Shimbun*, April 18, 2015.

9. Ōmura Internment Camp, also known as the Ōmura Detention Center, was established in 1945 in Nagasaki to deal with the endless flow of those illegally entering Japan from the Korean Peninsula. There were also Korean residents in Japan detained there who had committed crimes in Japan. The pro-North Korea group (General Association of Korean Residents in Japan), and leftist academics supporting the former Soviet Union, called for its closure and used me to attack the policies, especially in the latter 1970s.

10. *Nihon Keizai Shimbun*, March 21, 2017.

11. Sakanaka Hidenori, *Nihongata Imin Kokka no Sōzō* (Creating a Japanese-style Immigration Nation), (Tōkyō: Tōshindō, 2016).

12. "Immigration to Japan."

FOUR

Japanese Immigration Policy Is Preceded by Global Praise

FOREIGN PRESSURE AND OPENING JAPAN TO IMMIGRATION

In January 2011, I was approached by an American living in Japan, Nicholas E. Benes, of the American Chamber of Commerce in Japan (ACCJ), who has close ties to the United States Embassy in Tokyo. He told me that "the American government wants to support your immigration policy." After deliberating on this for several days, I replied that "it isn't the age of the black ships [when Commodore Perry arrived]. Opening Japan to immigration is the responsibility of the Japanese." In response, he said "please carry out ninety-nine percent of the immigration revolution. We'll support the last one percent." I can remember the exchange vividly.

***

The question of how Japan, the world's third largest economic power, will deal with its population and immigration issues is one of the greatest topics of interest among the countries of the world. Answering requests for interviews on Japanese immigration policy from the world's most prominent news media such as the *Washington Post*, the *Economist*, the *People's Daily* (of China), the British Broadcasting Company, and Agence France Presse should be the work of a politician. But there isn't a single politician in the world of Japanese politics or bureaucrats in the government with a well-informed opinion on immigration policy.

And so, the international media turned to me, Japan's "Mr. Immigration" who has shouldered Japanese immigration policy all by himself. As the director of a private immigration policy institute, I've laid out my vision of the immigration nation to the people of the world. I've been interviewed by the world's media more than fifty times (but far less by Japanese media). As a result, the vision of Japan as an immigration na-

83

tion—nothing more than my private idea—has spread throughout the world. A dynamic has been established where global opinion places pressure on the Japanese government to open the country to immigration.

This is a dishonorable thing for Japan, but the national trait and political framework of only being able to decide the country's destiny by submitting to foreign pressure—a method for deciding the country's basic policies that has frequently been seen in modern Japanese history—has become known throughout the world.

Having carried the banner of an immigration revolution, this breaks my heart. But given the current state of affairs where—even as the danger of a collapse of the population pyramid becomes imminent—our political leadership is hesitating to make the decision for a national commitment to immigration, I believe that the transition to an immigration nation will inevitably take the form of Japan opening itself to immigration in order to meet the expectations of the people of the world.

But even if the Japanese government reluctantly takes the plunge and opens the country to immigration with the encouragement of the people of the other countries of the world, the Japanese people shouldn't feel any shame at it. This is because it was I—the JIPI director regarded by the world's media as Japan's immigration policy expert—who established the theoretical foundations of the vision of a Japanese-style immigration nation that will become a model for the world. This isn't like when Japan succumbed to pressure from the world's powers and opened up the country in the late nineteenth century or when it had the "MacArthur constitutional draft" pushed upon it and created the current constitution. The world's intellectuals know that it was Sakanaka Hidenori, a Japanese man, who guided Japan's immigration revolution.

Lastly, I'd just like to say this. The proper path is for a nation's new shape to be derived from the autonomous decision of its state and people. However, looking back on Japan's modern history, it's a fact that "foreign pressure" has brought favorable results to Japan. It is undeniable that opening the country in the Meiji period and the postwar constitution provided the foundation for Japan's tremendous development. I believe that immigration nation Japan, having gestated during the *Heisei* period and been born in the new imperial era, will become something full of hope for the young.

MR. IMMIGRATION

Foreign correspondents in Japan were the first to appreciate my concept of an immigration nation and then transmit it to the world. I was working in the darkness domestically, but this cast a light on me. The vision for an immigration nation proposed by Japan's immigration policy specialist caught the attention of the world's journalists; I am confident that my innovative Japanese immigration policy is circulating through the world as well.

In the spring of 2014, I was told by another American, Kumi Satō, longtime CEO of a public relations firm in Japan, who held my immigration nation vision in high regard, that "it's amazing that there's a person like you, someone who came up with an immigration nation concept that's so unlike the Japanese. I'm interested in what kind of person you are." At the time I answered "I'm afraid I don't know the answer to that myself. I mean, I've never asked myself 'what kind of person is Sakanaka Hidenori'?"

I don't think of myself as the kind of person who accomplishes things of great importance to the nation. I'm just a normal Japanese with a strong sense of purpose. But the world doesn't do me the favor of viewing me like that. I've received the unsettling label of a revolutionary and the work I do has been the target of criticism and ridicule, from my initial essay in the 1970s to my immigration nation concept today. Isn't it rare for a Japanese to be criticized and jeered in such a widespread and extreme way, from both the left and the right, from both progressives and conservatives?

Domestically, where there are many Japanese with insular dispositions, there was almost no one who supported my open immigration policies. But the world's journalists were just the opposite and always served as my allies. They held in esteem the innovative vision for an immigration nation advocated by a Japanese knowledgeable about Japan's minority issues. I'll give an example. In January 2009, the *Washington Post* introduced me to the world as an "immigration expert" on its front page.[1]

Awe-inspiring adjectives have been applied to me by the world's intellectuals: "Mr. Immigration," "Savior," "Revolutionary." You could even say that these nicknames clash directly with my actual character and accomplishments. These honorifics are the highest decorations I've received from the world's intellectuals.

To Western scholars, I'm a "mysterious presence." It might be unbelievable to them that Japanese society—somewhere that great matters of state are determined through consultations between the powerful figures of the political world—would produce a Japanese man able to take on the perspectives of world and human history and create a unique vision for the immigration nation.

But while I am taking the global initiative in advocating a concept of world peace—the construction of a community of humankind society—I believe that the basis for my thoughts is basically the same as the peacefully inclined spiritual lifestyle embraced by the hunter-gatherer *Jōmon* people with their animistic worldview. I'm a clumsy Japanese who can only think about immigration policy. I'm an old type of person, a fossil of the *Edo* era. I might venture to say that it would be fairly accurate to describe me as "an immigration revolutionary in love with the aesthetic sense of the samurai."

Jessica Weisberg, an American freelance writer, visited Japan in the summer of 2015 to interview me about movements in Japan's immigration policy. During our two-hour discussion, she told me that she was moved when she read the aforementioned booklet *Japan as a Nation for Immigrants*. She also asked a number of questions about the "person" Sakanaka Hidenori, who advocates an immigration revolution in Japan: "I'm surprised that there's someone in Japan who thinks on such a large scale." She continued, "You've developed an ambitious theory of an immigration nation from the viewpoint of a theory of civilizations. What was the secret to writing this kind of book?" "What scholars most influenced you?"

I answered that I had never given serious consideration to what kind of person I was. Then, in a spur-of-the-moment thought, I got out of the question by giving the following answer (incidentally, I named Darwin, Max Weber, Keynes, Levi-Strauss, and Umesao Tadao as scholars who had most influenced me):

> While I'm an oddity among the Japanese, I've been given many names by foreign intellectuals. Aliases like "savior," "pioneer of the immigration revolution," "Mister Immigration," and "expert on immigration policy." These can be said to be signs of esteem from foreign intellectuals. You might be able to get a hint of what kind of person Sakanaka Hidenori is from these nicknames.

After the interview, I gave her copies of *Immigration Battle Diary* and *The Road to a Japanese-style Immigration Nation, New Edition*.[2] She said she had read them. I'm interested to see how an American, fluent in Japanese, who admires the aesthetics of Kyoto, portrays a mutant Japanese born from the traditional spiritual climate of Japan.

Let's change the topic. I participated in the World Economic Forum's "Conference of World Authorities on Immigration" that was held from November 29 to December 1, 2010, in Dubai, United Arab Emirates. This conference gathered twelve world authorities who have been formulating and implementing immigration policy for years, including people in charge of immigration and refugees from the Office of the United Nations High Commissioner for Refugees, European Commission, and World Bank. The purpose of the conference was establishing the theoretical framework for a new immigration policy focusing on the world of twenty years from now. This was based on the common perception that world immigration policy has been stagnant since the financial crisis.

I presented a short English-language paper ("Sakanaka Hidenori's Declaration of a Japanese-style Immigration Nation") at the conference and solicited critiques and advice from these world authorities on immigration policy. Specifically, I sought their opinions on devising an immigration policy for Japan and their views on the declaration of a Japanese-style immigration nation.

I received an unexpected comment from Demetrios G. Papademetriou, a world leader in immigration policy studies who acted as chair of the conference, in response (in an e-mail dated December 10, 2010):

> Your paper was the most fresh and creative paper I have thus far read in the field of immigration policy. This is because you're attempting to resolve the difficult problem of reconciling the acceptance of immigrants with social cohesion. Your proposal's strategy of "welcoming immigrants to Japan with language education, work training, and cultural education" not only has demographic merit, it has the wonderful point of focusing on young immigrants. It also emphasizes granting permanent residency (and ultimately citizenship) to immigrants; that is the best method for having immigrants understand that "Japan is prepared for the responsibility of accepting foreigners."

What parts of the immigration policy crafted by a Japanese did a world authority on the theory of immigration policy hold in esteem? This is just speculation on my part, but I believe he was surprised by the novel ideas that a "Japanese-style" immigration policy rooted in Japan's intellectual climate had.

***

Regardless of what side of the ocean you're on, great revolutionaries appear when the fate of their nation is in the balance, as if tasked with saving the country for its future citizens. It goes without saying that the most important task facing Japan today is escaping the danger of population collapse being caused by the rapid decline in the size of the younger population. If the government does not formulate and immediately enact a fundamental policy to stop this population collapse, the total collapse of Japanese society, economy, finances, and the livelihood of the public are unavoidable.

What is plausible as a "fundamental policy to stop the population collapse?" Since retiring as a national public official in 2005, I have asserted that population collapse will mean the collapse of our country unless the public and government unite and overturn the system closing Japan off from immigration and establish an immigration nation system,

However, until recently, not a single politician would lend my proposals an ear. And neither university professors nor journalists—both of whom can speak freely without the political calculations of an elected official or of his or her party—had the courage to take a firm stand and push for immigration policy.

As the outlook for immigration policy continued to look bleak, there was one event that provided a ray of hope for the future: the article previously mentioned entitled "Only Immigrants Can Save Japan" that ran in the *Japan Times* on October 21, 2012. The author of this article,

American Michael Hoffman, as I have mentioned, labeled me a "revolutionary" in it.

This *Japan Times* article gave me the courage to break through a difficult situation. I also realized that the idea that "immigration can save Japan" would be acknowledged inside and outside of Japan.

During my time as an official, I was part of the establishment and known for my interest in immigration control. But following the article I swore that I would live bearing the name "revolutionary" even if it clashed with the bureaucratic climate of Japan and my bureaucratic upbringing.

Why was I, who had a long career as a national civil official, named as the architect of the immigration revolution? It's because there was no other Japanese willing to take on the heavy burden of building a new country.

I will never forget October 21, 2012, as the birthday of "Sakanaka Hidenori, the revolutionary."

JAPAN, PRESIDED OVER BY AN EMPEROR WHO WARMLY WELCOMES IMMIGRANTS (*THE ECONOMIST*)

In August 2016, I was visited by the head of *The Economist*'s Tokyo bureau, Sarah Birke. In the interview, I explained recent movements in Japanese immigration policy and the essence of Japanese-style immigration policy, for lack of a better word. I mentioned the sense of crisis I felt about the moves toward anti-immigration sentiment in major immigration nations such as Britain and that now was the time for the Japanese government to raise the ideal of the human community and declare to the people of the world that we would welcome ten million immigrants over fifty years. I also noted that politicians had begun to make moves toward a national commitment to immigration.

The result was an article introducing my original immigration policy: "A narrow passage—Begrudgingly, Japan is beginning to accept that it needs more immigrants."[3] After introducing my "ten-million immigrant concept" and Diet Member Ishiba Shigeru's views on immigration policy, the same article concluded by referencing shifts in Japan on immigration policy in the following way: "Even Mr. Sakanaka and Mr. Ishiba think all migrants must learn the language and local customs, such as showing respect for the imperial family. But the economic case for a bigger influx is undeniable. For those, like [the prime minister] Mr. Abe, who speak of national revival, there are few alternatives."

The idea of connecting the imperial family and Japan's immigration policy wouldn't have occurred to a Japanese. It's the point of view of a British royal subject. I heard that this article, with its illustration of a *torii* gate and the Japanese flag and which hinted at an integral relationship between immigration policy and the tranquility of the imperial family, sparked a large reaction both overseas and within Japan. Thinking about it, the idea that immigrants would have to show respect the imperial family is consistent with global common sense.

The Economist's feature on immigration introduced the special character of Japanese-style immigration policy with its strong emphasis on education and the wonderfulness of the Japanese imperial family—which welcomes all the people of the world warmly without regard for differences of nationality, race, ethnicity, and religion. It pushed Japan toward a historic change in its traditional image as a country closed to immigration.

That's my perception of the significance of this article. I myself received the undeserved honor of having my vision for a Japanese immigration nation become the focus of the world's attention.

The article also made me begin to think deeply about the relationship between the Japanese imperial family and immigration policy. And now that the date for the *Heisei* Emperor's abdication has been set, I'm requesting that the Japanese government "crown the end of the *Heisei* reign with a declaration of an immigration nation."

At a press conference held on December 20, 2018, His Majesty the Emperor's birthday, the Emperor provided a statement that made the future of Japan brighter. He said on the acceptance of foreigners that "I hope that the Japanese people will be able to warmly welcome as members of our society those who come to Japan to work here." The historical significance of that statement cannot be overstated. I was deeply moved by His Majesty's wise words and my determination to create "a Japanese society which warmly welcomes foreigners" was renewed.

The following are the words of His Majesty the Emperor, who has thought deeply on the acceptance of foreigners. Upon hearing his words which convey his true feelings, I—someone who has walked at the forefront of immigration policy—realized that the immigration nation Japan will continue to shine eternally.

> This year marked 150 years since the beginning of Japanese emigration overseas. Over the years many Japanese people who emigrated have continued to work hard, with the help of the people in their newly settled countries, and they have come to play important roles in the societies there. Thinking of the efforts of those people of Japanese ancestry, we have made a point of meeting with them as much as possible when visiting those countries. Meanwhile, many foreign nationals have come to work in Japan in recent years. When the Empress and I visited the Philippines and Vietnam, we met individuals who were making efforts towards their goals of working in Japan one day. Bearing in mind that the people of Japanese ancestry are living as active members of society with the help of the people in their respective countries, I hope that the Japanese people will be able to warmly welcome as mem-

bers of our society those who come to Japan to work here. At the same time, the number of international visitors to Japan is increasing year by year. It is my hope that these visitors will see Japan with their own eyes and deepen their understanding of our country, and that goodwill and friendship will be promoted between Japan and other countries.[4]

"THE ESSENCE OF JAPANESE-STYLE IMMIGRATION POLICY" (*BBC NEWS*)

I was interviewed by a BBC reporter in February 2015 in busy Shibuya, Tokyo, with many people passing by behind us. The theme of the interview was "the recent state of Japanese immigration policy." The following is an outline of the points I raised:

> Japan is the first country in the world to have plunged into an era of population collapse. We have an extremely low rate of childbirth and our population is increasingly elderly. The shocking fact that the collapse of the population pyramid will be immediately followed by the collapse of Japan has become widely known among intellectuals since 2014 and a great debate over immigration policy has begun between anti-immigrant intellectuals and me. I propose that we accept ten million immigrants over the next fifty years via an immigration policy unique to Japan, one that cultivates human resources. This would bring us to an immigration population roughly proportional to that of Britain, Germany, and France (ten percent). Considering Japan's industrial capacity, solid higher education system, and the high educational level of the public, it's a quite realistic goal. Because the Japanese are a people who believe in the infinite *kami*, are religiously tolerant, and have almost no racial or ethnic discrimination, I believe that the acceptance of immigrants into Japan will be a success.

BBC World News broadcast this interview on television and radio on March 17. The essential points of my theory of immigration policy were also described on the *BBC News* website.

BBC World News is broadcast to more than two hundred countries and regions. The vision of an immigration nation formulated by a Japanese immigration policy expert thus became widely known among the world's intellectuals.

Since *BBC News* has a lot of influence in shaping world opinion, this reporting created a situation where many people across the world began to anticipate Japan opening to immigration. How did Japanese politics respond to these global voices hoping that Japan would begin accepting immigrants? That is still to be seen.

"PIONEER OF THE IMMIGRATION REVOLUTION" (*JAPAN TIMES*)

The October 21, 2012, issue of *The Japan Times* included the aforementioned article entitled "Only Immigrants Can Save Japan." The subtitle was "A new Japanese civilization will realize a multi-ethnic community, which no nation has ever achieved, and, in due course, it will stand out as one of the main pillars of world civilization," which paraphrases the 2011 version of my book *The Road to a Japanese-style Immigrant Nation*.[5] The conclusion of the article read "revolutionaries learn to live with that, firm in the conviction that their time will come."

This article was written by Michael Hoffman, who is knowledgeable about Japan, who has lived in the country for thirty-five years. After closely reading my *The Road to a Japanese-style Immigration Nation* and *Population Collapse and the Immigration Revolution*,[6] he dubbed me "the pioneer of the immigration revolution" and introduced the immigration nation concept that I advocate for to Japan and the world:

> Face of change: Hidenori Sakanaka, the former Justice Ministry bureaucrat and Tokyo Immigration Bureau chief fears the nation is on the brink of collapse and says: "we must welcome ten million immigrants between now and 2050." "The Japanese should become aware that they live in an era of a severe population crisis and that it is no longer possible to live in peace in a closed world only among Japanese nationals. There is no way for Japan to survive but to build a society of living with immigrants and hoisting a new flag: 'Immigrants Welcome'." "In Japan in the age of population decline, there is a need for a social revolution equal to that of the Meiji Restoration (the modernizing and Westernizing revolution that began in 1868)." "The very fundamentals of our way of life, the ethnic composition of our country and our socio-economic system will have to be reconsidered and a new country constructed." "I believe the (re-creation) of Japan as an immigrant nation is the ultimate reform, which will serve as a panacea for the challenges facing the country."

My concept of an immigration revolution running in Japan's foremost English-language newspaper sent a shock through the world's intellectuals. According to *The Japan Times*, they received a large response from overseas readers.

E-mails also arrived at the JIPI from people hoping for Japan's immigration revolution: "Today I read the article on Mr. Sakanaka's idea of an immigration nation and was very moved. It was the first time I'd heard that kind of idea from Japan. Mr. Sakanaka, please become the founder of a new Japan" (by an American with experience living in Japan).

Why was a former public servant of the Ministry of Justice Immigration Bureau—an organization whose goal is to maintain orderly immigration control—named a "revolutionary"? The label came at me like a bolt from the blue, but thinking about it calmly, it seems likely that it was because I was someone who, upon encountering Japan's once-a-millennium national crisis after devoting his life to formulating immigration policy, began advocating for ten million immigrants. In other words, an "era" of population crisis had suddenly made an expert on immigration policy necessary.

Having received the awe-inspiring label of "revolutionary," I decided that carrying out an immigration revolution was the only way to save Japan from its desperate situation.

"IMMIGRATION EXPERT" (*THE WASHINGTON POST*)

In January 2009, *The Washington Post* ran a related article on their front page. With the world recession deepening in the wake of the "Lehman Shock" of September 15, 2008, the paper told the world that the Japanese government's policy toward foreigners—establishing the "Foreign Residents Policy Promotion Office"—was "revolutionary."[7] My comments are quoted in the article:

> The government's effort to keep jobless foreigners from leaving the country is 'revolutionary'. Japan has a long history of rejecting foreign residents who try to settle here. Normally, the response of the government would have been to encourage these jobless people to just go home. I wouldn't say that Japan as a country has shifted its gears to being an immigrant country, but when we look back on the history of this country, we may see that this was a turning point. Sakanaka said the government's decision will send a much-needed signal to prospective immigrants around the world that, if they choose to come to Japan to work, they will be treated with consideration, even in hard economic times. Japan is finally realizing that it does not have a system for receiving and instructing non-Japanese speakers. It is late, of course, but still, it is important that the government has come to see this is a problem.

Because it appeared on the front page of one of America's most respected newspapers, it was likely also read at the time by newly inaugurated President Barack H. Obama and may have given him the impression that "Japan is a country friendly to immigrants." I believe that there's no question that at that time Obama, as the child of an immigrant, paid attention to Japan's immigration policy.

This *Washington Post* article rated my "theory of opening the country to immigration" highly. It introduced me as an "immigration expert" and spread my vision of Japan as an immigration nation emphasizing immigrant education among the world's intellectuals.

A 2008 *Washington Post* article, also written by the same reporter, Blaine Harden, pointed out that "Sakanaka's immigration proposal [for ten million immigrants], at least for the time being, has no serious backing among major political leaders,"[8] but the aforementioned 2009 article, the following year, said:

> There is a growing sense among Japanese politicians and business lead- ers that large-scale immigration may be the only way to head off a demographic calamity that seems likely to cripple the world's second- largest economy. A group of eighty politicians in the ruling Liberal Democratic Party said last summer that Japan needs to welcome ten million immigrants over the next fifty years. It said the goal of govern- ment policy should not be just to "get" immigrants, but to "nurture" them and their families with language and vocational training, and to encourage them to become naturalized citizens of Japan.

These two *Washington Post* articles show that there was a major change in the situation of Japanese immigration policy in the one-year period from late 2007 to late 2008.

In February 2010, Lee Hockstader, an editorial writer for *The Washing- ton Post*, visited Japan to interview me on the topic of changes in attitudes toward immigration in Japan. This was the third time I had been inter- viewed by the paper in as many years. *The Washington Post* has an above average interest in Japanese immigration policy.

He had carefully read my English-language booklet *Towards a Japa- nese-style Immigration Nation*,[9] and we had a rich discussion of its con- tents. The interview lasted for about two hours and we got along very well. We agreed that the only option for saving Japan from its demo- graphic crisis is adopting a bold immigration policy. When I saw him off, he gave me a firm handshake and said, "it's a lonely battle, huh."

The series of interviews with and reporting by *The Washington Post* led me to understand that the U.S. government is eager for Japan to open itself to immigration and that America's representative media—aligning itself with the inclinations of the U.S. government—supported my immi- gration policy.

The American government likely believes that Japan—its most trusted Asian ally—is not dealing with its demographic crisis appropriately and views Japan rapidly losing importance in the international community as undesirable in terms of America's Asian strategy. Or, more positively, perhaps they hope that Japan becoming an immigration nation sharing national ideals with America would deepen the alliance between the two countries. Those were my thoughts in 2010.

Judging from the constant interview requests from major American media outlets like *The Washington Post, New York Times, Wall Street Jour- nal*, AP, and CNN that continued afterward, I believe that my thinking at that time was correct.

"THE CHINESE IN JAPAN ARE A BRIDGE OF FRIENDSHIP"
(XINHUA)

In May 2006, my paper regarding Sino-Japan relations was published in the now-defunct Japanese diplomatic monthly issues *Gaikō Forum*.[10] The publication of the article provided an unexpected opportunity. On May 26, Xinhua, the Chinese state-run press agency, translated a summary of the paper (about a third of the length) into Chinese and released it in China. This was taken up by the Chinese media, including newspapers across the country. It was also introduced on about a thousand newspaper websites. The name "Sakanaka Hidenori, former head of the Tokyo Regional Immigration Office," became known throughout that country.

The focus of the article was asking what Japanese society should look like and attempting to change the image that Japanese have of Chinese living in Japan. I was surprised when I heard that it had caused a big reaction in China. While I don't know the intentions of the Chinese government, Xinhua faithfully translated my paper and introduced it favorably as news from their Tokyo desk. The Chinese government likely held the paper in esteem as it "created a stir" while Sino-Japanese relations were at their lowest point over the issue of Prime Minister Koizumi Junichirō's visits to Yasukuni Shrine.

I vividly remember a high official of the Japanese foreign ministry familiar with the domestic Chinese situation telling me that "it changed the Chinese view of Japanese people." The paper by a former immigration official who fairly appraised Chinese in Japan may have touched the heartstrings of mainland Chinese. At the same time, the Japanese foreign ministry, which had financialy supported *Gaik ō Forum*, created a complete Chinese translation of my paper, included it in *Yueyang Juji* (No. 13, July 2006), and distributed five thousand copies to government agencies in countries using the Chinese language, including China. My argument about Chinese people in Japan was used as a helpful diplomatic tool by both the Chinese and Japanese governments.

Looking back on the events of almost fifteen years ago, my theory of Chinese people in Japan took on a life of its own and there's a possibility that it played the role of a "catalyst" for the improved Sino-Japanese relationship at the time. Or it could be said to have made some contribution to creating a favorable image between the Chinese and Japanese peoples.

Personally, I learned once again about how the treatment of foreigners in Japan can greatly influence international relations. I hope those working in immigration matters today take this lesson to heart and engage in immigration administration in a just manner.

"JIPI DIRECTOR SAKANAKA HIDENORI" (*THE PEOPLE'S DAILY*)

An article entitled, "Tolerance and Equality 'Value Harmony' —Japan Immigration Policy Institute Director Sakanaka Hidenori," appeared in the international section of the November 24, 2007, issue of *The People's Daily*. It was a wonderful piece written in Chinese by the paper's Tokyo bureau chief, Yu Qing. The following is a translation of the article's major part:

> Sakanaka Hidenori (62) is a former Japanese national civil official who worked as head of the Nagoya Regional Immigration Office and the Tokyo Regional Immigration Office. He was involved in immigration administration for thirty-five years. He says that after retiring, he decided to continue researching Japanese immigration policy and began running the Japan Immigration Policy Institute to complete the work he had left. As a young man Sakanaka was fascinated with the world of Tang poetry and admired the sages and cultured men of ancient China who would meet in bamboo groves and have serious discussions about the world. The JIPI is the realization of a long-held dream for Sakanaka. Sakanaka's first opinion is that "immigration will save Japan from its crisis." Recently this opinion has drawn attention from the Japanese media and public. Japan has already entered an era of "low childbirth and an aging population" and can't stop its population from declining. According to experts' projections, the Japanese population will fall by forty million over the next fifty years. Sakanaka, who believes that Japan must accept immigrants if it wants to maintain a population of one hundred million, has proposed taking in ten million immigrants over the next fifty years. Sakanaka's other "new proposal" is creating a society based on multi-ethnic coexistence. When accepting this large number of foreigners, Sakanaka urges the Japanese people to be prepared to create a "society based on multi-ethnic coexistence" in which Japanese and those of other ethnicities live and respect each other. Traditionally, Japan has had a national character of respecting harmony. He says that Japanese must treat other peoples fairly in order to build friendly relations with foreigners.

In 2007, I felt bewildered at receiving such positive treatment in the official paper of the Chinese Communist Party. Now, twelve years later, I happily welcome it as one example of the world media's positive reception of the Sakanaka Plan of the immigration nation. Re-reading this article recently, I thought it is an outstanding analysis of my true nature. I also thought that it may have made some contribution to correcting the view that some Chinese had of Japanese people.

***

On the same day that *The People's Daily* was introducing my theory of immigration policy (November 24, 2007), I spoke at Tsinghua University in Beijing on "Aiming to Transform a Japan with a Declining Population into 'A Country Young People Wish to Emigrate To'." At the beginning of this lecture, a Chinese member of the elite spoke on "the future of Sino-Japanese relations." The following was the high point of my speech.

> What meaning does the decline in Japan's population have for its neighbor China? I believe that China can feel a sense of relief about it. This is because a Japan with a rapidly falling population will transform into a "mature society" in which all of Japanese society aspires to peace and stability and to maintain its place as one of the world's leading civilized countries through the latent strength of Japanese civilization. China is also rapidly experiencing a decline in childbirth and increase in age; within twenty years it will enter a period of rapid population decline. I hope that Japan's experiences grappling with the population decline issue will help China in the future. With a declining population, Japan needs to accept immigrations from the countries of the world as a matter of policy. When that happens, the immigrants who Japan has allowed to enter will have to learn how to properly read and write Japanese—that is, they'll have to learn *kanji*. It will be necessary to borrow the power of the Japanese language (*kanji*) in order for those of various ethnicities to become Japanese citizens. All of the philosophies and values of the Japanese people are contained in the Japanese language. I believe that those raised overseas will naturally integrate into Japanese society through learning the Japanese language. Throughout its history, massive China has used Chinese characters to bind together various ethnicities; this is the same principle. The Japanese will continue to treasure and protect the civilization of Chinese characters. In the modern world, the only peoples who use Chinese characters as their national language are the Chinese who invented them and the Japanese who learned *kanji* from the Chinese and devised hiragana. When I think of the future of Sino-Japanese relations I think sharing the civilization of Chinese characters is of great significance. This is because through *kanji* the Japanese and Chinese can communicate their thoughts, deepen mutual understanding, and foster friendship.

THE WORLD'S INTELLECTUALS VS. JAPAN'S INTELLECTUALS

There is a large gap in the views of the intellectuals of the world on Japan's immigration policy and those of Japan. The world's intellectuals have a high opinion of my vision for an immigration nation. On the other hand, those in Japan don't even give it a single thought. It's possible that Japanese intellectuals just don't know how to handle my theory of immigration policy, which seeks to fundamentally change one of the basic policies of the state.

I realized more than four decades ago that Japanese intellectuals are incapable of perceiving either eras or people. The *Zainichi* Korean policy theory that I wrote in 1975 was savaged by progressive people of culture and university professors for groundless reasons. I've been distrustful of Japanese intellectuals ever since. Recently I've felt disdain for university professors and "people of culture" who only follow the lead of politicians or perceived public opinion when it comes to immigration policy and don't think for themselves.

The situation where my revolutionary immigration policy has been ignored by Japanese intellectuals is a long-standing one, but if the government moves to make a national commitment to immigration, the gap in praise for my policy between those inside and outside of Japan will likely disappear. Opinion in Japan will immediately follow that of the rest of the world. And the unprincipled university professors and people of culture of the current generation will begin singing the praises of immigration. They will speak as if they have always been in favor of immigration policy. I don't look forward to seeing this flip-flopping of principles and arguments, but it's an attitude of intellectuals often seen in modern Japanese history.

***

I feel that there has been a huge difference between the world and Japanese intellectuals I've met in terms of their ability to discover people. In July 2007, I spoke with Terry E. MacDougall, a professor at Stanford specializing in Japanese politics who has a long connection with Japan. We dove into a conversation about what Japanese policy on immigration should be. I received words of great encouragement from this talented scholar who is writing his lifework, *The History of Japanese Immigration Policy* (tentative title): "The Japanese have a spirit of tolerance. There is a good tradition of making foreigners welcome through the Japanese spirit of harmony. I expect that the Japanese-style immigration policy that you propose will be successful." Incidentally, Prof. MacDougall is an expert on Japan who has read most of my writings. This praise from someone who has been watching Japanese immigration policy ever since my 1975 essay gave me confidence that the direction of my immigration policy is not mistaken.

In September 2014, as mentioned earlier, I was asked by Duncan Williams, director of the University of Southern California's Shinso Ito Center for Japanese Religions and Culture, to give the keynote address on the topic of "the future of Japan and its immigration policy" as part of the "Hybrid Japan" lecture series. I was also asked to participate in a symposium on Japanese immigration policy and social integration that gathered world researchers of immigration policy. While I don't know why I was chosen as part of "Hybrid Japan," Williams considered the author Murakami Haruki and movie director Miyazaki Hayao to be representative figures of "Hybrid Japan."

When he visited Japan after that in late 2014 to make preliminary arrangements for the speech, he appraised my writings that portray "the future of Japan as an immigrant nation" as "putting forth a vision of a true immigration nation" and having been "born from the traditional spiritual climate of Japan." His words—which came from a true sense of concern about the future of Japan—gave me courage. At that time, I set my mind to step forward into the world with my concept of a human community rooted in Japan's spiritual climate. Williams's mother is Japanese, and he is a Briton able to understand the hearts of the Japanese. A specialist in Japanese Buddhism, his name, "Duncan," is one often given to monks.

If I hadn't received support from foreigners with whom my vision of an immigration nation resonated, it's doubtful that I would have been able to climb so close to the summit of the immigration nation. With my more than thirty works being treated with silence by the Japanese intellectual community, I might have lost my will to fight against the sturdy barrier closing Japan off from immigration and given up on the work of creating an immigration nation.

The foreign intellectuals so beloved in Japan are more concerned about the future of Japan in an age of rapid population loss than the Japanese are. I will treasure my moving meetings with my friends from overseas for the rest of my life.

CAN JAPANESE JOURNALISM BE SAVED?

There is a huge difference in how Japanese immigration policy is perceived inside and outside of Japan. Major outlets of the global media such as *The Washington Post, New York Times, Reuters,* and *The Economist* have highly praised my theory of immigration policy for its originality. They've supported me as "Mr. Immigration." On the other hand, the Japanese media is not interested in immigration policy, as press clubs assigned to each bureaucracy and organization do not cover it. In other words, if the bureaucracy is not talking about it, or feeding the press clubs with delicious morsels of information, then they simply ignore the issues and do not cover them. Moreover, there are no reporters specializing in immigration issues and my immigration nation concept has not received any coverage in the last ten years. I take that as an unanticipated misfortune and tend to turn down interviews with any Japanese journalists who have not studied the issue. However, recently, there has been a greater awareness among these journalists, including Ōhira Makoto of the weekly *AERA* and the editors of the monthly journal *Sekai*.

The foreign reporters I've agreed to be interviewed by have consistently reported on my concept and evaluated my vision of the immigration nation as a fundamental solution to the grave population problem facing Japan. At the same time, Japanese journalists, with their lack of specialized knowledge on the Immigration Control Law and immigration policy, have not been able to do accurate reporting on the immigration nation concept, the most important political task for the country. And that's not all. Even though there is widespread discussion of immigration policy by young people online, the national papers and NHK are still hesitant to mention words like "immigrant" and "immigration policy." They also play a role in fostering anti-immigrant sentiment through their use of grotesque discriminatory language like "unskilled labor." Can Japanese journalism, which has lost the journalistic spirit of leading public opinion in the correct direction, be saved? Probably not.

My view is that no matter how they struggle, the possibility of Japanese journalism coming back to life in the era of the information revolution is low. I don't think Japan's major media outlets will adopt anti-immigrant positions. Taking xenophobic and anti-immigrant stances would only invite a backlash from those of the public who have sound judgment. It would make an enemy of global popular opinion and mean the death of Japanese journalism.

If our news media doesn't have the insight to grasp that the historic moment when Japan opens to immigration is coming and is content to just wait and see what the government—which remains obstinately opposed to this—does, then the turn toward becoming an immigration nation will be realized through the work of the proudly independent JIPI director. Immigration nation Japan will be born when the young people who—reading my books or the columns that I place on the JIPI homepage—resonate with my immigration policy rise up. This is because no matter how pigheaded our government leaders are, they will have to turn their ears to the voices of the young people who bear Japan's future.

Despite saying that, I deeply hope that the once-a-millennium immigration revolution will be accomplished as a "national revolution" based on the support of an overwhelming majority of the public, that a national consensus on accepting immigrants is shaped and we move towards becoming an immigration nation in a calm, relaxed manner. However, without the cooperation of the major media outlets, that hope will not be realized. I particularly admonish the print media to stir themselves to action. I request that they drastically reform their coverage. I want them to fill their pages with the cries of the public demanding the aid of immigrants.

Right now, Japan's immigration policy situation is shifting. The government is making strategic preparations for a national commitment to immigration such as when it decided in October 2018 to create the Immigration and Residency Management Agency as an external bureau of the justice ministry. The time had come for the prime minister to speak in the Diet about "realizing a society where we coexist with foreigners."

When the government decides this great national policy—a national commitment to immigration—Japanese journalism will completely lose face for falling behind the government. I want the Japanese media, which is so good at being the government's agent, to summon all its power and launch a campaign for opening the country to immigration. My view is that the government leadership, paying serious attention to shifts in national public opinion on immigration policy, would welcome such a move on their part.

"51% OF JAPANESE 'AGREE' WITH IMMIGRATION" (*ASAHI SHIMBUN*)

Even if a task of national importance is being ignored by everyone because it has virtually no chance of success, if we take it on with fierce tenacity anyway, there are times when a miracle occurs, and a path forward opens before us. And that has been the case with the research of immigration policy theory—my life's work. Ever since my 1975 essay, I've poured my entire soul into the formulation of immigration policy.

Now my many years of effort are bearing fruit. The public is awakening from the thousand-year-long hibernation of the closure of Japan to immigration. Having been guiding people along the path to an immigration nation, I feel spring is near.

In April 2015, the *Asahi Shimbun* released the results of a poll which found that fifty-one percent of those asked "do you agree with allowing foreigners who come to Japan hoping for permanent residency into the country as immigrants? Or do you disagree?" said that they approved. This was significantly more than the thirty-four percent who said they disagreed.[11]

When I saw the results of the poll—and the fact that the newspaper published them—I realized that the *Asahi Shimbun* was taking a stand and promoting immigration policy. I was convinced that history had begun shifting toward the creation of an immigration nation.

I have a long relationship with the *Asahi Shimbun* with regard to the formulation of immigration policy. I participated in a dialog on immigration that ran in the *Asahi Shimbun*'s "Three People, Three Arguments" column in 2007.[12] I consider this to have been a precursor for the theory of a Japanese-style immigration nation.

In this article of twelve years ago, you can see the prototype of the immigration nation theory, the policy theory that I would later flesh out. The *Asahi Shimbun* has my respect for having the courage to run an article on "accepting ten million immigrants through a human resources-cultivating immigration policy" in 2007 under the headline "Immigration Nation." The following is the essence of the immigration nation vision that was introduced in the *Asahi Shimbun*:

> During the long postwar period, the Japanese government admitted almost no foreigners. At the time, the guiding principle of immigration control was "preventing settlement." The fixed settlement or permanent residency of foreigners was disliked. Behind this were the social circumstances resulting from "a society that was overcrowded due to a growing population." "But now, Japan has entered a time of popula-

tion decline. From here on, Japan has no choice but to allow a certain number of foreigners in as a matter of policy. This is because there are many villages facing the danger of regional societal collapse due to underpopulation. There is also a shortage of caregivers for the aging population. If economic activity declines alongside the population, the social security framework will also collapse." "The argument has been made that we should accept more foreign workers, but I don't support that. I feel that this position carries the strong implication that we should accept these 'workers' and then get all the work we can out of them during a short period of time. Instead, Japan should explore accepting 'immigrants'." "It's a change to our foreigner policy, a model that encourages permanent residency with an eye towards making them future Japanese citizens instead of the usual method of accepting them and then kicking them out as suits our convenience." "Fifty years from now, the population will have declined by forty million. I believe that we can transition to being a society of one hundred million during that period if we work hard and accept ten million immigrants." "In that case, the system for acceptance will determine whether we succeed or not. Foreign workers with high-level skills want to work in English-language countries; they don't come to the *kanji*-using Japan." "We should accept this and adopt an immigration policy that "cultivates human resources." That is, make it so that foreigners can properly learn Japanese at schools in Japan and proactively support their occupations so that they are "cultivated" within Japan into being highly-skilled workers.

As shown above, I proposed my "ten-million immigrants concept"—the overturning of the fiercely protected national policy of closing the country off from immigration—in the *Asahi Shimbun*. I was prepared to be swamped in criticism but according to the *Asahi* at the time, there was absolutely no opposition voiced to this unprecedented concept. I was disappointed. It seemed like my concept was treated dismissively as a "dream" that had very little chance of becoming reality.

That was for the best. My "plan for a grand utopia" was able to be born without being harmed. Twelve years have passed since then. The Sakanaka plan on immigration policy has built up momentum. Support for immigration has rapidly increased, particularly among the younger generation. Influential global media outlets and world intellectuals are pushing for Japan to open itself to immigration. My perception is that the time is ripe for the government to make a historic decision.

I have a request for the *Asahi Shimbun*, which is in the position to become a Japanese opinion leader on immigration policy. I want the newspaper that ran the groundbreaking idea of creating "immigration nation Japan" in 2007 to stand at the forefront of building up popular opinion behind making Japan into an immigration nation today.

THE IMMIGRATION REVOLUTION AND THE INFORMATION REVOLUTION

While this was a bit late of me, I learned how to use a computer in the spring of 2013. I then began posting short columns (about 800 words or so) on the JIPI website and Facebook almost every day. Between these two outlets, I have easily written more than two thousand of these columns. These columns have had an outstanding effect in spreading my vision for an immigration nation. Since 2013, the number of young people who support immigration policy has rapidly increased. I believe it has also had an effect on young people outside of Japan.

I'll give an example. According to an aforementioned poll by the center-right *Yomiuri Shimbun* that was administered in August 2015, fifty percent of those in their twenties approve of accepting immigrants.[13] I have no doubt that many young people have studied immigration issues by reading "policy proposals" and the "electronic bookshelf" on the JIPI website and have come to understand the necessity of large-scale acceptance of immigrants. Recently there have been a remarkable number of junior high and high school students who have visited me wanting to learn more about immigration policy. I'm impressed by the passion that these young men and women have toward immigration policy. I want them to become more knowledgeable about immigration policy and try to be global citizens active in the world.

The depth of the spirit of tolerance possessed by young Japanese has to be among the top in the world. If the tolerant youth of Japan can have frank exchanges with those of other ethnicities as anti-immigrant sentiment increases among the youth of Western countries, the future of immigration nation Japan is limitless. I don't believe it to be just a dream to think that fifty years from now Japan can be an immigration nation standing at the pinnacle of the world.

Also, having read my immigration policy proposals, there is enthusiastic discussion of the immigration nation idea among pro-immigration youths on Facebook. The number of people supporting immigration policy is on the rise. For example, according to the Facebook investigation team on January 2, 2018, my essay (post) on immigration policy received 30,000 likes. This is a surprising number. I once again realized the necessity of making full use of the information transmission capabilities of computers when rebuilding the nation.

If the young generation, the children of the information revolution, complete the path to an immigration nation, future historians will note that "a new nation was created when the Japanese in their twenties rallied themselves to action during the *Heisei* era" and that "Japan's immigration revolution was a product of the information revolution" when they write "A History of Fifty Years of Immigration."

NOTES

1. Blaine Harden, "In a Shift, Japan Seeks to Help Laid-Off Immigrants Stay in the Country," *Washington Post*, January 23, 2009.
2. Sakanaka Hidenori, *Nihongata Imin Kokka e no Michi, Shinpan* (The Road to a Japanese-style Immigration Nation, New Edition), (Tōkyō: Tōshindō, 2014).
3. "Immigration to Japan: A Narrow Passage."
4. "On the occasion of His Majesty's Birthday," December 20, 2018, Imperial Household Agency.
5. Sakanaka, *Nihongata Imin Kokka e no Michi*, 2011 edition.
6. Sakanaka Hidenori, *Jinkō Hōkai to Imin Kakumei* (Population Collapse and the Immigration Revolution), (Tōkyō: Nihon Kajo Shuppan, 2012).
7. Harden, "In a Shift."
8. Blaine Harden, "Demographic Crisis, Robotic Cure?" *Washington Post*, January 7, 2008.
9. Hidenori Sakanaka, *Towards a Japanese-style Immigration Nation* (Tokyo: JIPI, 2009).
10. Sakanaka Hidenori, "'Sekai ni Hirakareta Nihon' o Mezashite: Zainichi Chūgokujin wa Kakehashi to Naru (Towards a 'Japan Open to the World': Chinese in Japan as a Bridge of Friendship)," *Gaikō Forum*, No. 215 (June 2006), pp. 52-59.
11. "Postwar Immigration—Japan-Germany Public Opinion Poll," *Asahi Shimbun*, April 18, 2015.
12. "Japan as an 'Immigration Nation'? Adopting a policy of cultivating human resources," *Asahi Shimbun*, February 9, 2007.
13. "Jinkōgen Shakai ni Kansuru Zenkoku Yoron Chōsa."

FIVE

Leader of the National Commitment to Immigration

THE FIELD OF IMMIGRATION POLICY IS MY SPECIALTY

Ever since the legislation creating a legal status for the *Zainichi* Koreans, I have devoted all my time and energy to formulating immigration policy. It's not an overstatement to say that the majority of my working life has been spent trying to tear down the system of closing the country off from immigration and establishing an immigration nation. Especially since retiring from the Ministry of Justice's Immigration Bureau at the age of sixty years old, I've been free and not had to do anything else. I've put all my energy into writing immigration policy papers with the goal of creating a full compilation of the theory of an immigration nation.

There might be some people interested in the background to the formation of my concept of an immigration revolution. I believe it's related to the fact that I wrote annotations for the Immigration Control and Refugee Recognition Act that established Japan's basic policies toward foreigners and am therefore well familiar with all aspects of the law, including its limits and issues. The innovative immigration nation concept was born from my thorough study of the law, I believe. That's where the ideas of an "Immigration Law" and the "human community" came from, things that couldn't be covered by the Immigration Control Law.

As I look back, no researchers aspiring to examine and promote immigration policy have appeared other than myself. I walk alone in the field of drawing up immigration policy and researching the legal system for immigration.

At some point, I became an authority on the research of immigration policy. I feel a strong sense of impending crisis about the fact that, even though gathering the strength of many experts is necessary when creating a new shape for a nation, I am the only expert knowledgeable about legislation related to immigration policy. And my misgivings have become reality.

Although debates over immigration policy have suddenly begun to occur in the Diet, they are unproductive, occurring between Diet members unfamiliar with immigration policy and the Immigration Control Law. They are just arguing based on their spur of the moment ideas or ideology. And the government is also unprepared and unable to act smoothly. Naturally, neither the government parties nor the opposition will make forthright statements laying out their own opinions on the necessity of adopting immigration policy. To my eyes, everything is being done with an attitude of great caution.

Why is this all being done in a way that embarrasses the country? Because until very recently politicians, administrators, intellectuals, and journalists all viewed the immigration question as taboo, not to be touched. Furthermore, not only does creating immigration policy require thorough knowledge of the Immigration Control Law and copious practical experience, it also demands a sense of mission about opening a new future for Japan and the burning passion to achieve that mission. And it requires the ability to create an idealized concept of an immigration nation and the spiritual power to withstand the criticism and ridicule that will come surging in from every corner. This, in other words, is why no Diet member, administrator, or university professor has appeared other than me to attempt a permanent plan for an immigration nation—even though it's something the fate of our nation depends on.

In fact, there's an even more serious problem than the above, a natural result of the government's avoidance of discussing immigration policy with the entire country for many years.

To jump straight to the conclusion, no one in Kasumigaseki, the center of the bureaucracy, and Nagata-chō, the political center of Japan like Capitol Hill is in the United States, is deliberating on the immigration nation vision devised by a former justice ministry official. Neither is anyone in the Diet. There has come no logical counterargument from Diet members. This is only natural. Speaking from the position of an expert in immigration policy, because politicians, bureaucrats, and university professors have almost no insight—no specialized or legal knowledge when it comes to immigration policy—they're unable to raise any arguments against me that are on-point.

As immigration policy has remained off the political agenda, the effort I alone spent on loudly shouting about the necessity and urgency of accepting immigrants has borne fruit. Public opinion has shifted from being somewhat opposed to immigration fourteen years ago to a majority being in favor today. The times have turned in the direction of opening the country to immigration.

What does that mean? The views of the public on how to proceed with immigration policy have become noticeably different from those of our politicians. The politicians need to be warned that governance that doesn't reflect the will of the people when deciding the basic policy of rebuilding our nation goes against the principles of democracy and absolutely cannot be allowed.

So, why is there no great debate among our government leaders over this grand concept that determines what the future of Japan looks like? I suspect that there are many who find this strange. The world intellectuals whom I've met have been flabbergasted that Japan is holding firm to its policy of no immigration, calling it "one of the seven wonders of the world." And in truth, as already stated, there is not one politician who is willing to stake their political career on immigration policy.

Naturally, there are also no politicians willing to go against the mood of the times and openly declare that they are opposed to immigration. The position of the immigration issue in the Japanese political world is the polar opposite of that in Western countries. Immigration policy has not become a political argument over which there is tumultuous public opinion. Things are still peaceful, like the calm before the storm. While this is just my intuition, it seems that some Diet members are afraid that—should full-fledged discussion of immigration policy begin in the Diet—the Diet will unanimously decide to open the country.

With the goal of spurring on serious reflection by the politicians who carry Japan's future on their shoulders and to rouse them to action, I have developed a thorough criticism of the current state of Japanese politics. I believe that the political leadership is paying careful attention to shifts in public opinion and will rouse themselves and endorse a national commitment to immigration once they perceive that public support for immigration has reached a decisive level. In other words, the great matters of state will be decided via the currents of public opinion.

In any case, if we are to undergo what I call the "Great Japanese Revolution," which will surpass the Meiji Restoration, when the country was opened to Western ideas and trade, in the sense of opening the country to all of the international community and its human resources, I contend that it will be necessary for the government to make the question of opening the country to immigration an issue in an election and ask the public what they believe. If the immigration nation is born having secured the support of a majority of the people, its legitimacy will be acknowledged both domestically and overseas.

We will likely not see clashes in the Diet between the government and opposition parties over the necessity of opening the country to immigration. Instead, it seems probable that legislation related to immigration policy based on popular consensus will be solemnly discussed in the Diet and then approved and passed unanimously.

The above state of the Japanese political world is naturally not a reflection of the maturity of Japanese politics. Looked at superficially, it
may appear like the ideal way to create a new nation and as fulfilling the
fundamental principles of democracy. It goes without saying that that
view is incorrect. It shows nothing other than the incompetence and poverty of Japanese politics. It is extremely unfortunate that this generation
of politicians has not inherited the spirit of the Japanese who fought
fiercely from the late Edo to Meiji eras over whether or not to open the
country.

The issue of deciding the new shape of the nation—whether it is to be
open or closed to immigrants—is the sole prerogative of politicians. Politicians make policy proposals, these are fiercely debated in the Diet, and
finally a decision is made through a majority vote. As with constitutional
revision, this is truly a political issue of such importance that the very
reason for the existence of Japanese politics could be called into question
if this is not done. But the many Diet members who do not correctly
understand the reason that politicians exist don't even feel any shame at
being left out of the loop when it comes to something that will determine
the fate of the nation.

So, who will play the primary role as we reach a new page of Japan's
history and the country faces a turning point? The wise public can clearly
see that it will not be the politicians who even now avoid engaging on
immigration policy despite it becoming clear that the generation of low
childbirth has no future.

The following describes a potential scenario leading to the immigration nation that is made based on the assumption that our politicians will
abandon performing the duties of their offices. In other words, one in
which a deeply sincere and patriotic Japanese public engages in thorough
debate—without the politicians—over this great national reform and
uses the overwhelming power of a people longing for immigration policy
to push through any political resistance, leading to the birth of an immigration nation.

If that happens, the politicians will have to accept that they only
played a side role in the creation of an immigration nation that will be
carved into the annals of Japanese history. Instead of the irresponsible
politicians, it will be me who—backed by public consensus and placed in
this position by fate because of my many achievements—becomes the
central figure needed for building the immigration nation. Japanese history textbooks will say that the *Heisei* immigration revolution was a
"democratic revolution" in which I took the initiative and the public—
distressed over Japan's future—arose.

I initially maintained an appropriate distance from politics and had no
intention of carrying out a role that should be the work of a politician.
However, having become fed up at our politicians' attitude and their
unwillingness to exercise leadership on immigration policy, I decided

that it is my responsibility as "Mr. Immigration" to carry out the central role now that we've reached the final phase in which the outcome of the public debate over a national commitment to immigration will be determined. And—exercising the influence that I've managed to gather through previous discussion on the immigration nation—I have put all my effort into furiously writing and engaging in public awareness activities so as to shape public opinion and secure a majority in favor of immigration.

***

To summarize the above, I, Japan's first researcher of immigration policy, have been placed in the position of being a leading figure in the creation of the immigration nation with the backing of the patriotic public.

I have spoken ill of politicians and it is possible that we will see the arrival of some who—ignoring their own irresponsibility—shamefully criticize me. As a mere volunteer activist, I have repeatedly exceeded my place and acted presumptuously. But I will leave the question of my responsibility to the judgment of future historians.

I have just criticized politicians bitterly. But it would be unfair of me if I did not amend that with the following: No politician has criticized my revolutionary concept of the immigration nation. And the political parties haven't been critical of immigration policy, either. In fact, I feel that individual politicians have watched over my immigration nation vision fondly. This fact is extremely serious.

Speaking solely in terms of immigration policy, Japan's politicians are fairly liberal compared to the Western politicians who openly voice their racist and anti-immigration views. They have absolutely not joined up with the forces of xenophobia. From what I can perceive, powerful figures in the political world may have decided early on that only the large-scale acceptance of immigrants can overcome the unprecedented population crisis.

If a mere civilian can step into the political sphere and provide some aid to the future of Japan, it is thanks to a tolerant political climate that permits an immigration revolutionary to act freely.

THE CREATION OF AN IMMIGRATION NATION TO SAVE JAPAN

I am increasingly concerned that if we do not resolutely embark on an immigration revolution within the next two years while the Japanese economy still has surplus strength, the Japanese people will not survive the time of population decline. We are now in a battle against time.

Global human resources will not come to a Japan in decline. It will do us no good to decide to become an immigration nation if we do so after the population has begun to disappear and our society, economy, and finances have died. The road to Japan's revival will have been completely severed.

Even after retiring as a civil servant, I have continued to maintain my spirit of public service and been anxious about where the country is headed. I have no doubt that the desire to save the country lives within my vision of an immigration nation. I devised my theory for the creation of an immigration nation in the hope to ensure the eternal security of Japan. It's a vision of the future, fixed on what the Japan and world of a century from now should be like. It's also a practical theory of immigration policy able to be put into practice immediately.

The ultimate goal of this revolutionary and his radical concept for an immigration nation is, put simply, preventing the Japanese from becoming an endangered species over the next two hundred years. It's to apply the brakes to the natural extinction of Japanese civilization, an irreplaceable part of world civilization.

The question is, has this ideal of the immigration nation that I have put my heart into creating gained universality and the understanding of a large segment of the public? Speaking frankly, I'm not confident of how far my sense of danger has penetrated into the minds of the Japanese people. The time has come for the people to rise up and establish an immigration nation, but I sense neither passion nor enthusiasm about this from the public, including politicians and business leaders. There are days when I feel that my efforts are in vain, that my argument is gaining no traction.

My last hope lies with the fact that the number of people supporting immigration policy is increasing rapidly, especially among young people and officials in their twenties. On the other hand, Diet members, leaders of big business, university professors, and journalists are slow to act. It seems there are still many, especially among the elderly, who feel uneasy about immigrants entering Japan. It will require further work for the idea of a Japanese-style immigration nation to capture the hearts of a majority of the public. I will continue trying to convince people until those in all areas of society have agreed on the necessity and urgency of adopting immigration policy.

I want to gain the understanding of a broad swath of the public that we should immediately make a national commitment to immigration. If we continue to reject immigration, we face a dark future of disappearing towns and villages, but if we accept it we will have a bright future.

It is my job to lay down the rails that lead to an immigration nation. It is the role of the government and the public to appropriately welcome immigrants.

In the dawn that follows the establishment of an immigration nation, it will be an unexpected joy to provide advice and frank truths to the government, public, and immigrants as an immigration policy research professional and a guide for immigration policy.

ESTABLISHING THE IMMIGRATION NATION SYSTEM BEFORE THE 2020 TOKYO OLYMPICS AND PARALYMPICS

Since retiring as a civil servant in 2005, I have dedicated myself to crafting my theory for the immigration nation. Even though I've been blessed with good health and have made it to the age of seventy-three, I'm not ready to let go despite my powerlessness. I want at least two more years of life. That is what's needed to lay the foundation of the immigration nation. I want that foundation—the preparation of the legal institutions for immigrants, for example—to be in place for the 2020 Tokyo Olympics and Paralympics—just a year away.

I'm prepared for the Tokyo Olympics and Paralympics to be the last chance for Japan to be resurrected as a vibrant nation. In light of the recent situation where Diet members have shown dynamic movement on immigration policy, I feel that it's possible that the goal will be met. But the world of politics is one where you never know what's going to happen until the very end.

Should my power be insufficient, and the immigration nation is not achieved by 2020, the weight of my failure will be such that I will deserve to die a thousand times over. The spiritual and physical loss it will bring to the people is incalculable. However, at this age I no longer have the willpower to commit *seppuku* as an apology to the public; I will have to live on in shame, mocked for the emptiness of my words.

Until this point, I have been looked down on by some intellectuals and derided for my pipe dream. But even if things don't go according to plan, I'm able to calm down with the thought that it's only a matter of time until my final mission is accomplished.

I earnestly pray that, in that situation, a great politician appears and immediately makes the decision for a national commitment to immigration, thereby establishing the immigration nation. That is the sole ray of hope that I have. At that time, I may be given another opportunity to step forward, should I still have the willpower.

***

Let's change the subject. I've recently found a new source of strength. Of late, daily accesses of the JIPI webpage have reached an average of 5,000. Some days, it's over 10,000. More than anything else, this is proof that the number of young people with whom my theory of immigration policy resonates is steadily increasing. This surprising number shows the great expectations the young have for immigration policy. I predict that the voices of those who support immigration policy will spread explosively online and become the driving force that creates a new future for Japan.

According to the aforementioned national poll in the summer of 2015 by the *Yomiuri Shimbun* on "a society with a declining population," "thirty-eight percent of people agree with accepting immigrants, with fifty percent of those in their twenties agreeing."

I was surprised by those results, as the public had paid no attention to my immigration nation concept in the preceding ten years. I was over-whelmed with happiness at the fact that a majority of those in their twen-ties—those who will carry Japan into the future—agreed with accepting immigrants. I became convinced that sooner or later the younger genera-tion would rise and build an immigration nation that will be a beacon in the world.

There has been a sea change from 2005, when immigration policy was absolutely not a topic of conversation, to today, when the number of young people who approve of immigration is rapidly increasing. The spell closing off Japan has been broken and we have set sail with the winds in our favor. The following is the scenario I propose.

By the 2020 Tokyo Olympics and Paralympics, the majority of the younger generation makes its support for immigration clear. Seeing this, the prime minister decides to endorse a national commitment to immi-gration. If the JIPI director—a man knowledgeable about the legal institu-tions for immigration—fulfills his duties, then immigration nation Japan will be inaugurated in the new imperial era, on the opening day of the Tokyo Olympics or subsequent Paralympics. It is essential that legislation related to immigration policy—the passing of an Immigration Law, re-form of the Immigration Control Law, and more—be passed in the Diet in 2019 to prepare a foolproof immigration nation system.

ESTABLISHING AN IMMIGRATION NATION THROUGH NATIONAL CONSENSUS

Making full use of my administrative experience in immigration policy, I am putting forth a realistic, concrete plan for immediately moving to-ward becoming an immigration nation. This includes the legal institu-tions for immigration such as enacting an Immigration Law, concluding immigration agreements with other countries, creating an Agency for Immigration Policy, establishing a Basic Conference on Immigration Poli-cy, and abolishing the Technical Internship Program. I am confident that it is a practical immigration policy that can be used to address the emer-gency situation we face: the collapse of the demographic order.

However, due to the absence of experts on immigration policy, my proposals for a Japanese-style immigration policy—laid out in my writ-ing from 2005 to the present—have not even been taken up for discussion within the Japanese intellectual community. Naturally, they have not be-come issues of political contention. For a long time, I felt chagrined at my own powerlessness.

But after many years of being the only one talking about immigration, a miracle occurred. In 2005, almost none of the population was interested in immigration. Today, fifty-one percent of people support accepting immigrants (according to an April 2015 *Asahi Shimbun* poll). We've entered a new phase where a majority of the population supports immigration policy.

While I believe that we're only one step away from accomplishing my goal, I strongly caution against being complacent and stopping. In order to overcome the sturdy barrier of politics—which attempts to distance itself from immigration policy—we need to aim for even more popular support.

The hurdles that we face are high. In truth, there's almost no sign of members of the public being proactive in creating a relationship of coexistence with immigrants. How can we break through this solid wall of public opinion and shape it, making it so proactive on accepting immigrants that the government has no choice but to decide to open up the country?

It is entirely my responsibility as an opinion leader on immigration policy. I will fulfill my responsibility to explain and gain the understanding of a great number of the public on the necessity and urgency of accepting immigrants. I will, for example, calmly explain the international significance of Japan opening to immigration, the heightened world expectations of Japan opening to immigration, the specific contents of the legal institutions for immigration, and the relationship between immigration policy and the social welfare system. Fortunately, I still have the will to create. I will continue to write powerful arguments and increase positive public opinion on immigration policy.

In fact, I hold the ambition of shaping public opinion so that seventy percent of the public supports accepting immigration. That support will shift politics. Discussion of a national commitment to immigration is inherently entangled with ethnic sentiment. It's not uncommon for it to lead to fierce arguments that can divide a country or conflicts that lead to blood being spilled. Japan has comparably less exclusionary ethnic sentiment than Western countries, however, and I believe that immigration policy will not lead to the public being divided as it has in, for example, America where President Trump has joined with white supremacy, or France where there has been a clear spread of Islamophobia.

If Japan can peacefully move to being an immigration nation through democratic means at the same time that the immigration powers of the West are closing their doors to immigrants, it will become a model for the world: a democratic revolution that establishes an immigration nation based on a national consensus.

LET'S DANCE BEAUTIFULLY ON THE STAGE OF THE FUTURE

While I never actually laid eyes on Umesao Tadao, I have looked up to him as my mentor since I was in my twenties. From among his copious writings, I was particularly influenced by *Hikaku Bunmeigaku Kenkyū* (Research on Comparative Civilizations), *Minzokugaku no Sekai* (The World of Ethnology), and *Chikyū Jidai ni Ikiru* (Living in a Global Age). Reading these books over and over, I learned the importance of writing policy papers that only a Japanese could write, that were more than just copies of those by Westerners. Whenever I write a new paper, I always choose a favorite from Umesao's writings and place it by my side. There are times when I think to myself that, with immigration problems becoming a global issue, now is the time to stand up and repay the intellectual debt I owe him.

This is a proverb from Umesao's final book, a collection of interviews published posthumously: "There are situations a person must not run from. And when that happens, it is necessary to dance properly. You need to be prepared and able to carry out your responsibilities."[1]

I've embarked on the adventure that is creating an immigration nation the likes of which no people in the world has accomplished. And I have never forgotten Umesao's last words to the Japanese people as I pursued my ideal model for that, not for a second. Umesao was an authority of ethnology that held a "love of the unknown" and steadfastly walked his course without wavering. I have no doubt that he is eagerly anticipating from his place in heaven the creation of a "Japanese-style immigration nation" and a "global human community."

Frankly, there are times when I feel like I want to flee from my responsibilities to the future of Japan. But I know that if Umesao was still alive he'd scold me, saying, "Never give up. Carry out your responsibility."

As the one tasked with ensuring a national commitment to the immigration nation, it is necessary for me to carry on Umesao's idea of global citizens, assume the leading role on the stage of creating Japan's future, and dance beautifully as I do so.

I don't know how far I can go in turning my pipe dream into global immigration policy, but I will carry out my responsibilities as a pioneer of the immigration revolution until the day I die.

At the very least, if I do not try to overturn the institutions closing Japan off from immigration, prepare the systems needed by the immigration nation, and help save the world from its humanitarian crisis, I will not be able to look Umesao Tadao in the face when I go to meet him.

PORTRAITS OF MODERNITY—JIPI DIRECTOR SAKANAKA HIDENORI

A long article introducing me ran in the "Gendai no Shōzō (Portraits of Modernity)" column of the weekly *AERA* in late 2018.[2] This excellent piece was carefully written by Ōhira Makoto. It might even be considered a pioneering piece that turns a spotlight on me, ending my long time in the shadows. I believe this biographical sketch, which came out just as discussion of immigration policy began in the Diet, was influential in many areas. The following are the portions of the article that stayed with me:

> The Ministry of Justice Immigration Bureau will be elevated to the status of an agency next spring and its immigration counters are trying to change significantly to match the expansion of its duties. It's just like trying to remove the chain from the sturdy gate closing Japan off from immigration and open a port for immigrants. Sakanaka Hidenori (73) is a unique career public servant who chose not to "read the room" and thereby gave the *Zainichi* Koreans a more stable legal status and saved the [Asian women who came to Japan to work in the 1980s] from the depths of despair. And he can see the town on the other side of that port. . . . Sakanaka's name became known in 1975 after his essay "On the Future of Immigration Administration" was chosen as the best entry in a contest commemorating the 25th anniversary of the Immigration Bureau. The main points of the "Sakanaka Thesis"—which is still talked about—were providing more secure legal status to the then-640,000 *Zainichi* Koreans, abolishing discrimination in employment, education, and housing, and creating an environment where it was easy to obtain Japanese citizenship while maintaining a minority cultural identity (such as non-Japanese names). This thesis, which Sakanaka had published in 1977 using his own funds, was met with protest from activist groups and progressive people of culture, most notably the Korean Residents Union in Japan (*Mindan*) and the General Association of Korean Residents in Japan (*Chongryon*). It was criticized as "a further progression of the policy of assimilation" and as "closing people off from being able to return to the Democratic People's Republic of Korea." The actual origins for the essay lay in the pure indignation of a young man with a strong sense of justice. It was the April after he had joined the ministry and he was twenty-five. Sakanaka recalls: "I did six months of hands-on training at what was then the Ōsaka Immigration Control Office. I was apolitical and had become a public servant for no particular reason. My image of foreigners at the time was of blond-haired and blue-eyed Westerners, so I was quite surprised that almost everyone I met at an [immigration] counter was a *Zainichi* Korean." Because of his essay, Sakanaka was entrusted with revising the law in 1981 while he was an assistant section head. This took shape as the "Immigration Control and Refugee Recognition Act" which was enacted on January 1, 1982 as a revision of the Immigration Control Order

that had been adopted in accordance with the Potsdam Declaration. The passage of this revision essentially ended *Zainichi* Koreans choosing to repatriate to the supposed "paradise on earth" of North Korea because they couldn't bear the discrimination they experienced in Japan. It's been more than forty years since the "Sakanaka Thesis" that served as a starting point. Seo Won Chul, secretary-general of *Mindan*'s Central Headquarters, sharply criticized the contents of the essay at the time but says that he now understands Sakanaka. Seo: "The term '*Zainichi*' came into usage in the 1970s and was coined by the second generation [of Koreans in Japan]. The feelings of that generation were a mixture of rebellion and being unable to endure any longer. The Sakanaka Essay expressed local feelings as they actually were, and that was a big shock. It was pure. The immigration policy that Sakanaka is working on is likely his final mission. Looking at the 150 years since the Meiji Restoration, there haven't been many like him. I'm impressed that someone like him was born." Prime Minister Abe Shinzō has repeatedly said that "there's no way that Japan will adopt an immigration policy," but in June of this year he announced that a wide range of foreigners would be admitted into the country to combat the labor shortage affecting small and mid-sized businesses. He changed course and proposed a substantial immigration policy out of consideration of gaining support for his third term as LDP president. There's no point if it's done without any discussion. The historic decision of adopting an immigration policy should be made into an election issue so that the people can be asked where their beliefs lie. If the people, on their own, embark on the creation of a new nation the likes of which has never been seen in the world, it doesn't matter how many years it takes. He doesn't care about money or fame. The convictions of Sakanaka Hidenori, the unyielding bureaucrat, will open the door to a new age.

SEEKING THE IDEAL IMMIGRATION NATION

There's no law that says that an elderly seventy-three-year-old cannot draw a heart-felt, beautiful picture on a white piece of paper like a young person would. And having great aspirations isn't a privilege reserved to the young. Old people who love to imagine what the future world should look like have eyes that see things from a broad perspective and the wisdom that comes from experience. There are utopian tales that only an immigration policy pro who has spent forty-nine years buried in speculation on the treatment of immigrants can write—the vision for a Japanese-style immigrant nation that would be loved by the global youth seeking a new world for immigrants, for example.

When I retired from the civil service in 2005, I resolved to devote the rest of my life to creating an immigration nation that would save Japan from its time of population decline. In recent years, I have seized upon the crisis of population collapse as a chance to throw our doors open to the people of the world and make a national commitment to immigration. I have actively advocated for my theory of the human community, a society in which the Japanese and the peoples of the world unify, for the idea for an immigration revolution that sprang to life in the head of a Japanese, a people with spirits rich in tolerance. There's still far to go on the path to the human community and the goal of eternal peace, but I believe that at the very least we've come far enough to clearly see their profile in the distance.

***

In the tenth chapter of *Immigration Battle Diary*, I expressed my contemporary feelings in a section entitled "Japan as a model nation for the world":

> While there are parts of Europe who are already experiencing the problem of population decline, there is no country in the world where the problem is so serious and the situation progressing so rapidly as in Japan. When thinking about this problem, it must be said that no country exists that can serve as a model for it. Accordingly, Japan will have to stand at the forefront of the world, investigate what a country facing a population decline should be like, and provide a vision of the future. I hope that the measures that the nation of Japan adopts to address its society with a declining population will provide a good precedent for the future world.[3]

Reading over this passage today nearly fifteen years later, it occurred to me that this was a declaration of resolve made as my life as an official was ending, and I was beginning a new life. To take responsibility for raising this issue, I founded the Foreigners Policy Institute (*Gaikokujin Seisaku Kenkyūsho*, the predecessor of JIPI) in August 2005 with the purpose of creating an immigration nation that could serve as a model for the world in the age of population decline. With that as my base of operations, I engaged in the work of fundamentally reviewing Japan's policies toward foreigners. And with the revised publication of *Vision of Immigration Nation Japan* in September 2018, I completed the basic theory for a Japanese-style immigration nation suitable for making Japan into a model for the world.

Having reached an age where it is time to conclude my life's work, I have reached the state of mind that I am settling things with fate. My determination to sacrifice myself to the great cause of saving the Japanese people from disappearing from the face of the earth has been renewed, and I constantly find myself thinking about the fate of my immigration nation vision and its ultimate goal of providing an example for the world.

There may be unforeseen difficulties waiting ahead as the goal enters view. I may come under unimaginable pressure. Can I overcome the wall of passivity that exists in politics over the question of accepting immigrants? Having walked the steep path toward an immigration nation alone, will my mind and body be able to withstand the demands when the crucial moment comes? Is it possible that the anti-immigrant sentiment extolled by President Trump will spread throughout the world? And will my dream of a human community collapse? Having been essentially on my own for so long, my mind is repeatedly assaulted by these kinds of nightmares, even if only temporarily.

But when this happens, these timid thoughts are immediately dispelled by stronger ones and my willpower rises up. Having come so far, there's no point worrying about these things.

And if someone from the current generation of Japanese doesn't establish an immigration nation system, we will be denounced by the Japanese of fifty years from now: "The Japanese of the *Heisei* period reduced Japan to the status of a second-rate nation." There are times when I'm caught up by that kind of threatening notion.

Spiritual conflict is not easily suppressed. But I am innately an optimist. I switch mental gears and resolve that now that the world's immigration policy has entered a time of turmoil is the very time for me to arrive and use the remainder of my strength to break through the difficulty.

The following is my action plan for the future, to make the most of what is left of my life:

1. To dedicate my body and mind and await the will of Heaven.
2. To believe that Heaven will aid the immigration nation vision that I have poured my heart and soul into.
3. To appeal to the world and Japan concerning the magnificence of the youth of Japan and their spirit of tolerance toward those of different ethnicities.
4. To step back from the front line before we enter the limelight.

AN IMMIGRATION NATION BLESSED BY THE WORLD

As a reckless revolutionary, I have come to believe that "the will of Heaven" and "sacred callings" are things that actually exist, and that my life up until this day has been intertwined with them. Why did I, the personification of rationalism, begin to embrace turning to God for help?

It's because I have taken on a task of historic significance for the Japanese people, the world, and humanity in general: the fundamental reform of what Japanese and human society looks like. It's because I'm fighting a problem that I could not even hope to budge through my own power. And, having done all that I could with Heaven's help, I believe that I have no choice but to entrust the rest to the will of Heaven.

As we move toward a new phase in which there is hope for a national commitment to an immigration nation, I have been able to spare the time to look back objectively on my tumultuous life. The will of Heaven and my sacred mission have given me an extremely happy life.

With Heaven always on my side, I happened across work that allowed me to trailblaze new history. I have developed a monumental theory of the immigration nation that has been well-received by the intellectuals around the world. I have broken through the sturdy wall closing Japan off from immigration that has existed since the *Heian* era (794-1185) and opened a path to becoming an immigration nation. And as if in response, the youth of Japan have raised their voices in support of immigration. The government has begun to stir itself to action, adopting policies that lead in the direction of a national commitment to immigration.

Thinking back on the road that got me here, it was a long, thorny path that seemed to stretch on endlessly. I took on the issues that will determine Japan's survival in an age of population decline, wrote immigration policy papers that were on-target, and showed the public how to solve the problem. While taking to heart that I could not stray from the right path because Heaven was watching, I did what I wanted to do in the way I wanted.

For a long time, I had to persevere alone against trials and difficulties, but my fortunes changed in 2015. The trends of the times have turned in favor of my vision of a Japanese immigration nation. I have reached a place where I can catch a glimpse of a Japanese-style immigration nation.

When I was in school, I was just a normal student. There was nothing special about me. After graduating from university, I chose to be a civil servant because I wanted a stable job. I entered the Ministry of Justice's Immigration Bureau, a modest office with jurisdiction over minority issues. I had no idea that a cutthroat life awaited me where I would spend all my time battling against issues that were taboo. Only God knew what the future held for me.

My life as a civil servant came to an end in March 2005. I am someone whose only ability is to formulate immigration policy, and in the hard world of modern Japan, there was no workplace for that kind of optimist. Unable to find an appropriate workplace for my second life, I chose to devote myself to researching immigration policy as a volunteer. I'm thankful for that. No one impeded my research. I was able to run single-mindedly down the course of immigration policy research unfettered.

It's been almost fifteen years since I retired from the justice ministry. I made the creation of an immigration nation unparalleled in the world as my goal, my only reason for living. For me, it truly was a sacred mission. It could also perhaps be said to be perfect as a post-retirement job.

Then came January 2017. Having completed the theoretical backing for the Japanese-style immigration nation, I encountered an unexpected event. America, the world symbol for an immigration nation, turned into a country that limited immigration following the inauguration of the Trump administration. Seeing this, I intuitively knew that the time had come for Japan to open itself to immigration and save the world from its plight.

If the Japanese government declared itself an immigration nation just as things were looking grim for immigrants, it would be a Heaven-sent opportunity for Japan to really stand out. Immigration nation Japan would receive intense support from the young people the world over and be blessed by the spirits of the world.

GREAT FLOWERS COME FROM GREAT DREAMS

"Forgoing dreams yields no fruit, but conjuring great dreams leads to great flowers." This is my favorite saying. Embracing the grand ambition of creating a new state, my dreams have gradually expanded as I get older. For that reason, it becomes harder and harder to realize my dreams. So, have I had a happy life? In truth, that can't necessary be said. For most of the 2010s, the realization of my dreams only seemed to become more distant. I frequently wanted this life of only pursuing dreams to end.

However, over these last three years I've been defiant. I've roused myself and churned out policy papers, telling myself that now is the time for the decisive battle. The supreme expression of my tragic but brave determination is the new edition of *Vision for an Immigration Nation Japan,* which I published in September 2018. With the major Western immigration nations largely closing their doors to immigrants and refugees, I wrote this book with the determination to take the lead in immigration policy not just for Japan but for the world. Expending all my body and soul, I have extolled an ideal immigration nation that will serve as a pillar for my vision of a human community.

Recently, there have been times when I have been optimistic that the time when my many years of effort will be rewarded is close. The times have changed so much that now a majority of youth in Japan have expressed support for admitting immigrants. I am proud of them. They are prepared to truly welcome immigrants while those elsewhere in the world have embraced anti-immigrant movements. The future of the immigration nation is a bright one and these broad-minded young people serve as the locomotive that pulls it forward. An immigration nation in which the youth of Japan play a leading role would serve as a beacon among the immigration nations of the world, as they have learned to be global citizens.

Having travelled eighty percent of the way along the path to an immigration nation, I feel reassured. The government seems to have settled on a policy of shifting toward an immigration nation. Debate over immigration policy has begun in the Diet. The immigration issue has become an urgent political task that Japanese politics will need to address. The era when I fought on alone has ended.

I want to work hand-in-hand with capable young people to complete the remaining twenty percent of work needed to create an immigration nation that becomes a model for the world. I want to cause a beautiful flower to bloom on the Japanese archipelago.

***

My other dream, the creation of a human community, is the long-felt desire of humanity for eternal world peace. The intellectuals of the world will have to take on the challenge of realizing it in the several centuries to come. If I, who have taken the lead thus far, may be allowed one wish, it would be for the youth of Japan—the only country to experience the use of nuclear weapons in wartime—to take the lead in this.

Today, we've plunged into an era when the existence of weapons of mass destruction—capable of destroying all living things including humanity—has become a true threat. The future existence of the human race depends on the success or failure of the human community. Human society cannot dismiss the concept of the human community—the antithesis of nuclear war—as a mere "paradise dreamed up by a Japanese." I believe that it will develop into a realistic and global task which the humans living in the global age of the twenty-second century will join together and take on.

It will be a world where humanity—the most intelligent of all the world's creatures—unifies and rises together to realize a society based on the human community, returning to our biological starting point of "humanity as all comrades of the same species." It will be a world that blooms in full glory with diverse flowers as humanity and all of creation coexists on the earth. I might be the happiest person on the planet when I fantasize about that land of peace where all of creation lives and flourishes together

NOTES

1. Umesao Tadao, *Umesao Tadao Kataru* (Umesao Tadao Speaks), (Tōkyō: Nihon Keizai Shimbun Shuppansha, 2010), pp. 213-214.

2. Ōhira Makoto, "Sakanaka Hidenori, Imin Seisaku Kenkyūsho Shochō: Nyūkan Issuji, Hankotsu no Motokanryō (Sakanaka Hidenori, Japan Immigration Policy Institute Director: A Longtime Immigration Official and Bureaucrat Who Fought Authority)," *AERA*, No. 1716 (December 17, 2018), pp. 56-61.

3. Sakanaka, *Nyūkan Senki*, p. 237.

SIX

The Spirit of the Japanese-style Immigration Nation

THE PHILOSOPHY BEHIND THE POLICY

Generally speaking, young people in today's Japan lack vitality. Perhaps this is because they feel insecure about their futures. I've heard that the number of Japanese who study overseas for long periods is falling. My personal impression is that the number of young people with an interest in the world is declining and that many are withdrawing into Japan. Will the Japan of the era of population decline be an introverted country?

As Japan enters an unprecedented period of population decline, the demographic crisis looms over all of society. In particular, a dark cloud hangs over the future of those few children who have been born into this generation (those thirty and younger). The burdens on them look to only grow heavier as time passes.

What should those in positions of responsibility—politicians, bureaucrats, business leaders, and intellectuals—do to eliminate their feeling of being trapped? How can they create a future society in which the young burn with hope? My answer will come as no surprise. They should throw open the doors of the country to the talented of the word and admit "ten million immigrants" into Japan. Our population's problems—an extremely low birthrate and an aging society—are unparalleled in the world in their severity, but they can be overcome through a national commitment to immigration. This is the only national vision that can capture the hearts of those born in this time of low childbirth, those who carry Japan's future on their shoulders.

A suitable "immigration policy" to promote the acceptance of immigrants is indispensable to creating an immigration society in which Japanese and immigrants coexist. I am proposing a "Japanese-style immigration policy" that trains foreigners to become capable human resources, provides them with stable workplaces, and accepts them as permanent residents. The reason I say this is a "Japanese-style" policy is because it emphasizes education and takes the approach of "cultivating" foreign talent rather than "securing" it.

If we are to accept immigrants on an unprecedented scale, it will be necessary to fundamentally reform how the country treats foreigners. We must change to a style of administration that is considerate of immigrants, who are in the position of being a minority. The administrative focus of this immigration policy is placed on Japanese language training and employment support to promote the smooth adaptation of those foreigners accepted as immigrants to being part of Japanese society. It will also be necessary to establish a new system under which those immigrants who wish to take Japanese citizenship are able to do so easily.

Regarding the ten-million immigrants number, it should be kept in mind that even if that many immigrants are admitted over the next fifty years, the population will still decrease by thirty million. My basic position is one that emphasizes having a "shrinking society," one that moves toward being a smaller Japan in accordance with the natural decline in the population. I believe that we should accept that the population will continue to decline for at least the next fifty years and make our national goal leaving a beautiful natural environment and a stable society for the Japanese of fifty years from now.

This ten-million number will also include immigrants' families. Judging from the West's experience with immigrant families, in addition to the initial group of immigrants who enter Japan with the intention of working and residing here permanently, we can also expect a fair number of them to marry or call on their families to join them.

"Ten million immigrants" is just a temporary guide. Over the fifty years we should move toward becoming an immigration nation where "ten percent of the population is made up of immigrants," as is the case in other developed nations. While even under the current immigration system we can predict some increase in the number of foreigners residing in Japan as the population crisis becomes more serious, this will be accomplished by devising a firm immigration policy. We will accept immigrants in an orderly fashion, establishing a plan for how many to accept each year, taking into account what progress has been made in adapting them to Japanese society. In doing so, we must avoid immigration policies that are lopsided toward any particular nationality or ethnicity. We will invite public backlash if we follow an immigration policy similar to that in place today, where most permanent residents are Chinese or Korean.

If we adopt an immigration policy that accepts people from a diverse range of the countries in a balanced manner, it will not only benefit us from a diplomatic and security standpoint but also make multiethnic national unity comparatively easy to accomplish.

In order for the large-scale admission of immigrants to proceed smoothly, we will need transparent and fair immigrant acceptance standards that are made public to the world.

For example, how about a point-based system like that used in developed immigration nations such as Britain and Canada? In this kind of system, criteria such as a potential immigrant's academic history, age, and language ability are converted into points in accordance with that country's standards, and foreigners who reach a certain number of points are granted the ability to apply for immigration. Specific screening items such as language ability, academic history, work history, and ability to adapt to Japanese society would be established and made public.

THE DISTINCTIVE FEATURES OF A JAPANESE-STYLE IMMIGRATION NATION

The distinctive feature of the Japanese-style immigration nation system is that it makes the most of the country's higher educational and workplace training institutions to cultivate superior human resources from the immigrants who enter Japan. It then provides these immigrants with vocational support, permanent residency, and a rapid path to citizenship. The decline in childbirth means that that there will be a surplus of educational facilities such as universities and agricultural and other vocational high schools. These can be used to educate immigrants and train them.

Domestically cultivating individuals with specialized knowledge and skills means that we won't be robbing developing countries of their precious human resources. Because the "immigrants" we will be welcoming will be foreign talented individuals who have received good training (including in the Japanese language) at universities and similar institutions, the deterioration of public safety that the public is worried about will not happen. Based on my experience working in immigration for thirty-five years, I can say that immigrants who adapt to Japanese society and have stable workplaces don't cause problems.

I'm opposed to the acceptance of "guest workers" or "foreign workers" (including foreign technical interns). This is because this term carries a strong implication that someone has been brought into the country to help alleviate the industrial labor shortage and work for low wages. There's also the inference that these workers will be allowed into Japan while the economy is good but thrown out if it enters a downturn.

The Japanese population will continue to steadily decline. Meanwhile, the population of several Asian countries will continue to increase, at least for the immediate future. The biggest concern is that foreign workers will enter the country illegally, in a disorderly fashion. Industry

wants to hire foreign workers and pay them low wages, but we absolutely must avoid that. Permitting it will invite the large-scale illegal entry of
foreigners into Japan and nearly destroy our immigration control systems.

I propose that a "foreigner vocational training system" be created to
take the place of the Technical Internship Program. We would thereby
replace a program that was created during the time when Japan's population was increasing and has caused a host of problems with one that will
help us survive the era of population decrease.

This system would make use of agricultural, industrial, and fishery
high schools (all sectors that will continue to suffer from labor shortages
as the low rate of childbirth continues) and other vocational training
facilities to establish a three-year "foreigner vocational training curriculum" under which foreigners would be taught specialized knowledge
and skills (including the Japanese language). Those who complete this
curriculum will be provided with the opportunity to undertake a further
year of on-site practical skill training.

Under this system, foreigners who have completed this four-year program and wish to work in Japan will be granted a status of residence by
immigration officials that permits them to do so—on the condition that
they are employed as full-time employees (such as by the companies that
provided the vocational training).

I propose the following to prepare the foundation for a Japanese-style
immigration policy: enactment of an "Immigration Law" that outlines the
basic ideas of the policy; revision of the "Immigration Control and Refugee Recognition Act," a "Nationality Law" to ensure consistency on immigration policy; and the creation of an "Immigration Policy Agency" so
that the country's policies on immigrants are enforced uniformly. I also
seek the passage of a "Basic Law on Social Cohesion" and an "Ethnic
Discrimination Prohibition Law" to promote social cohesion and multiethnic coexistence.

My above proposals were accepted by the LDP's National Strategy
Headquarters' "Path to a Japanese-style Immigration Nation" project
team in June 2008 and were incorporated into "A Country Open to Human Resources! The Path to a Japanese-style Immigration Nation," a report, mentioned earlier, that was submitted to Prime Minister Fukuda
Yasuo.

THE GOAL SHOULD BE A "BALANCED MULTIETHNIC SOCIETY"

Today, Japan stands at the crossroads of history and is in urgent need of a
thinker who can clearly show it the way forward. Unfortunately, however, no such thinker—someone who can picture what Japan and the world

will look like a century from now—can be found among the current generation of Japanese

We have no choice but to give up on the hope that someone will emerge from the multitude in Japanese society who looks upon our unbroken blood purity with pride, someone who can devise a long-range plan for Japan that perceives the human society of a century from now, brings global human resources to Japan, and leads us to a world bursting with talent.

With the survival of Japan in a global age on the line, the time has come to change into a "society in which diverse ethnicities can coexist," one that welcomes the people of the world as immigrants (future citizens). If Japan accepts ten million immigrants as future citizens and the Japanese transform into a nation with diversity, it can survive in a tumultuous global age.

Enacting an Immigration Law is indispensable to creating a multiethnic society with a population rich in diversity. The government will, in a fair manner, determine guidelines for how many immigrants of each nationality to accept each year based on the stipulations of the Immigration Law and ensuring that certain countries or regions are not disproportionately represented. Government bodies such as the justice and foreign ministries will strive to secure diverse human resources from across the world in accordance with those guidelines, expanding Japan's immigration agreements globally and granting permanent residency flexibly via the Immigration Control Law.

Looking at Japan's current population of permanent residents, it could be dubbed an "East Asian-centered immigrant community." Chinese and Korean permanent residents (immigrants) make up the overwhelming majority. We will need to quickly amend this state in which those racially similar to the Japanese hold an oligopoly if we are to create a balanced immigrant community.

If we emphasize fairness as we greatly expand our immigration policy, we will create a "model multiethnic society" that includes all of the world's major ethnicities. We will move from a highly uniform Japanese society where an overwhelming number of Japanese are of the same race and script to an immigration society rich in diversity where people of different races, religions, and customs live with each other in mutual understanding.

I'd also like to emphasize that immigration policy is an indispensable part of national security. If the government engages in proactive immigration diplomacy, makes the fair acceptance of the peoples of the world the basis for Japanese immigration policy, and concludes immigration treaties with friendly countries, then Japan will build close relationships with the countries those immigrants come from. Japan's national security system will become stronger.

And the candidates for future citizenship who enter Japan from friendly countries via these immigration agreements will likely passionately study the Japanese language, strive to learn Japanese customs, and become Japanophiles who revere the imperial family.

"Human movements" between Japan and the countries of the world will increase, "interactions" will expand, and the "circle of friendships" will widen. "Immigration" will become a bridge of peace between Japan and the world.

And if the government resolutely implements a policy of permitting absolutely no immigrants with anti-Japanese ideologies into the country, it will be able to appropriately control the immigration of people from countries with fiercely anti-Japanese educational systems like China and South Korea that the public is concerned about.

ON THE DEFINITION OF "IMMIGRANT"

When I use the word "immigrant," I do so in accordance with its internationally accepted common sense meaning of "a foreigner who has received permanent residency [or *eijūken*] in accordance with immigration law." This is the same meaning that a green card holder has in American immigration law.

But while the concepts of "immigrant" (a permanent resident) and "citizen" are related, they are legally distinct.

Looking at the history of how Western countries admitted foreigners, they initially brought them in as slaves and later accepted others as labor. In the modern world, it is normal to welcome foreigners as immigrants (permanent residents) and humans. Immigration policy is considered the best method for humanely admitting foreigners.

For example, Germany—which took in foreigners as a labor force throughout the postwar period—announced in 2005 that they would become an immigration nation. Afterward, they proactively expanded their immigration policy of admitting foreigners as permanent residents and are now regarded as the top immigration nation in Europe.

Industry sees foreigners as labor. When times are good, foreign workers are allowed in, but when they turn bad, they are expelled. In many cases, they are not treated as people but rather as low-cost labor to be driven hard. In reality, there are cases when their treatment isn't that different from slavery.

Immigrants are foreigners who will reside in Japan permanently. They are foreigners with a good chance of quickly obtaining citizenship. As members of society, immigrants fulfill their obligation to pay taxes and are enrolled in the social security system. They possess all rights except those constitutionally restricted to citizens: the right to vote, the right to run for office, and the right to seek employment as a national public official.

If asked what foreigner policy is right for Japan with its rapidly declining number of citizens, I would answer that it is a policy of immigration as it directly leads to an increase in the number of citizens. The proper policy toward foreigners for a country with a society of declining population is to permit the admittance of immigrants and their families into the country as consumers, workers, and future citizens.

Recently, the word "immigrant" has become commonplace among politicians, bureaucrats, scholars, researchers, and journalists, and essays and books using the words "immigrant" and "immigration policy" have become numerous. In the media and online, "immigrant" has become mainstream, displacing the phrase, "foreign worker."

And the government, which has been negative toward the acceptance of immigrants and has emphasized in official documents that it "would not adopt immigration policy," has played a role in publicizing "immigration policy." Then, in October 2018, the curtain was lifted on discussion of immigration policy in a plenary session of the Diet.

As the director of the JIPI, I have released many papers and works that made free use of the terms "immigration," "immigration policy," "immigration revolution," "immigration nation," "Japanese-style immigration policy," "the ten-million immigrant concept," "demographic collapse and the immigration revolution," "global spread of immigrant countries," and "vision for a Japanese immigration nation" over the past eleven years. Additionally, the Japanese-born vision of an immigration nation has been freely debated daily online using these words since the spring of 2013. I've maintained the same posture I always have in interviews with domestic and international media outlets. I have absolutely no use for the term "foreign worker."

THE HEART OF AN IMMIGRATION POLICY THAT CULTIVATES HUMAN RESOURCES

During my time at the justice ministry, I was known as someone who came down harshly on foreigners who were in Japan illegally. I've heard that I was called the "demon Sakanaka" by some among the foreigner community in Japan.

It is true that I dealt with them in a rigorous—but impartial—manner as an administrator in accordance with the Immigration Control and Refugee Recognition Act (otherwise known as the "Immigration Control Law") which states that "impartial immigration control" is to be performed.

The Japanese people's perception of foreigners is the key to determining whether the country can successfully become a society in which Japanese coexist with foreigners. That society cannot be created if they associate them with negative elements such as crime or terrorism. And I believe that the work of immigration control—preventing illegal entrance into the country—is important for preventing the public's view of foreigners from worsening.

For example, following 9/11, America—a country that had been tolerant of immigrants ever since its founding—changed dramatically. It became a country that strictly limits entrance into the country by immigrants.

America is a country that was created by immigrants in the first place. The active acceptance of immigrants was a national policy. Terrorism drastically changed its posture toward immigrants. When this happened, I took it to heart that the historical change in America's immigration policy had to be seen as a lesson for Japanese immigration control.

During the long period prior to the amendment of the Immigration Control Law in 1990, the Japanese government admitted virtually no foreigners into Japan for the purpose of work or residency. The guiding principle for immigration control at the time was "prevent residency." Newly employed immigration control officers had it pounded into them by their seniors that preventing the permanent residency of foreigners was a mission that had been given to the immigration control administration. The social situation behind this policy was that Japan was "an overcrowded society with a growing population."

But today Japan is leading the world in population decline. It is now necessary for Japan to systematically admit ten million immigrants. Many towns and villages in areas with primary industries are already experiencing rapid declines in population. Unless we decisively adopt immigration policy, they will be in danger of disappearing. With the rapid decline of the consumer and productive populations, it is obvious that we will soon enter a period of negative economic growth. And that's not all. Financial collapse, bank failures, and collapse of the social security system are all becoming more likely by the moment.

Some make the argument that we should admit foreigners as workers, but I'm opposed to that. This is because the position that they will be admitted as "workers" carries with it the strong implication that they will be short-term "migrant labor" that is treated poorly. With its declining population, the foreign human resources that Japan needs are not "foreign workers" but rather "immigrants." It is essential that we change to an immigration policy that accepts foreigners as members of Japanese society from the start and provides them with guaranteed stable legal status and treatment, and the possibility of becoming future Japanese citizens. It is only through accepting immigrants that the realization of a society in which Japanese and immigrants coexist will become a national task.

I believe that given the high education level of the Japanese people and their spirit of tolerance toward other ethnicities, accepting ten million immigrants over the next fifty years in a planned fashion and maintaining a society of one hundred million people based on multiethnic coexistence are national objectives that we can accomplish.

The framework put in place for accepting immigrants into Japan will determine whether that effort succeeds or fails. Japan should adopt an immigration policy that "cultivates human resources." Foreigners should learn the Japanese language and high-level skills in Japanese schools and be trained into being "capable people" here. The industries that take in immigrants will make good use of the abilities they possess. Status and salary will be determined based on ability without regard for nationality or ethnicity.

"Japan Culture Centers" should be established in the major cities of the world. Japanese language and culture will be taught to young people all across the globe that have an interest in Japanese culture. The promising youths thus discovered will be accepted at government expense, matched with educational institutions and employers, and rapidly given permanent residency and Japanese citizenship.

The cooperation of universities will be essential to training the foreigners that Japan admits into highly skilled individuals who can be active in all areas of society. It will be necessary for them to play an important role as higher educational institutions for foreigners newly arrived in Japan and for the children and family of permanent residents (immigrants). I believe it will eventually be necessary to construct a system of higher education where millions of foreigners can study. Whether or not Japan's human resource-cultivating immigration policy succeeds or not will depend on how well the system for accepting international students can be expanded and used.

There are past examples of accepting foreigners that Japan can reflect upon—namely, the 1983 plan to accept 100,000 international students and the acceptance of Brazilians of Japanese ancestry from 1991 on.

Of the students who came from China (a majority of the total), many did so via loans of as much as three million yen (approximately $30,000) from brokers such as "snakeheads." Having difficulty paying back these loans, many of these students stayed in the country illegally and continued to work. The root cause of this problem was the implementation of a policy of accepting international students on a large scale without also expanding the systems that would support them, such as those for scholarships and dormitories—despite the great economic disparity between China and Japan.

***

In 2000, when I was head of the Nagoya Regional Immigration Bureau, I saw the actual conditions of the Japanese-Brazilians working at factories related to Toyota Motor Corporation. The living conditions of their children were wretched. Because they only understood Portuguese, only forty percent of the children of Japanese-Brazilians attended Japanese elementary schools. Being unable to write or read Japanese, these children couldn't go to college or find employment. Some turned to crime.

Japan has not provided foreigners with hopes or dreams. For example, in practice, foreigners employed by Japanese companies are generally only used as cheap labor, and often for the so-called "3K" work— *kitanai* (dirty), *kiken* (dangerous), and *kitsui* (hard). Their abilities are not properly assessed, and they are not given the same treatment as Japanese. And this is one of the reasons that I'm wary of the call for "expanded admission of foreign workers" heard from the business world.

Just looking at the position of foreigners in Japan now should make the necessity of an immigration policy that emphasizes education understandable.

TRAINING SKILLED HUMAN RESOURCES THROUGH AN IMMIGRATION POLICY THAT EMPHASIZES EDUCATION

To admit ten million immigrants over the next fifty years, we will need to discard the fantasy that the world's highly skilled human resources will automatically choose to come to Japan. Looking at the track record of our immigration control policy over the past twenty-nine years, it is clear that it has ended in failure.

In the age of immigration, Japan needs to understand that foreigners with specialized knowledge and advanced skills will not come to the *kanji*-using Japan; they will attempt to enter countries in the Anglosphere such as America, Britain, and Canada. Japan needs to use its higher educational institutions to cultivate skilled human resources. If we actively develop the ability to cultivate human resources and make that the cornerstone of our immigration policy, then the large numbers of immigrants who enter Japan and are trained to be highly skilled will be active in every area of Japanese society.

This is a policy of cultivating advanced human resources domestically. Ambitious foreigners will attend Japanese universities and similar institutions where they will be thoroughly educated in the Japanese language, taught specialized knowledge and advanced skills, and actively provided with government support in finding employment. By viewing this as a national undertaking and mobilizing our educational institutions' instructors for immigrant education, we will be able to provide society with excellent human resources. And our immigration authorities will quickly grant permanent residency to those foreigners who have found stable employment.

It is, in other words, a system that sustainably makes immigrants out of international students. Isn't this an immigration policy perfectly suited to the national character of Japan and its passion for education? Importantly, this policy is also conducive to making effective use of our educational institutions. Those educational institutions that have fallen upon hard times due to the lack of children will be placed in charge of immigrant education.

I have a request for the implementation of immigrant education. At no level—from elementary school to university—can this education be designed to mold them into becoming Japanese. We cannot kill off the unique ideas and rich sensibilities that the immigrants bring. It is essential that as we introduce this immigration policy with its emphasis on education, we comprehensively rethink our current educational system intended to produce uniformity. We need to make a change to the kind of education that respects the immigrants' cultures and cultivates human resources with individuality.

There is something I am concerned about regarding the admittance of advanced human resources—namely, whether Japan's universities, think tanks, and private research organizations have any interest in offering posts to these people. To my eyes, they don't seem to have the mentality needed for free competition—the desire to invite excellent human resources from across the world and join with them to produce research results.

Our universities need a breath of fresh air. The closed-off system where almost all professor positions are held by Japanese must be remedied. To raise research standards and improve the education level of Japan's universities, an effort should be made over the next ten years so that foreign nationals hold ten percent of professorships. Open up Japan's universities to young foreign researchers. If our universities prepare professor positions for accomplished foreign researchers, the great minds of the world will compete to come to Japan.

With the increasingly severe lack of children, we will soon enter an era where the large number of universities who have rested on their laurels face closure. Any university not willing to spill some of its own "blood" in the process of reform has no future.

I am proposing a "Japanese-style immigration policy" under which foreigners are trained to be capable human resources, provided with stable workplaces, and granted the status of permanent residents. But at the same time, this is also a policy to aid our excellent higher educational institutions.

The outcome of an immigration policy that cultivates human resources will depend on whether or not we can draw the youth of the world to Japan's higher education institutions such as vocational schools, universities, and graduate schools and train them to be capable human resources.

There's something I'd like to say to those affiliated with universities. I want you to undertake a "university revolution," not just for the sake of leading Japan's immigration policy toward success, but also so that our universities survive.

First, we must rapidly develop a robust system for admitting 300,000 international students and develop a strategic international student policy that admits international students in a fair manner and is backed by a system that educates them to the world's highest standards.

A prerequisite for doing this will be to drastically rethink the oligopolistic state of affairs where Chinese students make up nearly sixty percent of international students in Japan and reduce the proportion of Chinese students to ten percent or less over the next ten years. If that isn't done, our policies on international students and immigration will both draw backlashes from young people in Japan and the world. And we won't be able to become an immigration nation where global human resources diverse in race and ethnicity are able to become actively involved.

Second, after rapidly implementing this 300,000-international student plan, the country will plan for its actual goal: admitting one million international students. The system for a million international students (a figure that includes the second generation of immigrants who will study at Japanese universities) will be the central pillar supporting immigration nation Japan. Universities will discover and educate global human resources and send them out into Japanese society. Excellent human resources from around the world will flock to our universities where so many international students learn.

If the system for one million international students is put in place, seventy percent of these students find employment in Japan, and these are granted permanent residency, then the ideal immigration nation in which ten million skilled human resources are added as immigrants (candidates for citizenship) will be established.

THE HISTORICAL SIGNIFICANCE OF THE BASIC REGISTRATION SYSTEM FOR FOREIGN RESIDENTS

On July 9, 2012, the alien registration system was abolished and the basic registration system for foreign residents was launched in its place. Having been involved with the *Zainichi* Korean issue since the 1970s, I found the abolishment of the Alien Registration Law—a symbol of the management of their residency—a deeply emotional event for me.

On that day, the era of the *"Zainichi* Koreans"—the symbol of foreigner issues in postwar Japan—came to an end. Now the main focus of Japan's foreigner issues shifted toward "immigrants."

The implementation of a basic registration system for foreign residents correctly views foreigners as members (residents) of regional society and heralds the beginning of new stage for the administration of foreigners.

Foreign and special permanent residents (other than those on short-term visas) are issued certificates of residence by the local municipality where they reside. In addition to listing their name, date of birth, gender, address, and so on, these certificates of residents also include items unique to foreign residents such as their nationality/region of origin, residency status, and term of residency. Foreigners registered as residents can receive copies of their certificates of residency at their local government office the same way that Japanese can.

With the introduction of the new system, foreigners residing in Japan can provide these copies to relevant organizations and receive various administrative services such as for education, health care, welfare, and housing. My assessment is that this system, which treats immigrants as members of society, will act as a driving force behind the adaptation of immigrants to society as we head toward an age of immigration.

I believe that the basic registration system for foreign residents will not only improve the prospects for immigration policy. It will also have a large psychological impact on immigrants, letting them know that they are residents just like the Japanese are.

I'd like to note here that this system anticipating an era of immigration was created through the administrative leadership of the Ministry of Justice and Ministry of Internal Affairs and Communications. It is the responsibility of Japanese residents to make the most of the spirit of this groundbreaking system and build relationships of coexistence with the immigrants in their local communities.

JAPANESE-BRAZILIANS RETURN FROM A COUNTRY IN ECONOMIC COLLAPSE

Beginning in the late Meiji era, Japan made the dispatch of numerous Japanese overseas a national policy. But even though this had been a state policy, it must be said that both the Japanese people and their government were quite cold toward these emigrants once they had left Japan. The many people who emigrated to Brazil are symbolic of this.

As Japan experienced its bubble economy in the late 1980s, there was an increasing need for foreign workers, particularly within the industrial sector. The Immigration Bureau came under criticism for "closing the country off from labor." The question of whether or not to admit foreign workers ultimately developed into an argument that divided the country.

Meanwhile in Brazil, the value of the currency had been devastated by hyperinflation, rocking the domestic economy. Japanese television shows feature scenes of Brazilians engaging in hysterical consumption as the assets that they had accumulated became less valuable by the moment.

The economic chaos that Brazil was experiencing due to the record level of inflation naturally had a serious impact on the livelihoods of the descendants of those who had emigrated from Japan. And it's not hard to imagine that—to their suffering eyes—Japan, their ancestral homeland on the other side of the world (which was then at the peak of its bubble economy), appeared to be a golden country.

Japanese newspapers reported that immigrants to Brazil from countries other than Japan (Germany and Italy, for example) had begun abandoning Brazil and returning home. Given the aforementioned demand for labor in Japan and the living conditions of the Japanese-Brazilians in Brazil, I came to the conclusion that the time had come to extend a hand to these descendants of the Japanese who had crossed the sea as emigrants.

An amendment to the Immigration Control Law was unanimously passed by the Diet in 1989 and went into effect in June 1990 (I played a leading role in its drafting). With this, two new categories of status of residence that I had long wanted were incorporated: "Spouse or Child of Japanese National" (self-explanatory) and "Long-Term Resident" (for those of Japanese descent).

The dreams of the descendants of immigrants to return to the homeland of their parents and work there had finally been granted. Through this revision of the law, a path had finally been opened to allow those with Japanese relatives and those who considered Japan their homeland to enter the country.

Finally, I'll take this space to say one thing. We Japanese have to warmly welcome the Japanese-Brazilians as comrades tied to us by blood. It is especially necessary to provide their children with an education in the Japanese language so they can adapt to society. We also need to put effort into providing workplace support such as vocational training to provide them with stable lives. The country needs to be responsible and quickly create a system for implementing these two tasks.

With this in mind, I regard the Cabinet Office's establishment of its "Long-Term Resident Policy Promotion Office" in January 2009 as a groundbreaking step. With this, a system was prepared to provide employment counseling, Japanese language education, and vocational training to unemployed Japanese-Brazilians and their families.

PROVIDING "PERMANENT RESIDENT" STATUS TO THOSE OF JAPANESE ANCESTRY

When I became director of the Nagoya Regional Immigration Bureau in 2000, the first thing that surprised me when I visited the bureau was that its counters were unusually crowded.

Going to see why on earth this was so, I found out that it was flooded with Japanese-Brazilians going through the procedure to extend their stays. I was also surprised that there were many elementary school-aged children among the visitors. These children weren't at school. They had come with their parents to the immigration office. There were also children acting as interpreters for their parents because their parents couldn't speak Japanese well enough.

Approximately fifty-two percent of *Nikkei* Brazilians, or Brazilians of Japanese descent, are concentrated in the Nagoya area, also known as the Tōkai region. With so many people frequently coming to the bureau, it was only natural that the counters would be extremely crowded.

When I saw this, I immediately thought of a solution. The legal status most suitable for the Japanese-Brazilians—a group with close ties to Japan—was surely that of "permanent resident." Not only that, but—unlike other foreigners—those with Japanese descent can easily obtain permanent residency under Article 22 of the Immigration Control Law. Most of them were unaware of this, however. If they obtained permanent residency, these Japanese-Brazilians would no longer need to come to the bureau to extend their stays.

And obtaining the legal status of permanent resident would also have the benefit of increasing their credit in Japanese society. They would be able to secure home loans from banks, for example.

Realizing this, I immediately engaged in an information campaign to persuade Japanese-Brazilians to apply for permanent residency. Speaking with the Brazilian consul in Nagoya, I arranged for the consulate to disseminate the information that Japanese-Brazilians could easily obtain the more secure status of permanent resident. We prepared an information pamphlet in Portuguese for that purpose.

As a result, a large number of Japanese-Brazilians became permanent residents, as can be clearly seen from the numbers: in 1999, the year before I joined the bureau, a mere 313 people in the jurisdiction of the Nagoya Regional Immigration Bureau were granted permanent residency. This jumped to 1,388 people in 2000 and then increased six-fold to 7,180 people in 2001. It maintained a level of more than 7,000 people a year for a while after that. It is clear my predecessors were content with just doing routine work and not seeking remedies.

IMPROVING THE TREATMENT OF JAPANESE-BRAZILIANS

With the revision of the Immigration Control Law in 1990, two new categories for status of residence were established: "Spouse or Child of Japanese National" and "Long-Term Resident" (for admitting those of Japanese descent). With the ability to work extended to third-generation descendants of Japanese, the number of Japanese-Brazilians who entered the country increased dramatically. They numbered 300,000 at their peak and made three great contributions.

The first was to the Brazilian economy. Sending money they earned in Japan back to Brazil was one factor in getting the Brazilian economy back on its feet.

The second was supporting the Japanese economy by working diligently in subcontracting factories, mainly in the automotive industry which is centered in the Nagoya area, during the difficult economic times that followed the bursting of the bubble.

The third was their contribution to just immigration control. In the 1990s, the number of people in the country illegally had increased to nearly 300,000. That number has since fallen to roughly 60,000. This is because people of Japanese descent have been admitted into the country as proper workers and taken the place of those here illegally.

There are many things that need to be improved, however. The education of children in particular is the most inadequate aspect of Japan's acceptance of the Japanese-Brazilians. As Japanese elementary and junior high schools have little experience teaching children who can't speak Japanese, they can't function as a system for educating foreigners. This is why some of these children don't attend elementary or junior high schools (which are the years of compulsory education in Japan), and few go on to high school (which is not compulsory and generally costs money to attend). The government should rapidly implement a system for properly providing basic education for the children of foreigners. I especially want a system for teaching the basics of reading and writing Japanese to be prepared immediately.

I also have a request for their parents. For the sake of your children's futures, you should decide to live permanently in Japan. If you prepare yourself to live in Japan permanently, your life will become more stable. I also want the companies that employ Japanese-Brazilians to properly regard them as immigrants and accord them proper treatment—such as making them full employees. If that is done, the economic independence and social status of the Japanese-Brazilians will improve and they will become a model for what the admission of immigrants to Japan should look like.

***

As the global recession stretched on into April 2009, the Japanese government implemented a system that provided a certain amount of money to support the return of Japanese-Brazilians who had given up on finding new jobs in Japan and had decided to return home—on the condition that they would not apply for residency in Japan again on the basis of their ancestry.

At that time, I believed that while there was nothing inherently wrong with providing funds for the Japanese-Brazilians returning home, the immigration control measure of not allowing those who received these funds to reenter Japan had major constitutional issues. I pointed this out in an announcement on the JIPI homepage. I wrote it in the hopes that it would spur on reflection by the Ministry of Justice Immigration Bureau, the government agency that trained me.

> Under this system, those of Japanese descent who have returned to their countries and then attempt to reenter Japan with a valid passport will be denied entry by immigration officials, even if they can establish the validity of their entry into the country as the descendant of Japanese through documents (such as copies of one's *koseki*, the family registry recording births, deaths, and marriages). Under the Immigration Control Law, so long as a foreigner bears a valid passport, there is a residency status that applies to them, and there is no reason for denying them entry, they must be allowed into Japan. It is completely unthinkable and goes against common sense to think that accepting funds for going home would be an applicable reason for denying them entry the way that a criminal record would be. To not allow them entry to the country as an administrative operation measure is to refuse entry to only certain foreigners (those of Japanese descent who have received money to support their returning home) even though there are no applicable reasons for such refusal; this not only goes against the principle of equality enshrined in the Japanese constitution (as different entry procedures apply to other foreigners), it also violates the basic principles of legalism. Those of Japanese descent, especially Japanese-Brazilians, were admitted to the country as long-term residents with the establishment of that status of residency in the 1990 revision of the Immigration Control Law. They supported the post-bubble Japanese economy by working diligently. There are people of Japanese descent who returned to their second homeland Japan but then had no choice but to leave due to the global recession that followed the Lehman shock. If they wish to once again come to Japan, they should be warmly welcomed by the Japanese government regardless of whether or not they received financial assistance to leave.

ACCEPTING SYRIAN REFUGEES

Japan accepts extremely few refugees, which has led to it receiving international criticism for being a country closed to refugees. One reason for this is that, during its era of population growth, Japan was a country closed to immigrants and admitted almost no foreigners for permanent residency. All of the world's refugee powers are also immigration nations. The severe inflexibility with which Japanese immigration officials interpret refugee treaties can also be given as a reason for the extremely low ratio of refugee recognition.

Having now entered an era of population decline, however, Japan has no choice but to accept immigrants on a large scale. I therefore propose that conventional refugees (those for whom the refugee treaty is applicable) and resettlement refugees requiring humanitarian consideration should be considered within the framework of immigration—that is "conventional refugees" and "resettlement refugees" should be accepted as immigrants, should they so choose, as part of immigration policy.

I am calling for Japan to accept ten million immigrants over the next fifty years so that it can overcome the danger of demographic collapse. And when it does so, 500,000 of these should be humanitarian immigrants (refugees). This is because Japan's global image as a country cold or indifferent to refugees will not be wiped away unless we do so.

In September 2015, I proposed accepting one thousand Syrian refugees a year, mostly women and children. When I did so, politicians shifted their position on refugee policy, opening up a crack in the wall closing off Japan from refugees.

In a plenary session of the House of Councillors in January 2016, Yamaguchi Natsuo, president of the ruling coalition party junior partner Kōmeitō, asked a timely question of "Why don't we accept Syrian refugee children as international students to educate them in Japan?" Prime Minister Abe answered, "We will explore the possibility of accepting children who carry the future of that country."

Ultimately, the government decided in May that year to accept 150 Syrian refugee children as international students over the following five years. (It is unclear at this time how many have been accepted, if any.) The number is lacking, but this system for accepting refugees can still be considered the first success for a Japanese-style immigration policy.

As the European immigration powers such as Germany and France close their doors to Syrian refugees, I have expectations that this groundbreaking system will greatly expand. I would like the government to take this opportunity and be more flexible in admitting refugees into Japan and granting them residency than it has been in the past. Even if they don't qualify as refugees under the convention, they are still people in need of humanitarian consideration.

WE CANNOT ALLOW ANTI-JAPANESE FOREIGNERS INTO THE COUNTRY

The biggest question when it comes to Japanese immigration is "What if only people from countries with large populations come?" But the truth is, by implementing an immigration policy, we will actually be able to correct problems that are already occurring, such as the large numbers of Chinese entering the country which heavily skews the national origins of our foreign population.

First, the government will encourage the smooth acceptance of immigrants by establishing that the fair acceptance of people from all countries in the world is a basic tenet of Japanese immigration policy and conclud-

The Spirit of the Japanese-style Immigration Nation

ing immigration treaties with many countries. At the same time, it will enact a new "Immigration Law" which ensures that "fairness is an iron-clad rule of Japan's immigration policy."

And it will rapidly correct the state of affairs where Chinese make up an overwhelming majority of the foreigners in Japan. An immigration policy that is biased in favor of China will cause a backlash from the public. And it goes without saying that it is not to Japan's benefit in terms of diplomacy and national security, either.

The government—taking into consideration factors such as the international environment encapsulating Japan and the opinion of the public toward its immigration policies—will establish a plan for annual immigrant acceptance.

This plan will be drawn up by the cabinet and approved by the Diet. In formulating the plan, the number of immigrants to be accepted from each country annually will be decided with consideration given for those countries that produce immigrants that are highly adaptable to Japanese society or are favored by the Japanese public.

If immigration policy is implemented in a way that balances how many immigrants come from each country, the multiethnic nature and societal diversity of the population will be increased even further.

There is another foreigner issue that the Japanese public is concerned about: whether the entrance of anti-Japanese foreigners into the country can be strictly regulated. "Pro-Japanese" people in South Korea have been the target of fierce attacks from the entire public throughout the postwar period. Pro-Japanese politicians and intellectuals are labeled "traitors," forced into silence, and soon banished from society.

What has been the result? In today's South Korea, the entire population, from the president down, show signs of being anti-Japanese. There are few signs of any pro-Japanese people or policies. It has become a highly abnormal situation in which almost the entire country seems to pride itself on its anti-Japanese sentiment. As someone with close ties to Koreans, I am very sad about this.

Are anti-Japanese slogans the only thing the South Koreans can unify themselves around? Building a true relationship of friendship between our countries will be forever impossible so long as the South Korean popular opinion is against Japan and the country is incapable of raising pro-Japanese people.

Looking at immigration policy from across the world, the government will establish a framework for accepting immigrants by nationality, comprehensively taking into account factors such as relations between the Japanese people and immigrants and diplomatic relations.

If the government consistently follows a policy of not permitting immigrants with entrenched anti-Japanese thought into the country, then immigration from countries like South Korea and China with a zeal for anti-Japanese education (in part as a way to secure the legitimacy of the respective governments) will be strictly restricted under Japan's immigration policy. At the very least, the current "unsupervised inflow of foreigners" would end.

I have been subjected to hate speech—called a "traitor"—for attempting to push immigration policy forward. But I will clearly state that establishing a legal system for immigration that implements appropriate quantitative restrictions on nationalities will actually allow us to better prevent the entry of "anti-Japanese foreigners"—those possessing anti-Japanese sentiment and embedded anti-Japanese educations—into the country and instead welcome more friends of Japan.

IMPREGNABLE DEFENSES TO DEFEAT LARGE-SCALE ILLEGAL IMMIGRATION

When Japan begins admitting immigrants on a large scale, we will open the front gate of the country and actively accept them in conformance with the national immigration plan. But at the same time, it will be necessary to thoroughly crack down on terrorists, criminals, and others who attempt to sneak in through the back door. In particular, we must resolutely prevent the entry of terrorists into Japan in order to protect the lives of the public from terrorism. I want government authorities—immigration control authorities in particular—to adopt a flawless immigration control system that doesn't allow even a single terrorist in. But at the same time, they need to correctly perceive that terrorism and immigration are separate issues and continue to push forward with immigration policy with unwavering determination.

Next, there is something that I—an old immigration control hand that was feared as the "demon Sakanaka" by Chinese planning to enter the country illegally from the late 1980s to the early 1990s—would like to emphasize: the presence of China, a massively populated land which will attempt to push its surplus population onto us. Illegal immigration from China is the issue of national security that Japan needs to be most wary of. I want the authorities, beginning with the Immigration and Residency Management Agency, to recognize that the control of illegal immigration is an indispensable part of Japan's national security and prepare impregnable defenses against the illegal immigrants that will press in from China.

With a state of emergency threatening the national border management system, it is vital to make the utmost of the benefits that being an island nation offers for immigration control: immediately put the trump card of Article 3 of the Immigration Control Law (the provision that prohibits illegal immigrants from landing on Japan) into effect, gather the total strength of the Immigration and Residency Management Agency, Japan Coast Guard, Maritime Self-Defense Force, and police and completely prevent illegal immigrants from China at the water's edge. As soon as groups of illegal immigrants enter Japanese territorial waters, arrest them on suspicion of illegally entering the country and send them all back to China. We cannot permit even one person to violate our territorial waters or illegally land on Japan.

We won't be able to secure the public's understanding and cooperation on immigration policy unless immigration control performs sufficiently on the issues of terrorism and illegal immigration from China. If the Japanese perception of foreigners becomes tied to negative elements such as terrorists and illegal immigrants, the acceptance of immigrants will stagnate. The government must come together and control the illegal entry of foreigners to prevent the public's image of immigrants from worsening.

***

As there is no end to the foreigners who will attempt to enter the country illegally by crossing the seas from nearby countries, Japan is the country most in need of a legal system for immigration control that can appropriately restrict these foreigners at the point when they enter our territorial waters. It was with that viewpoint that the Immigration Control and Refugee Recognition Act, the basic law governing immigration control of foreigners, makes a clear distinction between the "entry" and "landing" of foreigners and includes provisions for dealing with each so that the necessary immigration control can be provided. In other words, the "landing" and "entry" of foreigners are established as separate concepts under the Immigration Control Law. And "foreigners who do not possess a valid passport" and "foreigners with the intention of landing illegally" are prohibited from entering Japan's territorial waters (Article 3, Immigration Control Law).

There has been a case where this provision was applied, and the illegal landing of Chinese people was prevented in advance. In August 2012, fourteen people (activists from Hong Kong and others) entered Japanese territorial waters. Five of them landed on Uotsurishima in the Senkaku Islands. The 11th Regional Coast Guard and the Okinawan Prefectural Police arrested all fourteen people on the boat (including the five who had landed) for violation of the Immigration Control Law. The Fukuoka Regional Immigration Bureau certified that the fourteen fell under the criteria for forcible deportation under that law and all were then deported to Hong Kong.

While I'm indignant that they were somehow able to physically land on Uotsurishima in the first place, the Japan Coast Guard, police, and immigration strictly enforced the Immigration Control Law, and I consider the incident to have shown the country and the world that Japan is in effective control of the Senkaku islands. It's worth special notice that all of the activists who had entered Japanese territorial waters were arrested as entering the country illegally, whether or not they had landed on

Uotsurishima or not. I consider this to have set a good precedent. I believe that the provisions of Article 3 of the Immigration Control Law will
also show their effectiveness when illegal immigration is pushed toward
Japan on a large scale by our neighbors.

SEVEN

Economics, Finances, and Immigration Policy

IMMIGRATION POLICY IS THE BEST ECONOMIC POLICY FOR A SOCIETY WITH A DECLINING POPULATION

A country's society and economy need a good balance of children, adults, and elderly people to exist healthily. No matter what economic or financial policies are adopted, if the number of workers and consumers in a country is rapidly falling, then the economy can only decline.

For the past six years, I have repeatedly stated that—given the conditions of rapid population decline—Abenomics would not be able to put the Japanese economy on the path to growth unless it included an immigration policy. While the Bank of Japan has introduced bold monetary easing measures such as negative interest one after another, it has not been successful at expanding domestic demand or stimulating the real economy. This is only to be expected. The government has the wrong approach of primarily relying upon the Bank of Japan's monetary policy to revive the economy. It has not taken a scalpel to the issue of population decline, the root cause of the weakening of our economy.

So long as the government obstinately maintains its ideology of closing Japan off to immigration, it will be unable to formulate a growth strategy that produces results. Our prime human resources will continue to become fewer and consumption will remain low. In fact, if it remains fixed to the position of not ameliorating the rapid decline in the productive and consumer populations through immigration policy, the Japanese economy will not expand. It will contract. And once an economy has begun contracting, it is extremely difficult to return it to growth. There is a high probability that zero or negative growth will become the new normal.

But if the government resolutely decides to open the country to immigration—by, for example, accepting immigrants on at least a scale of 200,000 a year over the next ten years—the Japanese economy will regain its vitality. First, direct investment in real estate (which provides housing to immigrants) and the food service industry (which provides food to immigrants) will increase. And because immigrants are consumers, in addition to necessities, they will also purchase expensive items related to their lives such as cars and electronics. The cost of educating their children will also be a fair amount.

Immigrants will have a large demand creation effect. Furthermore, overseas investors will change their patterns of investment in Japan as they anticipate the effects that securing young human resources and new consumers will have on the Japanese economy. There's the possibility that investment in Japan will dramatically increase. In the mid and long-term, if ten million immigrants are added as consumers and producers, a virtuous cycle between immigration policy and the economy will be created and the Japanese economy will be placed on a stable course.

In the short-term, it is increasingly likely that there will be a world-wide recession due to factors like the departure of Britain from the European Union and the Trump administration's "America First" economic policies (both of which the immigration issue is their root cause). It's quite plausible to think that—as America, Britain, Germany, and France increase their restrictions on immigration—the world's institutional investors will welcome the birth of Japan as an immigration power, turn to actively investing in Japan, and cause Japanese stocks to skyrocket.

JAPANESE IMMIGRATION POLICY AND THE FOREIGN INVESTMENT STRATEGY FOR JAPAN

I met with leaders of four of the largest American investment firms in March 2014 as they were interested in shifts in Japan's immigration policy.

After first explaining the historical significance of the February Diet testimony in which Prime Minister Abe called for "public discussion on admitting immigrants" and the essence of my ten-million immigrant concept, I stressed the necessity of Japan establishing the foundation for becoming an immigration nation prior to the opening of the 2020 Tokyo Olympics and Paralympics.

Next, I discussed the connection between Japanese immigration policy and shifts in foreign investment in Japan with these global investors. Below are the main points they made at this time:

> The reduction of the productive and consumer populations has meant that we haven't considered Japan a good place to invest in for the past ten years or so. We became disillusioned with the country and its in-

ability to come up with an effective solution to its population crisis. Because they wouldn't even discuss immigration policy, we gave up, thinking that the Japanese government wasn't even interested in trying. Your concept for admitting 200,000 immigrants annually is insufficient to make up for the rapid decrease in the productive population. While it will be necessary to further increase the number of immigrants going in, for the time being, Japan likely has no choice but to make up for the shortage in the productive population by utilizing women and the elderly as well as immigrants. Japan's immigration policy is closely tied to the issue of financial collapse, Abenomics' long-term strategy, and global investors' investments in Japan. Foreign investment strategies towards Japan have a particularly large impact on the Japanese economy and these investors are keeping a close watch on the country's immigration policies. I hope that your concept for an immigration nation is quickly achieved.

Through my discussion with these foreign investors, I was able to confirm that major global investment groups' investment strategies toward Japan are closely linked to the country's immigration policy. I was also able to verify that if Japan becomes an immigration power, global institutional investors will move to buy Japanese stock, something that will send the Japanese economy into a new phase.

I'll state my views simply: if the Japanese government resolutely decides to open the country to immigration, the foreign investors who have been waiting and hoping for the birth of a new immigration power will actively invest in Japan. This will trigger a new rush of economic energy that will support the expansion of the economy. Stock prices will skyrocket, real estate prices will rise, deflation will cease, the immigration market will expand, and more. Talking to these investors, I realized that the positive economic environment that would be created by opening the country to immigration would have an immeasurable effect on the Japanese economy.

In late-2019, I believe that the economic effects would not end there. The current global economy appears to be heading toward a recession due to the combination of a number of factors including the stalling of the Chinese economy as its population peaks and then declines, Britain's pending exit from the European Union, America's rejection of the free-trade system, and the intensifying Sino-American trade war. I believe that Japan—as a long-standing economic power and a rising immigration one—may be able to play a role in revitalizing it.

ABENOMICS' MISSING ARROW: IMMIGRATION POLICY

In June 2011, an opinion column I'd written appeared in the *Wall Street Journal* (Asian Edition) under the title, "An Immigration Stimulus for Japan."[1] In it, I had the following to say about the relationship between population, immigration, and the economy: "The only solution is to import more workers. I estimate that Japan needs to welcome some ten million immigrants over the next fifty years to avoid the negative consequences of population decline. Such numbers would spur growth because there would be new markets and demand for clothing, food, education, labor, finance, tourism, and information."

A week later, a related editorial appeared in the paper:

> The whole of Japan is going to meet with tragedy unless someone immediately shows us the path forward to a Japanese resolution and we resolutely follow it. With the aging of the Japanese population, the public finances that support the Japanese government's expenditures will go bankrupt. The public that was always encouraged to save is going to stop buying government bonds and instead begin using their savings to support their retirement. As pointed out by Sakanaka Hidenori in this column last week, the decline in the size of the working population will likely apply new pressure on the government to adopt a revolutionary immigration policy. It is necessary to reform our foreigner policy. In particular, it is essential that we shift to an immigration policy that admits foreigners not as migrant workers but as permanent residents. The longer that the government puts off this reform, the more difficult it will be to avoid a difficult choice. Whether it was the Meiji Restoration or rebuilding after the Second World War, Japan was able to overcome painful changes in the past and develop. If a leader with the correct perception of things arrives and implements the correct reforms, Japan can regain its former prosperity.[2]

June 2011 was shortly after the Great East Japan Earthquake. My opinion piece and the paper's editorial agreed that an "immigration revolution" was the way to save Japan from the economic and financial collapse that would accompany demographic collapse. This editorial gave me strength. I vowed that I must use immigration policy to bring life back to a Japan that had become despondent following the Great East Japan Earthquake and make it a healthy country again.

***

I was interviewed by *Wall Street Journal* editor Joseph Sternberg in Tokyo on June 20, 2013. He and I have known each other for a long time. Our discussion focused on the relationship between population collapse, immigration policy, and Abenomics (especially its growth strategy). We share the view that with Japan facing an impending population collapse, immigration policy is an essential part of formulating a strategy for growth.

The main points I made were the following: "While I'm not someone who believes in economic growth at any cost, Prime Minister Abe cannot avoid accepting immigrants on a large scale if he wishes to achieve economic growth even as the child rate falls and society ages. The economy of a country with a rapidly declining population will continue to weaken no matter what economic or fiscal policy is put in place. The only way to put the Japanese economy on a stable course in the mid to late term is to fully implement immigration policy (and thereby directly increase the population size) before the fundamental strength of the economy dwindles."

Six days later, a commentary by Sternberg ran on the paper's opinion page.[3] The title, spot-on, was bold: "Mr. Abe's Missing Arrow—The absence of immigration reform from Abenomics bespeaks a deeper problem":

> If there's one reform that's symbolic of Prime Minister Shinzo Abe's eponymous program to rejuvenate the Japanese economy, it is immigration. Japan needs as many as ten million immigrants by 2050 to offset natural population decline, according to Hidenori Sakanaka of the Japan Immigration Policy Institute. Many of Mr. Abe's other goals ultimately depend on immigration. For instance, unanswered in Mr. Abe's plan to open thousands of new child-care centers so that mothers can return to their careers is the question of who will staff them. Immigrants are the most plausible solution.

This op-ed hit home on the weaknesses of a Japanese economy amidst a declining population and put pressure on the Japanese government by arguing that "immigration policy is essential to formulating a long-term strategy for Japan's economic growth." I believe it had an influence on the Japanese business figures and economic officials.

THE BUSINESS WORLD AND IMMIGRATION

Why does the industrial world fail to stand explicitly in favor of immigration policy despite being directly affected by the low rate of childbirth and the country's declining future prospects? It is completely beyond my understanding. As far as I'm concerned, by increasing the productive and consumer populations, immigration policy is the answer to the industrial world's prayers. What are they so afraid of? I can't help but be critical of them and think that they are perhaps afraid that the introduction of immigration policy—the correct and ideal system for accepting foreigners—will mean the end of the Technical Internship Program—a system under which foreign workers are driven hard for low wages and which the international community has criticized as "Japanese-style slavery."

In other countries, it is generally the business community that seeks to make things more open for immigrants. And yet, there doesn't appear to be a single business leader who has the foresight to see what the future of Japan should be like from a national standpoint. There are only small leaders concerned only with their companies' profits. I feel depressed at the reality that there is no influential figure within the business community who will directly tell the prime minister to open the country to actual immigration.

While politics is also extremely lacking in human resources, the problem is even more serious in business. The people there can't look one hundred years into the future or consider things on a global scale. They are unable to escape from their seclusionist mentality or keep pace with a tumultuous world. I can only say that, with these kinds of business leaders at the helm, the future of the Japanese economy is desperate.

Generally speaking, the business community is not opposed to immigration. Nor should it be, as it means not only more workers but also more consumers. Asked what they really think, they'll tell you that they're "in favor of immigration policies which can be expected to bring global human resources and expand domestic demand." As the human resource shortage becomes more serious due to the lack of young people, it's utterly implausible that the financial world—the top of Japanese management—wouldn't consider immigration policy that revitalizes and stabilizes the Japanese economy attractive.

But if the business world wants immigrants, they need to correct their treatment of foreign workers first. More than anything else, correcting the current state of affairs—where foreign employees experience working conditions inferior to those of Japanese employees—is a prerequisite for accepting immigrants.

To make a further request, I want a business culture where status and compensation are determined based on ability without regard for nationality, ethnicity, or gender. I want management policies that make the most of the abilities of global human resources to be promptly established in order for Japanese companies to be able to compete on an equal footing with global corporations in the global labor market and to secure human resources rich in diversity.

In general immigrants will be people who move to Japan to achieve success here. They will work hard, establish roots in local society, and make contributions to regional revitalization. Before long the majority will take Japanese citizenship. In other words, if the nation turns to immigration policy, the brakes will be applied to a certain degree to Japan's negative economic growth and rapid decline in the number of citizens.

When employing these "immigrants" (which are, after all, future potential citizens), I want the business community of the coming era of large-scale immigration to adopt the principles of "full-time employment" and "equal pay and equal work" as societal responsibilities and strictly follow them. They definitely must not do anything to widen the economic disparity between Japanese and immigrants.

I caution that any executives who do not do so will make enemies of the ten million-strong immigrant community (with its giant consumer power and rich human resources) and soon face bankruptcy.

COMPANIES WITHOUT GLOBAL HUMAN RESOURCES HAVE NO FUTURE

It has long been pointed out that the smaller local factories that provide the backbone for Japanese industrial and technological strength are going out of business one after another due to personnel shortages and difficulty in finding successors. Unless human resources are abundantly supplied to these smaller companies, the continuation of the Tōkai industrial belt—Japan's historical industrial heritage—could even be endangered.

For example, some of the companies and subcontractors under the umbrella of Toyota—the leader of Japanese industry—have gone bankrupt because they were unable to secure workers. The impact of that extends out to all of Japanese industry.

Toyota has said that it will absolutely continue to produce three million cars a year domestically. As a nation, we need to respond to Toyota's patriotism. To support Toyota's domestic industrial system, we should welcome manufacturing engineers from overseas as immigrants and allocate them to smaller companies affiliated with Toyota. The ten million immigrants who come to Japan will be consumers. We need to resolutely decide to open the country to immigration to increase the consumer population that purchases cars.

At the summer forum hosted by the Japanese Business Federation, or *Keidanren*, in July 2015, President Sakakibara Sadayuki referenced Japan's policies on immigration, saying that "because the worker shortage in a wide range of fields such as construction, healthcare, and manufacturing will continue to become more serious, it is essential that we expand our acceptance of immigrants." This statement has significance because it's basically a request from the top of the business community to the government and public to accept immigrants.

With the automotive industry suffering a shortage of workers, why not have Japan train the youth of the world to become skilled workers at Japan's industrial technical schools? Once they've found work, they can be given the new residency status of "Manufacturing Technician" and then, after five years of abiding by the laws of the country, permanent residency.

From the aspect of immigration control administration as well, this should help revive manufacturing by smoothly providing talented, qualified foreign human resources (who have entered the country legally intending to gain permanent residency) to meet the demand of the small and mid-size enterprises that support Japanese manufacturing.

***

Here I would like to make a suggestion regarding the state of Japanese companies' success in the world, speaking from the perspective of an immigration policy specialist.

Companies who do not have personnel familiar with the tumultuous world situation might be left behind in the global marketplace. In particular, because we Japanese are unable to escape our "island country mentality" and tend to be unacquainted with ethnic and religious issues, companies composed of solely Japanese employees can't compete with global enterprises that have employees of many nationalities and backgrounds. We cannot properly respond to issues such as terrorism, hostage-taking, and civil wars that come from ethnic and religious conflict, for example.

When attempting to operate in overseas markets, it is necessary to seek help from cultural anthropology experts who can research the relationship between culture, ethnicity, religion, and the economy from a global perspective. If a company doesn't have any experts well-versed in the tastes and values of different ethnicities, it won't know what its foreign customers want and what products will sell. Similarly, risk assessment and mitigation should take into consideration those cultural aspects.

The Japanese, who don't give much thought to foreign traditional cultures and how foreigners think about things, can't compete with the internationally minded personnel of multinational corporations. I want the managers of smaller companies who have the grit to try their luck in the world to do so by joining forces with international human resources knowledgeable about the cultures (and risks) of other countries.

If these companies do hire foreigners, they should provide them with salaries and promotions in a way equal to that given to Japanese employees. Unimpeded competition and meritocracy should be the guiding principles. Have Japanese and foreigners begin at the same starting line and then choose the more capable employees without concern for their nationality. Open a path for new foreign graduates to make it to the top of the company.

As long as the business culture isn't open to the global talent, the elite of the world won't even look at Japanese companies. I want these companies to make plans for hiring foreigners and international students with an eye toward the increasingly globalized world market and a Japanese society with its rapidly declining population so that they will still be around fifty years from now.

FINANCES AND IMMIGRATION

While the population of Japan is headed toward being the first in the world with an average life expectancy of ninety years, the fourteen-and-under population is projected to continue to shrink rapidly. This kind of society—one with very few children and many elderly people—has never before been seen in human history.

Right now, in the early months of 2019, Japan's accumulative long-term debt (both national and local) has surpassed one quadrillion yen. The debt carried by the country will continue to snowball as these social trends continue. Fifty years from now the productive population will have been cut in half and the per capita share of the national debt will be unimaginable.

The few children who are born will do so burdened with massive debts. Fifty years from now, Japan will have become a "society from which the children have disappeared." There will be 4.4 elderly people for each child, and I have no doubt that the youth of Japan will regret having been born here. I can truly understand why the young people of the current generation are hesitant about having children.

The politicians and bureaucrats don't have the bravery to explain what the future state of the country looks like: a vision of hell with collapsed financial and social security systems. But they can't be allowed to keep it a secret forever. If they do not directly take on this issue—a financial collapse triggered by the destruction of the demographic order—and immediately take effective, appropriate steps, it is certain that that nightmare will be realized within the next ten years.

The only path to avoid financial collapse and protect a minimal social security system is to have a total of ten million immigrants bear part of the burden of taxes and social security costs and for the government to undertake wholesale reform of the social security and taxation systems. And even this will have the prerequisite that the public willingly shares the pain and hardship together.

To summarize, we might be able to avoid the financial collapse if we add ten million immigrants (most of whom will need to be in their late teens and twenties when they enter the country) as new taxpayers and contributors to the social security system—assuming we undertake fundamental systemic reform to adjust to a society with a rapidly declining population and implement a long-term austerity budget.

Even then, experts will likely earnestly debate the necessity of admitting even more immigrants to further increase the youthful population in order to ensure financial rebuilding in the near future.

***

One more tragedy is waiting for our country plagued with debt: increasingly intense conflict over the ever-increasing burden of social security costs between the young (who will shoulder the costs) and the elderly (who will receive the benefits). Intergenerational conflict—not the simple difference in values but one over dwindling financial resources—will erupt. In the worst-case scenario, it's possible that there will be family discord on a national scale. Few things in the history of the world could be considered as frightening and miserable as that.

And that's not all. The spirit of harmony cultivated by the Japanese people, respect for the elderly, and our admirable tradition of helping each other in emergencies will all be damaged.

Is there a way to avoid Japan's tragedy? A national commitment to immigration is the only method of escape that I have been able to think of. An effective immigration policy to supplement the rapidly dwindling young population is the only method to prevent splitting the country in half. And Japan's substantial social security system is attractive to immigrants as well as Japanese. It will also be necessary to maintain the framework of the social security system in order to get immigrants to come to Japan and make it their home.

The change to an immigrant society is essential to avoiding demographic collapse and financial ruin, and for leaving a minimal social security system in place for future generations of citizens. It is the duty of our politicians to secure popular agreement for this. Maintaining popular unity for the purpose of managing the interests of different generations will be the highest priority task in Japanese politics.

But I do not know any Diet member who speaks of the importance of popular unity. I've proposed the urgent introduction of immigration policy to prevent public divisions but received no response from the political world. It's truly unfortunate but there is no one among the current crop of politicians who truly thinks of our children's future.

I will predict that there will absolutely come a time when the foolishness and culpability of the current generation of politicians—those who stood idly by in the face of demographic collapse and continued to close the country off from immigrants—is condemned. I have no doubt that the Japanese people of the late 21st century, having achieved minimal intergenerational conflict, will explode in anger at the foolish politicians of the *Heisei* era who forsook their responsibility to future generations.

Even in this age of extremely low childbirth, three thousand children are born every day. What are we leaving behind for our children and grandchildren, who are the treasure of Japan? That's a question that all Japanese should seriously consider.

REGIONAL BANKS ARE IN DANGER IF WE DON'T ACCEPT IMMIGRANTS

In July 2015, I was given the opportunity to deeply consider the relationship between immigration policy and the state of Japan's banks. I gave a speech on the topic of "Solving the Problem of Population Decline" at the Deloitte Tohmatsu Financial Business Seminar 2015. About seventy bank leaders participated in the session on immigration. Rapid population decline is exhausting rural economies, leading to the disappearance of borrowers and the creation of a harsh fiscal environment. These leaders of financial institutions nodded along as they heard me appeal to the necessity and urgency of immigration policy—the most effective solution to the population issue.

For lenders (banks), reductions in businesses borrowing is a grave matter for their operations. Financing depends on demand for funds. But what on earth are local banks to do with borrowers disappearing one after another? I can imagine that my speech struck close to home for some of the bankers. They seem to have taken it seriously as raising a shocking problem. I expect there to be increasing calls for immigration from local businesses—with the local bank leaders with whom my theory of immigration policy resonated leading the way.

After my lecture ended, I chatted with experts well-informed on the current state of financing. They knew that banks, local economies, and immigration were all closely related due to the issue of population. It suddenly occurred to me that local economies could likely be revitalized through the synergy of immigration policy and strong financing.

If Japan is reborn as a country that has made a national commitment to immigration and takes in abundant immigrants in their prime, then regional economies will have healthy industrial bases, increase production and consumption, and become sources of vitality. Local industry, on the verge of death, will be brought back to life through the power of immigration.

At that time, the local banks that support these local economies will play an important role. It will be the time for these financial institutions to provide the necessary funds for advancing local industry and preparing the living environment (such as housing) for the immigrants entering Japan.

THE IMMIGRATION BANK

I want an immigration bank created to perform the role of a circulatory organ for the immigration economy. This bank—the like of which has never existed in Japan—will have as its main business lending money, collateral and interest-free, to immigrants without relatives in Japan, the money necessary for renting a home and laying the foundation for their life in Japan, studying at school, or starting a business, for example.

The following is an overview of the bank. It will be launched using one trillion yen provided by the government and institutional lenders as its starting capital. Its customers will be immigrants and their families, ten million people at most. The maximum that can be borrowed by a single person will be three million yen, with repayment postponed for five years after they've entered the country.

As immigrants will be consumers, they will have a healthy demand for financing. For example, in addition to costs associated with the necessities of life, they will also need to pay for education for their children. Because the Immigration Bank will provide the financing to immigrants that will prime the pump for the vitalization of the immigrant marketplace, the immigrant economy will be able to get under way.

And with the creation of the Immigration Bank, a system will have been put in place to provide comprehensive management and oversight for "overseas remittances" (the transfer of money from immigrants to their home countries). Illegal dealings such as money laundering will therefore be prevented, and a framework can be created where the money sent by immigrants will aid in the economic development of their home countries.

As a specialist bank supporting the long-term residency of immigrants, the Immigration Bank will attract global attention. As a powerful ally of newcomer immigrants, it will no doubt receive the thanks of the immigrant community. Furthermore, if immigrants find employment and work diligently, they will begin saving at the bank as their lives become easier. If the ten million immigrants can diligently work and save, it staggers the imagination to think of what the total savings of these immigrants as a whole could reach.

That's not all. The Immigration Bank will support the ten million in the immigrant marketplace and therefore contribute to the development of the Japanese economy. It will also play an important role in leading Japanese-style immigration policy—which emphasizes the education of the children of immigrants—toward success.

NOTES

1. Hidenori Sakanaka, "An Immigration Stimulus for Japan," *Wall Street Journal* (Asian Edition), June 15, 2011.

2. "Editorial: A New Plan for Japan," *Wall Street Journal* (Asian Edition), June 22, 2011.

3. Joseph Sternberg, "Mr. Abe's Missing Arrow—The absence of immigration reform from Abenomics bespeaks a deeper problem," *Wall Street Journal* (Asian addition), June 26, 2013.

EIGHT

Population and Immigrants

THE PLAN FOR 300,000 FOREIGN CAREGIVERS

If we do not admit immigrants, what on earth are we to do for the field of nursing care in a Japan with very few children and an increasingly elderly population? We're becoming a society where we will have to work for our entire lives, even if we live to be eighty or ninety. However, that doesn't mean that all of the elderly are able to work healthily. We're becoming a society where many elderly people die all alone without anyone looking after them only to be discovered days, weeks, or months later.

Meanwhile, there's the possibility that the young generation born in an era of low childbirth will have the burden of supporting the elderly population pushed upon them. There will be a torrent of young people who despair for their lives. And the problems do not stop there. It would not be suitable to concentrate the precious human resources of a society where only a million children are born annually into the field of caregiving. It would also be impossible. There's a need for young human resources to also be provided to public security organizations such as the Self-Defense Forces and the police, and to the regional and national public sectors. And of course, industry will be calling for fresh human resources.

We must rapidly draw up a "plan for 300,000 foreign caregivers" with a mid-term target of 2030 and devise a system for securing the necessary foreign human resources.

First, we should conclude "immigrant caregiver agreements" with Southeast Asian countries such as Indonesia, the Philippines, Vietnam, and Myanmar. Second, immigration control will grant the "Caregiver" status of residence to foreigners who enter Japan based on those agreements. In principle, permanent residency will be granted five years later, and citizenship granted by the Ministry of Justice's Civil Affairs Bureau after seven years if so desired.

The caring spirit of humanity is universal. Many Filipinos married to Japanese and Japanese-Brazilians have entered the field of nursing care and, having spoken with the directors of caregiving facilities, I can say that foreign staff have a good reputation with the elderly. They have the spirit of respect toward the elderly that the Japanese are losing. Moreover, they like to talk and sing cheerfully. They communicate emotionally as well as through the Japanese language. The elderly are happy with them.

It is not just the elderly people who receive heartfelt care from foreign staff who are thankful toward them; their families are as well. I think that therein lays a hint for how to make the acceptance of immigrants successful.

Perhaps Japan should consider the field of caregiving—one where foreign nursing staff and elderly Japanese are together harmoniously—as a model case for a Japanese society based on multi-ethnic coexistence.

LABOR UNIONS AND IMMIGRATION

In January 2009, *Gekkan Jichiken* (Local Autonomy Monthly), the magazine of the All-Japan Prefectural and Municipal Workers Union (*Zennihon Jichi Dantai Rōdō Kumiai*, or *Jichirō*), included a special feature on "Our Towns' Populations." The journal's approach to the story was "Searching for scenarios leading to policy change: we will soon be a society with a shrinking population. With household changes and social uneasiness also becoming more common, what future should local governments pursue for their areas?" Included in this special feature was a short essay by me entitled "A Proposal for a Japanese-Style Immigrant Country."[1] My points were as follows: I proposed that we accept ten million immigrants over the next fifty years. That's how we can break out of the trapped state we find ourselves in because of the fall in childbirth and aging of society. We need to train foreigners, provide them with stable employment, and accept them as permanent residents.

It's possible that this essay had a significant influence on local government employees. At present, areas with agricultural villages are directly confronting the threat of population collapse that accompanies extreme low childbirth. It's a certainty that we will soon face a crisis where local communities in areas with primary industries will begin disappearing, one after another. Naturally, many of the officials who work in the local governments of these areas will meet the sad fate of being laid off. I feel that the day when *Jichirō* sheds its labor union antipathy toward immigration and takes a leading role in driving immigration policy is close.

The following is a portion of the essay that ran in *Gekkan Jichiken*:

> Japan has entered an unprecedented era of population decline and all
> of society is under heavy pressure from the population crisis. Particu-
> larly dark clouds loom over the future of the generation born in the era
> of low childbirth (those thirty and younger), as their burden will only
> grow heavier as time passes. How can we break out of this unspeakable
> trapped situation that our society finds itself in? How can we open a
> path to a brighter future? Boldly open the country and welcome ten
> million immigrants over the next fifty years. The world's "human re-
> sources" should be incorporated into our country. Taking on the popu-
> lation issue through a "national commitment to immigration" is a na-
> tional vision that can capture the hearts of the low childbirth genera-
> tion, those who will shoulder Japan's future. Unless we borrow the
> strength of immigrants, the labor shortage being experienced by agri-
> cultural areas will worsen and we will face the danger of regional
> collapse. But if we are to use the energy of immigrants to revitalize
> agricultural village communities, we must treat them like future citi-
> zens. Fundamental reform of agricultural management (such as mov-
> ing to large-scale farms) is also necessary to provide these immigrants
> with stable jobs. This will not be without its difficulties. Resistance
> from vested interests is likely. But even so, immigration policy pro-
> vides human resources, solves the issue of Japan becoming forty per-
> cent self-sufficient for its food supply, and provides an opportunity for
> reviving agriculture.

REGIONAL REVITALIZATION THROUGH IMMIGRATION

Having entered an era where domestic population movement has stag-
nated due to there being extremely few children, Japan should find its
means of escaping in international population movements (immigration).
It should cast its eyes on the human resources of the whole world rather
than just competing over those found within the Japanese archipelago

I believe that if we establish a large-scale system for properly accepting immigrants into Japan and educating young foreigners at our agricultural and fishery high schools, then our primary industries—with their
well-developed infrastructure and accumulated industrial technology—
will draw promising young people from around the world. And I see the
residents of the countryside—who still have warm compassion toward
others—welcoming these immigrants.

As the introduction of immigration policy proceeds, I anticipate a
great wave of migration from urban areas to agricultural villages as the
immigrants living in rural areas and the youth of Japan rise up together
under the banner of "rejuvenating our countryside." There's no question
that the introduction of fresh immigrants will trigger local rejuvenation. I
want the young people of Japan and the world to join together and carry

on Japan's industrial, cultural, and natural heritage. And our national and local governments should provide full assistance to the local rejuvenation activities of these young people with their hearts full of patriotism.

The agriculture, forestry, and fishing industries are our historical industrial heritage. The industrial technology they contain has been passed on and expanded on by the Japanese people ever since the *Jōmon* period, producing food, catching fish, and cultivating trees while giving thanks to the blessings of nature. It is a mistake to view these primary industry occupations as having little value. It profanes Japan's rich natural environment and goes against the view of nature that has been passed on to us by generations of our ancestors: the belief that everything in nature has a soul.

If we devastate the spiritual home of the Japanese, then that spirit will waste away. It is necessary to protect "landscapes where humans can draw close to and live with nature" (of which *satoyama* and *satoumi* are representative examples) so that the Japanese spirit (at the root of which lies the philosophy of coexisting with nature) can continue to be passed on forever.

I sincerely hope that we see the appearance—one after another—of Japanese who have been drawn by rural life, where humans can live with full satisfaction.

THE GREAT EAST JAPAN EARTHQUAKE OF 2011 AND IMMIGRATION

Even before the 2011 Great East Japan Earthquake, I was calling on the Japanese people to establish an immigration nation, saying that that was how we could revive Japan from the brink of death and prevent the systemic collapse that will come from the great population shift we are experiencing. No one points it out, but no reconstruction plan will produce results unless it sets targets for recovering our rapidly decreasing productive and consumer populations. As long as immigration policy is not used to end population decline in the areas affected by the Great East Japan Earthquake, it will be difficult for us to completely recover from it. That is what I believe.

Today, eight years after the Great East Japan Earthquake, I have another request for the government. I want it to immediately declare that Japan will become an immigrant nation. I want the government to show the nation and the world how determined the country is to recover from the earthquake.

If Japan takes up the banner of rebuilding from the earthquake and is reborn as an immigration nation, our economy and finances will become more sustainable because we can expect domestic demand to expand and for our immigration population to increase. Immigrants will rush to areas affected by the earthquake from across the world, and—thanks to their efforts—their rebuilding will proceed steadily.

Japan, already in the midst of a deepening population crisis, was struck by a once-a-millennium natural disaster. Now its fate rests on nothing less than simultaneously (and successfully) undertaking a national commitment to immigration and revolutionizing the agriculture, forestry, and fisheries industries.

That is, we must completely change the management structure of these industries as we push forward with an immigration policy that welcomes the promising youth of the world into Japan. Instead of being managed on the family level, they will be made into large-scale operations capable of being hosts for these immigrants.

The people in these areas will welcome the immigrants who rush to help them from the bottom of their hearts. And they will absolutely never forget their feelings of gratitude for the support they received from the people of the world. I suspect that the world's young people—with their love for traditional Japanese culture and the Japanese spirit—will get along well with the inhabitants of Tōhoku who have carried on the blood and spirit of the people of the *Jōmon* period.

If the government opens Japan to immigration and adequately supplies (primarily young) human resources to these disaster-affected areas, their communities and economies will regain their lost vitality.

Even after the Great East Japan Earthquake, areas throughout Japan have frequently experienced earthquakes and flooding. The victims of these disasters are increasingly in areas with elderly populations and few young people in their teens and twenties. As the collapse of these local communities progresses rapidly, it is becoming increasingly difficult for areas with agricultural and forestry industries to hold on against natural disasters. The government should immediately resolve to open Japan to immigration and send fresh immigrants into these agricultural and mountain villages.

IMMIGRATION WILL RESTORE ABANDONED FARMLAND

In recent years, policy proposals have been repeatedly suggested for reviving the agricultural sector: raising food self-sufficiency to fifty percent, reviewing the policy of reducing the amount of land used for rice, revising the Agricultural Land Law and promoting having ordinary companies join agricultural production corporations, and attempts at eliminating abandoned farmland.

All of these are essential and necessary policies for revitalizing agriculture. However—speaking from the standpoint of what is actually achievable—as long as these efforts are not accompanied by an effective method for increasing the number of people engaged in agriculture, their goals are mere pipe dreams.

Focusing on the fact that the fundamental reason why the agricultural sector has weakened is the reduced size of the farming population, I believe that Japanese agriculture has no future unless agricultural reform is undertaken that has a plan for securing new farmers.

I therefore propose my "Agriculture Immigrant Special Zone" concept as a policy to bring Japanese agriculture back from the brink of death. This involves accepting 50,000 agricultural immigrants over the next ten years and returning the entire roughly 400,000 hectares of abandoned farmland back to use.

First the cabinet will—based on applications from local communities—designate certain areas "agricultural immigrant special zones." These will be centered on the abandoned farmland in each prefecture, of which there are significant amounts. At the same time, it will also designate specially authorized "agricultural production corporations" (hereafter, "designated agricultural producers") to employ agricultural immigrants in these special zones. Ordinary companies who are the majority shareholders and primary managers of agricultural production corporations will be appointed as designated agricultural producers.

The country will promote measures—including in the areas of taxation and financing—to allow designated agricultural producers to accumulate small-scale farms and farmland and forests owned by absentee landlords who do not adequately manage them.

At the same time, young people from other countries who want to work in Japan's agricultural and forestry industries should be admitted to and educated at Japanese agricultural colleges and high schools. We already have a sufficient number of agricultural colleges and high schools, although their staff numbers continue to decline due to the falling admissions (there are 43 agricultural colleges in the country with about 4,000 total staff and 400 agricultural high schools with about 8,000 total staff. These colleges offer one or two year-long courses of study, while the course at the high schools is three years long). This concept does not waste the valuable resources of these specialized agricultural schools but instead uses them to educate foreigners so they will support Japanese agriculture. Foreigners who have graduated from foreign agricultural high schools will enter agricultural colleges; the rest will enter agricultural high schools.

Immigrants should be educated in Japanese at these colleges and schools. They would study a bioresource circulating style of agriculture that emphasizes the connections between the three areas of agriculture, forestry, and livestock. Furthermore, according to my proposal, an "Agricultural Immigrant Fostering Fund" will be created and funded by the government, the Norinchukin Bank (for *Nōrin Chūō Kinko*), and designated agricultural producers to provide the funds necessary for educating these agricultural immigrants.

Designated agricultural producers will employ foreigners who have graduated from Japan's specialized agricultural schools as full employees. This will of course be done with the principles of equal work and compensation with Japanese employees in mind. The foreigners' status under the Immigration Control Law will be "Student" while they're studying and "Agriculture" after they've found employment. Once employed, they will rapidly be granted permanent resident status. In other words, they'll be recognized as "agricultural immigrants," following a proper, comprehensive cultural, language, and technical education.

Designated agricultural producers will use land such as abandoned and fallow farmland and mountains and forests with absentee landlords and engage in intensive, flexible agriculture and forestry. They will also develop multi-faceted business including food processing, timber processing, and breeding livestock.

They will jointly engage in agriculture and forestry, taking care to ensure that agricultural immigrants have work throughout the year. In principle, agricultural immigrants will engage in agriculture from spring to autumn and forestry in the winter.

Agricultural immigrants will live in core towns equipped with the necessities of daily life such as residences, schools, hospitals, and stores. They will commute from there to the areas of production in the low uplands or remote areas. The government will establish industrial parks in these core cities for the concentrated placement of agriculture and forestry-related factories such as food and meat processing, dairy products, timber processing, and the manufacture of biofuels.

Designated agricultural producers—using the best of Japanese agricultural technology and selective breeding—will export high quality, delicious rice, fruit, and meat. They will stand at the forefront of the effort to expand Japan's agricultural exports. If this agricultural immigrant special zone system goes well, competition will arise and it will become increasingly common for medium-sized farmers to form joint corporate organizations, begin large-scale operations, and actively employ agricultural immigrants.

The government, in cooperation with designated agricultural producers, will formulate a plan for the reuse of farmland, bringing the approximately 400,000 hectares of abandoned farmland in the country into active use over a period of ten years. Of the 100,000 agricultural workers estimated to be needed to achieve this plan, 50,000 will be agricultural immigrants. Thus 50,000 Japanese are also projected to be employed.

The farmers who provide land will be welcomed as agricultural technology instructors (teachers who pass Japan's agricultural technology on to agricultural immigrants) in the new agricultural corporations.

How will accepting 50,000 agricultural immigrants affect the future of agricultural and mountain village society? The rural areas where large numbers of agricultural immigrants live will regain the energy that they used to have. These residents of foreign origin—who love Japanese food and will actively participate in Japan's traditional activities such as festivals—will form close relations with the Japanese there.

THE GROUNDBREAKING AGRICULTURAL SPECIAL ZONE IN OGATA VILLAGE

While working as a regional bureau director for the Ministry of Justice Immigration Bureau from 1997 to 2005, I was shocked as I witnessed up close the actual conditions in rural areas from where Japanese are disappearing. I truly felt the threat posed by the era of population decline already under way in rural areas and stressed at a conference held by the Ministry of Justice that there were two paths that a country with a declining population could follow: a "path of decay" (not accepting immigrants regardless of population decline) and a "path towards a stable, vigorous society" (in which immigration is used to make up for the shrinking population).

Speaking from the position of an expert on immigration policy, I now propose that immigration be actively used to save our primary industries which are endangered by the rapid decline in the working population. That is, I propose the introduction of immigration policy that will admit foreigners and grant them permanent residency. Local residents will warmly welcome these immigrants as fellow humans, as consumers, as members of society, and as future Japanese citizens.

As humanity has always coexisted with nature and worked with it to produce food, the agricultural, forestry, and fishery industries are all traditional industries that have existed in Japan for 15,000 years, ever since the *Jōmon* period. They require knowledge and technology that combine the wisdom of generations of Japanese. They are absolutely not the "unskilled labor" that they are commonly referred to as.

The question we face is, is it acceptable for us to allow the people who have inherited the industrial technology that the Japanese people have maintained for all this time to disappear, for settlements in areas with primary industries to disappear one after another?

In the agricultural and forestry areas where the size of the working population continues to plummet, farmland is increasingly abandoned. The rice paddies and forests that the Japanese people have diligently maintained are going to ruin. We must save these agricultural and mountain village communities from their life or death crisis no matter what it takes. I say this not only from the focus of securing food and natural resources but also from the perspective of land and environmental safety.

The same is true of our fisheries. Even though we're surrounded by the sea and blessed with aquatic resources, both the number of people working in the field and the size of catches continue to decline.

Unfortunately, it seems that the youth of today like urban life. What will become of the future of Japan when the country is inherited by those of the low childbirth generation, most of whom were born and raised in cities? It goes without saying that the young people from other countries won't want to migrate to areas where there aren't any young Japanese. It'll be too late. There will be nothing to be done. The situation will be desperate. If the youth of Japan and the world can come to find attractiveness in rural Japanese life, however, we may be able to find a ray of hope.

We've plunged into an era when the productive population is rapidly decreasing; the only method remaining at this point that can save our primary industries from ruin is immigration policy. The government needs to immediately make the decision to introduce immigration policy and make good use of global human resources. If we don't make that decision now—while the elderly are still alive to teach industrial technology to immigrants—it will all be in vain.

It is therefore necessary for us to fundamentally reconsider the frail state of primary industry when managed on the family level and reshape it to have a management structure that will attract urban youth and guarantee the livelihood of immigrants. I will point out that if we do not implement a revolution of our primary industries, we will have no chance of winning the international competition over securing human resources.

If the Japanese of this era do not have the drive to fundamentally reform the agriculture, forestry, and fishery industries, the number of immigrants coming here will stall and Japan's primary industries will tumble down a path toward destruction alongside the natural decline in population. I have no doubt that should these industries which the obstinate Japanese have maintained since ancient times be driven to ruin, then future generations of Japanese will be furious at us for our shiftlessness.

***

The long-awaited agricultural revival project has begun. In October 2016, the government put forward the concept of an agricultural special zone to admit foreign agricultural specialists and save the agricultural industry of Ogata Village in Akita prefecture, an area where there is a great shortage of people to take over farms. A document released by the government at that time made special mention that "to solve these problems, we will actively bring in 'foreigners.' However, because these problems are beyond the capabilities of 'technical interns,' we will make it possible for 'specialist human resources in the field of agriculture' to be hired!"

When I saw this official document, I interpreted it as the introduction of an "agricultural immigration special zone system" granting a (new) "Agriculture" status of residence and permanent residency to foreign agricultural technicians.

This idea of an agricultural special zone in Ogata Village, Akita, will quickly spread to the farming and mountain villages across the country as a model for helping agricultural areas recover from the brink of death. At the same time, the Technical Internship Program—which has been an obstacle to reviving agriculture—will hopefully rapidly become obsolete. A groundbreaking system for accepting immigrants has been inaugurated and the saying that "the good drives out the bad" has been validated. I now see the possibility of Japanese agriculture being placed on a stable course.

FISHING IMMIGRANTS WILL REVIVE THE SANRIKU FISHING INDUSTRY

March 11, 2011, 2:46 p.m. The Great East Japan Earthquake struck with its epicenter off the Sanriku coast of Miyagi prefecture. Immediately afterwards the Pacific coast of Tōhoku was attacked by a giant tsunami. The cities, towns, and villages along the Sanriku coast—a leading Japanese fishery—were reduced to a pitiful sight.

What has become of the fishing industry in this area since suffering this massive blow? Even though eight years have passed since the disaster, reconstruction of the Sanriku coastal area has not proceeded as planned. In fact, I've heard that the decline of the fishing population has accelerated as younger people continue to leave the occupation.

The reality is that a massive earthquake and tsunami caused the sudden reduction of a working population that was already declining due to chronic difficulty in finding successors. It's clear that the greatest bottleneck to recovery has become the shortage of human resources needed to support the fishing industry in the future. With most of the current workers in their sixties and seventies, this devastated local industry cannot be expected to recover. It's possible that the worst-case scenario will come to pass. It will not recover from the great damage caused by the disaster and regional society will disappear.

But there's an effective way to escape from this desperate situation. First, make good use of "immigration policy" to welcome the young and energetic global human resources as immigrants (future citizens). Second, reconsider the fishing industry's fragile management structure based around families and reform it into a managerial structure able to properly accept immigrants.

In order the revive the Sanriku coastal fishing industry—which contains good fishing grounds where the Oyashio and Kuroshio currents meet—fishermen's cooperatives and ordinary companies will invest in fishing industry corporations (a type of joint-stock corporation). These will hire young foreigners who admire Japanese fishermen and develop a large-scale and diverse fishing industry capable of competing on a global level. A prerequisite for this will be that foreigners in their late teens and twenties enter Japanese fishery high schools, are taught the know-how of the Japanese fishing industry, are trained into qualified fishermen, and that local residents warmly welcome immigrants (and their families) as pillars of the fishing industry. Fishing immigrants will work in the open sea fishing, coastal fishing, aquaculture, and seafood processing industries.

If immigration policy is introduced, the Sanriku fishing industry will be brought back to its old vitality through the good work of elderly Sanriku fishermen and young fishing immigrants. And the national fishing industry will recover as the Sanriku fishing industry serves as a model for revival elsewhere.

LARGE-SCALE TOURISM PROJECTS AND REGIONAL REVITALIZATION

The government has been making efforts toward regional revitalization since the autumn of 2014, but it has not yet found a practical policy to act as a decisive blow. I have a good idea: with the explosive increase in the number of foreign tourists, regional residents should seize the initiative and establish new enterprises related to foreign tourism. The sudden rise of a new industry full of regional ideas will lead to regional vitality and positive economic effects.

The increase in the number of foreign tourists is remarkable, reaching thirty million in 2018. Because this trend of increase is expected to continue, why not have the prefectures compete over massive projects aimed at enticing foreign tourists, the construction of resort hotels and the development of new tourist resources that showcase the attractiveness of local areas, for example.

This would increase investment related to regional public works. After these projects have been completed, they will act as bases for regional foreign tourism businesses. They will have positive effects on employment and regional economies. For example, jobs will be created such as for hotel chefs and clerks, tourist bus drivers and guides, and souvenir shop employees. And the local economy will prosper from the large amounts of money that residential foreign tourists will spend staying in hotels and going to restaurants.

Immigration policy will also contribute by admitting global human resources into the country to act as project team leaders, managers, chefs for non-Japanese cuisine, hotel clerks, tourist guides, and interpreters.

Local residents will welcome these workers as members of society and future immigrants.

The national government will give full cooperation to local governments on the financial and technological aspects of developing and planning tourist resources to attract foreign tourists. It will also prepare a system for admitting foreign tourists. With their region's survival on the line, local government leaders will join together with local residents and strive to promote local industries through sound business strategies.

TOKYO IS ESPECIALLY IN NEED OF LARGE-SCALE IMMIGRATION

From Meiji to the early postwar period, surplus population was a serious problem for Japan's agricultural areas. Large numbers of young people moved to cities to find work. These diligent youths from agricultural villages joined the industrial working population and supported the development of the Japanese economy. Japan was able to achieve an amazing level of high-speed economic growth.

Today, however, there are towns and villages in areas with primary industries that are on the verge of collapse due to the rapid decrease of their residential population and a lack of people to take over for those who have died. Rural areas drained of people have no one to send off to the cities. After 150 years, the domestic population migration from agricultural villages to the cities has come to an end.

What does that mean? It's the beginning of the withering of the Japanese economy. Economic vitality is disappearing throughout the Japanese archipelago and the Japanese economy is on such a steep path of decline that it is as if it was falling down a hill.

The capital Tokyo is no exception. While excessive centralization in Tokyo is also becoming a problem, if young people stop moving there for social mobility, then Tokyo—which has the lowest level of childbirth in the country—will soon have its population decrease.

If the policy of closing Japan off from immigration continues for another fifty years, Tokyo will likely become filled with ghost towns, places where there are high-rises but no one living in them. I frequently assert that Tōkyō is in need of large-scale immigration to avoid declining.

Tōkyō should take the lead and seek to become a global city like New York with "immigrants making up ten percent of city residents." Following Tokyo's lead, large cities like Ōsaka, Nagoya, Yokohama, Fukuoka, Sapporo, Sendai, Hiroshima, Kyōto, Kōbe, and Kanazawa will also rise with a goal of becoming global cities with "ten percent immigrants." I believe that it will be necessary to use the majority of the ten million immigrants who enter Japan to prevent the decline of these large cities.

Japan has no choice but to wager the fate of the nation on a national commitment to immigration. This way, when domestic population movements slow, we will be able to find an escape route in global population movements (immigration) and Japan as a whole will prosper through the introduction of global human resources.

IMMIGRATION POLICY AS AN EFFECTIVE COUNTERMEASURE TO THE DECLINE IN CHILDBIRTH

In 2017, some 600,000 couples got married, the lowest number of the postwar period (according to a welfare ministry report).

Is there a magic bullet for increasing the number of births as the birthrate remains low and the population of young people of marriageable age continues to fall?

As an expert on immigration policy, I have a good idea for how to increase the number of births: adopting an immigration policy intended to cultivate human resources—that is, one that educates the young people of the world at Japan's high schools and universities and trains them to be full members of Japanese society. As a by-product of this policy, Japanese and international students will study together, become good rivals, form friendships, and eventual relationships.

The majority of these immigrants will be international students in their late teens or twenties as they enter the country. It's not difficult to imagine that marriages between these immigrants will be common as will be marriage with Japanese people.

Incidentally, humans naturally possess feelings of admiration and curiosity toward other ethnic groups. The young people of Japan in particular tend to feel attracted to people of other ethnicities and races. They aren't necessarily opposed to the idea of marrying a foreigner.

If ten million immigrants come to live in Japan, we can expect that marriages between Japanese and immigrants will increase explosively, a large number of second-generation immigrants will be born, and the young population will increase.

An immigration policy that emphasizes education will thus be extremely effective at increasing childbirth. How about the government makes good use of immigration policy and makes it a pillar of its countermeasures against low childbirth? With a relatively large number of people in Japan viewing international marriages positively, I believe that immigration policy will contribute to increasing the birthrate.

All of the developed nations with birthrates at the relatively high level of 2.00 or so are countries with immigration: America, Britain, France, and others. In all of those countries, however, the birthrate for white people remains low. Experts on global population issues all share a common understanding that there is a correlation between immigration policy and a rise in the national birthrate.

NOTES

1. Sakanaka Hidenori, "Nihongata Imin Kokka no Teian (A Proposal for a Japanese-Style Immigrant Country)," *Gekkan Jichiken*, Vol. 51, No. 592 (January 2009), pp. 49-54.

NINE

The Human Community—Global Citizens—Hybrid Japan

WHY WILL FOREIGN PERMANENT RESIDENTS FALL IN LOVE WITH JAPANESE CULTURE?

From my experiences having friendly conversations with foreign permanent residents of various nationalities (notably *Zainichi* Koreans)—first as
a national public official charged with foreigner administration and, since
retiring, as the director of the JIPI—I've felt that Japan has a mysterious
ability to draw foreigners to it and help them integrate themselves into it.
How on earth was the nation of Japan able to acquire the power to capti-
vate foreigners? The following is the hypothesis I've developed over the
course of many years.

The "spirit of harmony with nature" which arose during the *Jōmon*
period, during which life continued peacefully for 15,000 years, is also
engraved deeply into the souls of the modern Japanese people. And the
infinite, immortal *kami* are enshrined within our hearts. These aspects
have been continuously passed on, almost like "genes of tolerance" that
allow us to accept diverse values and existences. And isn't this likely
what has led to the formation of a strongly assimilative society, one that
the foreigners permanently residing in Japan naturally merge into over
many years?

Here I would like to emphasize the captivating power of the Japanese
language and how it can make Japanese culture enthralling for those
from foreign countries. To give one example, the *Zainichi* Koreans—some
who were originally strongly anti-Japanese—have naturally assimilated
into Japanese society with the passage of time. In particular, second and
third generation *Zainichi* Koreans raised within the linguistic environ-

171

ment of the Japanese language and its emphasis on vowels have almost perfectly assimilated into Japanese society.

Meanwhile, examining the Japanese view of foreigners, our fortunate history of avoiding large-scale influxes of peoples from other cultures and invasions or occupations by foreign powers means that we have relatively little fear or xenophobic sentiment toward others.

The Koreans, Chinese, Indians, and Americans I am close to love and respect the Japanese for their good manners, humility, tolerance, attentiveness, and mild character. They like the nature here which is rich in changes with its four seasons, the scenery of our beautiful rice paddies and *satoyama*, our unified society, and the way society maintains peace and order. They love Japanese *anime*, cuisine, fashion, festivals, and/or its culture as a whole.

From the second generation on, the children of immigrants will study in Japanese elementary and junior high schools and grow up in Japanese society with its lack of discrimination toward other races and religions. They will feel an attachment for the Japan in which they were born and raised, and their hearts will blend together with those of the Japanese. I believe that in the near future we will see glimpses of the establishment of the world's first human community.

In recent years, I've exchanged opinions on Japanese immigration policy with foreign permanent residents of various nationalities. They all tell me the same thing: "With their spirit of tolerance, the Japanese will accept immigrants well," and "If the Japanese and immigrants cooperate, they can create the world's first human community." They also give their enthusiastic support to an immigration policy filled with the Japanese spirit of harmony. Within the permanent resident community in Japan, there are heightened hopes that the country will open to immigration.

They recognize that compared to the rest of the world's peoples, the Japanese are neither arrogant nor aggressive. Looking at the ancient history of Japan, it seems that beginning in the *Jōmon* and *Yayoi* eras, the indigenous people and new migrants were able to build a relationship of coexistence. There was very little fighting between the indigenous people and those who came from across the sea. Neither side attempted to wipe the other out. This is directly attested to by the fact that there are a fair number of the descendants of various ethnicities in Japan today such as those of the *Jōmon* and *Yayoi* peoples.

Due to Britain's frightful experiences being invaded by various other groups, it sometimes seems that the British people take a cool view toward foreigners. Meanwhile, as the descendants of the British Empire, they are proficient at controlling other ethnic groups, such as by inciting wars between them in order to profit from the sidelines.

While the Han Chinese built the Great Wall to prevent invasions by other ethnic groups, they've also maintained an attitude based on Sinocentrism of looking down on other peoples. The modern Chinese are the world champions of ethnocentrism and remain fixated on Sinocentrism. Under the Chinese Communist Party regime, minority policies — such as those applied to the Koreans, Uighurs, and Tibetan Buddhists — are pursued via coercive means.

Unlike these two peoples, the Japanese accept "different ethnicities" with a warm gaze. Long ago, the Japanese welcomed those who came from other countries across the sea with love and respect as guests. Even when the country was closed during the Edo period, sailors from other countries who washed ashore were treated humanely.

And the Japanese have nothing like "Sinocentrism" or the sense of being a "chosen people." Unlike the Americans, Russians, and Chinese and their notably arrogant attitudes, the Japanese can be classified among the world's major ethnicities as a humble and calm people.

Looking back across human history, it is a series of wars caused by ethnic and religious differences. However, if we look only at the history of warfare on the Japanese archipelago, the Japanese have no experience fighting those of other ethnicities or being occupied by foreign armies other than after the last world war. It seems fair to say that being an island nation has worked to our advantage and allowed for the formation of the Japanese ethnic character that causes us to greet those of other countries with a pure heart.

We Japanese have accepted foreign cultures and religions with a broad spirit, rearranged them in accordance with Japanese tastes and made them our own. I have no doubt that immigrants will also be welcomed with a spirit of kindness and that good relations will be established.

JUNIOR HIGH SCHOOL AND HIGH SCHOOL STUDENTS INTERESTED IN IMMIGRATION POLICY

(1) In August 2014, I was visited by a 12th grade student who attended a high school in the city. She was writing a ten-page-long graduation paper on the topic of "Japanese immigration policy and Japanese language education." She had passionately read the "Sakanaka Proposal" available on the JIPI homepage and understood the importance of Japanese language education for immigrants. She had also grasped the essence of an immigration policy that cultivates human resources. As we talked, I soon realized that I had little to teach her. We discussed the necessity of developing teaching methods for Japanese in English and other foreign languages, the importance of Japanese education that considers the viewpoints of immigrants, and the spirituality of the Japanese who believe in the infinite kami and how this is related to accepting immigrants. It was an enjoyable and lively conversation.

She had become interested in immigration issues after the teachers at her high school and cram school had asked their students, "What do you think about accepting immigrants?" I was happy to hear that accepting immigrants has become a topic of discussion among high schoolers. We promised to meet again after she entered university and then we parted.

(2) In November 2015, I was visited by an 8th grader. He said he was writing a report on the immigration issue to submit for class. He had read about the immigration nation concept on the JIPI homepage and understood the necessity of immigration policy. He was also very interested in the issue of population collapse. He asked insightful questions about the relationship between immigration policy and the decline in population, and the important points of my theory of immigration policy. We were able to have a high-level discussion for about ninety minutes. I was very impressed that a fourteen-year-old junior high schooler was able to grasp the essence of the Japanese-style immigration policy. It was an enjoyable time. He was also a very capable young man. I gave him copies of *Immigration Battle Diary*, *The Road to a Japanese Style Immigration Nation (New Edition)*, and *Japan as a Nation for Immigrants* and we promised to meet again.

(3) In November 2016, I was visited by three students interested in immigration policy as a solution to the population problem. The three were students at Sōzan Junior High School in Okayama Prefecture, where their general education class had been given the name the "Future Directions Project." Each student was to research a topic of their own choosing and collect their findings into a twenty-page graduation paper which they would then present. The three junior high school students thought that Japan should introduce immigration policy to solve Japan's population problem and had chosen the immigration issue as their topic. The following were the main points of their questions. They were all good questions that got right to the core of the issue:

> (1) If we accept immigration in large numbers, it's possible that there will be cases where people who came as immigrants become isolated. For that reason, we thought that we should accept many children. By coming into contact with Japanese culture from a young age, they will be able to dismantle cultural barriers. If we accept children, what region do you think we should accept them from? (2) Currently refugee problems are spreading globally. I believe that by accepting troubled children such as those without parents from these kinds of poverty-stricken areas, we will solve their problems and at the same time be able to move Japan in the right direction. (3) We can see anti-immigrant movements in the world's immigration nation. Does that not affect your thinking that Japan should proactively accept immigrants?

Their understanding of the issues and insight were wonderful. Based on these great questions, the conversation went into specialized areas, but they were able to engage smoothly. We were able to have a ninety-minute, meaningful discussion.

When I told them that, even if the immigration powers of the West change course and turn against immigration, my belief that we should pursue immigration policy wouldn't change, they smiled. I handed them my most recent work, the privately published "The Japanese-style Immigration Nation will Change the World," and recommended they read it. As they left, I said "please continue your research into immigration policy."

The junior high and high school students who apply themselves today to the study of immigration policy are the "golden eggs" that will open up Japan's future. The immigration nation Japan that these kind young men and women lead will immediately become "the country that immigrants most want to live in."

HYBRID JAPAN: THE EASIEST COUNTRY FOR IMMIGRANTS TO LIVE IN

Nearby, I have a copy of Kenneth Boulding's book, *The Meaning of the Twentieth Century*.[1] I repeatedly read it in the 1960s as a student. It's filled with red and blue underlining. The following section is particularly well highlighted. There's no question that this passage greatly influenced me as a young man: "The different races of mankind have a sufficient sexual attraction for each other so that in the absence of any geographical or cultural obstacles to genetic mixture it is highly probable that in the course of a few thousand years the human race would become racially uniform, and the existing differences between races will be largely eliminated."

I read over that passage many times after I entered the ministry. I soon came to think seriously about the relationship between immigration control and international marriages. I also came to pay attention to fluctuations in the number of marriages between *Zainichi* Koreans and Japanese.

In the synusia called humanity, different races are sexually attracted to one another and they repeatedly mix. As a result, the future is one where the diversity of humanity is gradually being lost. And a thousand years from now, a global society will be born where barriers of race, ethnicity, and nationality have disappeared.

That's the sort of fantasy that—set off by Boulding's wonderful writing—I immersed myself in during my twenties. Today, fifty-three years later, I passionately advocate for the human community concept to the people of the world as the director of the JIPI.

But is modern humanity progressively becoming more racially unified as Boulding suggested? At the very least, it's a fact that—as acknowledged by the way that the global youth of today view life and how to live—we've entered an age of "large-scale international population movements" where hundreds of millions of people migrate across borders every year and where marriage between different ethnicities and racial mixing is increasing explosively. The youth of Japan are no exception. Aren't they among the top groups in the world in terms of the number of international marriages?

I want to propose that one effective measure for successfully introducing immigration policy to Japan is for marriages between Japanese and immigrants to increase and deepen the blood relations between the two groups.

In my controversial "Sakanaka Thesis," I paid attention to shifts in intermarriage between *Zainichi* Koreans and Japanese and the correlating population changes in the number of people (children) with mixed blood. I used this as a sign of improved relations between the two groups. Generally speaking, marriage is something undertaken by people of their own individual free will who have been mutually brought together by affection. The increase in marriages between *Zainichi* Koreans and Japanese is, more than anything else, evidence that relations between the two groups have become close. I viewed the (mixed blood) children produced by these marriages as symbols of this reconciliation.

In the section entitled, "The Treatment of the *Zainichi* Koreans," I said the following regarding future trends for marriage between *Zainichi* Koreans and Japanese and their children: "Relations between *Zainichi* Koreans and Japanese have come closer in terms of blood ties as well; if current trends continue, it is predicted that within several generations a majority of *Zainichi* Koreans will have a Japanese blood relative."

Looking at movements in marriage since then, the ratio of *Zainichi* Koreans married to Japanese has progressed at a speed faster than that predicted in my essay; today, more than ninety percent of *Zainichi* Koreans are married to Japanese.

The history of *Zainichi* Korean and Japanese growing closer—that is, the path through which these two ethnicities that were initially in a relationship of conflict improved relations through the spread of marriage— will be spoken of as a model for multiethnic co-existence in the coming era of large-scale immigration.

The above example of marriage and blood relations rapidly spreading between the minority and majority groups in a society and so-called minority problems being peacefully resolved in a short period is something that is largely unheard of in the history of the world's minorities.

***

But because Europeans have deep-seated racial and religious discrimination, intermarriage between citizens and immigrants has not progressed very far in the major European countries.

Germany accepted several million Turks as foreign workers during the postwar period, but the marriage rate between Germans and Turks is unusually low, less than one percent. The English—also of Anglo-Saxon ethnicity—have about the same low rate of international marriages as the Germans.

I've heard that intermarriage between white French people and those of African descent is more than twenty percent. Since ethnic discrimination is not that bad among the French, France is a possible country where a society based on multiethnic coexistence could develop. However, the difficult problem of overcoming Islamophobia and colonial mindsets for persons of the older generations remains.

The 16th-century Spanish and Portuguese Christians engaged in the large-scale slaughter of the native inhabitants of the areas of the South American continent that they colonized. That's not all. The ethnic make-up of the various countries of South America today—where the descendants of the native women raped by Spaniards and Portuguese make up the majority of citizens—is a situation brought about by this historic tragedy.

The history of the Europeans—who from early modern times to the mid-twentieth century regarded ethnicities of different religion, race, or customs as at best inferior (and at times, less than human) and treated others in cruel ways utterly unthinkable for a human—leaves a dark stain on the history of humanity.

Now, looking at international marriage trends in Japan, the ratio of Japanese married to those of different races, ethnicities, religions, and nationalities is relatively high as symbolized by the aforementioned overwhelming number of *Zainichi* Koreans who have married Japanese people.

Recently, there was a delightful event. A Japanese woman with Japanese and black parents was chosen as Japan's representative at the Miss Universe pageant. I couldn't help but be surprised that the Japanese view of beauty had changed to be international enough to think that someone of mixed race was beautiful. And, of course, they are. Race and ethnicity have nothing to do with external beauty, only the perceptions of it.

The path has not been easy, however. "Half," as mixed-race children are often called, was long considered or used as a derogatory term by the older generation, but quite often it is used by younger people in an admiring way as presumably being bi-cultural, bi-lingual, and/or possessing the best features of both races. The world's best female tennis player, Ōsaka Naomi, is of mixed race—her mother is Japanese and her father, an American, originally from Haiti. Symbolic of the generational change, however, Ōsaka's Japanese grandparents supposedly had great difficulty accepting the union, according to a story about the family. They have since come around, and Ōsaka herself is a role model for many young people.

Recently, there have been examples of young people close to me marrying people of different races. I will entrust the future of immigration nation Japan to the younger generation who feels attracted to those of different races. Don't Japanese young people, who have very little racial and religious discrimination, have the potential to create a "Hybrid Japan"—the easiest country in the world for immigrants to live in?

If Japan opens its gates to immigration, attractive immigrants from around the world will migrate to Japan. And the young people of Japan will also be attractive to immigrants.

Japanese women are the target of admiration from men throughout the world because Western intellectuals and artists have spread word of their virtue and the images of beautiful women in *ukiyoe* prints around the world from late 19th century to today. And Japanese men haven't fallen behind; the image of the "Seven Samurai" has been inputted into the heads of people all over the world.

The following is the vision of Japan that I see in my dreams, a Japan of one hundred years from now: "As the result of a thorough policy of opening Japan to immigration, twenty million descendants of immigrants live in the country. The young people of Japan and the world intermarry in a way that is seen as completely natural. These unions of beautiful men and beautiful women are producing plentiful beautiful mixed children. The immigration power of Japan is at the forefront of the world, following the path of Hybrid Japan."

ALL PEOPLES ARE THE DESCENDANTS OF IMMIGRANTS

Among those opposed to immigration, there are those who assert that if Japan adopts immigration policy the purity of the Japanese race and culture would be damaged. However, that type of thinking is fundamentally mistaken. Neither the Japanese people nor our culture have developed in a pure way. They are an amalgam formed with people and ideas from foreign countries mixed in.

That Japanese culture is loved by so many foreigners is precisely because it is a hybrid culture created by voraciously integrating and honing global culture. Japanese culture—which became increasingly elegant and refined through repeated cultural exchange—is a universal culture praised by the entire world.

There is virtually no ethnicity on the face of the earth that is "pure" and contains absolutely no blood from other ethnicities. The history of humanity is one of population movements. People expanded their habitat in pursuit of food and repeatedly married and mixed with different ethnicities as they adapted to the climate of those new lands and split off into different ethnicities.

The various ethnicities of today—living divided into the various nationalities of the world—are all descendants of immigrants. The Japanese—living in a country that has not experienced a large-scale influx of another ethnicity since before the *Heian* era—can be said to be a relatively pureblooded ethnicity. But even then, the Japanese are still a crossbred ethnicity incorporating the blood of the peoples (such as the *Jōmon* and *Yayoi*) who came to Japan from elsewhere in the world during the time between the *Jōmon* and *Heian* eras.

Let's take a look at human society a thousand years from now. By that time, geographical, national, and cultural barriers will have completely disappeared, marriage and mixing between people of different ethnicities will have increased explosively on a global scale, and humanity will be converging into a single ethnicity. Even if one person or one generation resists, future generations may not.

This will be the "backward evolution" of humanity—which originated as just one race before repeatedly dividing into different ethnicities—and can be regarded as a step along the path toward becoming one extremely ethnically mixed global people. Likely long before that era is reached, Japan will have led the way as "Hybrid Japan" and a "human community" will have been realized on the Japanese archipelago.

JAPANESE CULTURE HAS BECOME SOMETHING THAT BELONGS TO THE PEOPLE OF THE WORLD

Japanese traditional culture is something familiar and attractive to the immigrants who are permanently living in Japan. It is no longer "something that the Japanese have to themselves." It's "something that the people of the world have." For example, *anime*, flower arranging (*kadō*), and the tea ceremony (*sadō*) have become part of a universal culture that many people in the world respond to. What does that mean? Japan's cultural power will be a driving force behind the national commitment to immigration.

Yokozuna (senior rank) sumo wrestlers from Mongolia are fine. *Geisha* with blue eyes are fine. It's fine for Asian beauties to appear in Takarazuka plays. It's fine for young foreigners to carry *mikoshi* (portable shrines carried on shoulders of villagers in festivals, etc.) in the Hakata Gion Yamakasa festival. It's fine for young people of other cultures wearing multicolored folk clothes to dance in the Awa Odori (famous festival in Tokushima Prefecture). It's fine for permanent residents to go on the pilgrimage of Shikoku. It's fine for Westerners to study Zen Buddhism at Eihei-ji Temple.

My heart leaps as I picture that nirvana, filled with the hearts of people of different ethnicities merging and becoming one as they carry *mikoshi*, dance, and drink *sake* together. And won't an awareness that all of humanity are comrades be formed in the hearts of those global citizens at that moment?

The Japanese cultural heritage that moves the young hearts of the world—such as festivals and *kabuki* (classical dance-drama)—and the beautiful scenery of *satoyama* and terraced rice paddies can be found throughout our country. Let's uncover the cultural and natural heritage that attracts the people of the world to Japan and use it to appeal to the world. Why should not the foreigners permanently living in Japan take on that role? Through their uniquely foreign sensibilities, they will discover new cultural resources and spread them through the world.

The increases in foreign tourism and the number of Japanese who support immigration policy are closely linked. If the number of foreign tourists increases, so will the opportunities for close interaction between Japanese and foreigners. An atmosphere will be fostered among the Japanese people where they will welcome the foreigners who come to live in Japan. And there will be those among these foreign tourists who feel affection toward the Japanese people with their emphasis on courtesy, their calm nature, and their considerate hearts. It will spur an increase in the number of foreigners who wish to live in Japan permanently.

***

It is foreign wrestlers who are supporting Japan's national sport of *sumo*. The public must acknowledge the reality that a representative part of Japanese traditional culture is being protected by foreigners.

Sumo—traditional Japanese wrestling in which advancement is dependent on actual ability—opened its doors to foreigners early on and wonderfully became a symbol of "a Japan open to foreigners." And the sight of foreign wrestlers earnestly striving to assimilate into Japanese society moved the hearts of the Japanese people and contributed to them forming a positive view of foreigners.

As eloquently spoken to by the overwhelming presence of foreigners in *sumo*, it is no way the case that those that inherit Japan's traditional culture and pass it on to the next generation have to be Japanese. There are young people across the world that are well-versed in areas of Japanese culture such as *anime*, fashion, Japanese literature, *kabuki*, *Zen* meditation, *kadō*, and *sadō*.

The times have changed. Japanese culture has become something that is "cherished by the people of the world." The fact that foreign tourists who love Japanese culture have increased explosively in recent years shows that better than anything else.

It is necessary that we Japanese acknowledge the universality of Japanese culture and the way it attracts the hearts of foreigners. If there are still Japanese who believe that there's no way that foreigners could be capable of understanding the essence of Japanese culture, their way of thinking is out of date. Indeed, it may demonstrate an ignorance not only about the outside world, but about the culture they think they are trying to protect.

Practitioners of Japanese traditional arts and crafts are having difficulty finding successors. If foreigners charmed by Japanese culture are provided with places to shine in these areas, they will play a part in the preservation and development of that traditional culture. The government should treat foreigners with deep knowledge of Japan's traditional culture as leading immigrant candidates. The proper state of immigration policy is to rapidly grant permanent residency to Japanophiles who have a love and respect for Japanese culture and grant citizenship to them if they so desire.

I have a request for the Ministry of Justice. I would like new categories of residency status to be established for "Traditional Arts" and "Traditional Crafts" so that foreigners who would inherit traditional Japanese skills can be welcomed as immigrants.

EXPANDING "NIGHT-TIME JUNIOR HIGH SCHOOLS," THE OTHER WORLD FOR FOREIGNERS

On March 2007, I attended the graduation ceremony for a night-time junior high school as the guarantor (*hoshōnin*) of a student. That student was a twenty-two-year-old woman who was born in North Korea as the child of a Japanese mother and later escaped to Japan. A very energetic and hardworking young woman, she worked various jobs during the day and attended junior high school at night for two and a half years without rest. Looking back on those days, she told me with a smile that "I have only happy memories of my days at night junior high school." I attended her graduation wanting to praise the hard work she had put into safely completing Japan's mandatory education requirement.

It was there that I realized the contemporary significance that night junior high schools have. Of the fourteen graduates, only one—a seventy-year-old woman—was Japanese. The others were either foreigners or of foreign origin. Their nationalities were diverse: Chinese, South Korean, Filipino, Mongolian, Cuban, and stateless. Night-time junior high schools have been transformed into educational institutions that warmly welcome the long-term foreign residents of Japan.

At the end of the ceremony, each of the graduates gave farewell remarks. It was a display filled with emotion; in addition to words of gratitude to the teachers who taught them with kindness, they spoke of the close friends they had made and how they had experienced a full school life. Listening to the graduates talk about their happy memories, such as those of school trips and cultural festivals, in fluent Japanese, I realized that night-time junior high school must be like a paradise to long-term foreign residents. It's "another world" free of discrimination and bullying, a "*dōjō*" where minorities living in Japan with a desire to learn can come together and "train." It's a place of education based on multicultural coexistence where people of different ethnicities and cultures learn things like reading and writing Japanese through friendly competition.

I was able to understand that the foreigners who graduated from night-time junior high school had studied diligently, filled with dreams and hopes for their future lives. Indeed, the majority of the graduates spoke of their aspiration to go on to high school. There were also those who aimed to go all the way to university. No doubt their time at the junior high school gave them confidence about living in Japan.

Incidentally, the young woman I was there to support would later enter and graduate from a part-time high school, and then go on to university.

In the above way, night-time junior high school plays an important role in the education of foreigners. Unfortunately, however, it seems that the number of these schools is falling. At the ceremony, I heard that only eight junior high schools in Tokyo had night classes.

So, will night-time junior high schools fall behind and lose their reason for existing? Absolutely not. We are entering an age where the number of foreign permanent residents will increase, and it will be necessary to establish more evening classes for them.

There are currently serious foreigner problems that are connected to the children of foreign permanent residents: truancy, delinquency, and crimes. One of the reasons that there are many crimes committed by foreigners is that—once foreigners have been allowed to enter the country—they are provided with essentially no support for education or employment. Left isolated, foreign youths feel excluded from Japanese society. It's reasonable to believe that this is one factor that drives them to crime.

With our population declining, it will be necessary to prepare a system for aiding foreign permanent residents in adapting to Japanese society if we are to solve our foreigner problems and move toward a "society that coexists with immigrants." The first step will be outfitting the education system for young foreign permanent residents. And making good use of night-time junior high schools should be considered one of the most effective ways of implementing that.

Under this concept, the very kind and detailed teaching methods of the "night junior high schools" will be expanded nationwide and made part of the system for accepting immigrants. The goal will be to rapidly adapt young foreign men and women who desire permanent residency in Japan to our society and enable them to be independent.

INTERNATIONAL STUDENTS WHO MAKE JAPANESE FRIENDS WILL STAY IN JAPAN PERMANENTLY

I have a request for the government. I want the emphasis of the policy toward accepting international students to be moved from "quantity" to "quality."

The emphasis should be on preparing an environment in which excellent international students can devote themselves to study, not just increasing their number.

And the special support provided by the education ministry for international students should be changed from the current system — which benefits university administrations — to one that aids the students themselves. The current system for accepting international students — which operates under the assumption that they will work themselves ragged doing part-time work — needs to be rapidly reformed.

Why not, for example, seriously consider providing them with stable lives by increasing the ratio of international students receiving scholarships from the Japanese government from ten percent to thirty, establishing a framework for these students through immigration agreements with other countries, and building five hundred international student dormitories (enough for 20,000 students) across the country?

Immigration officials need to reconsider the current state of affairs where the "Student" status of residence has effectively become a work visa. They should revise the policy that generally permits international students to work and return to one where, in principle, they are only permitted to do so in exceptional circumstances and for short amounts of time.

Providing an environment in which international students who want to devote themselves to study are able to do so to their hearts' desire will be an urgent task if we want to draw global human resources to Japan during the era of extremely low childbirth. It is likely that there are many administrators at universities, colleges, and vocational schools who will seek to use international students to survive their financial difficulties by having them make up for the rapid decrease in Japanese students that has accompanied the low birthrate.

However, that is a terribly mistaken idea. I will caution that the universities, colleges, and vocational schools who attempted to do that in the past experienced serious foreigner problems (such as illegal working). They were criticized by the public, and were ultimately abandoned by Japanese students, leaving them no choice but to close.

And educational institutions that the youth of Japan have turned their backs on are unlikely to be able to accept foreigners who desire to study and provide them with an appropriate education in the first place.

I will warn that, should Japan maintain its approach to international students while adopting a policy of accepting them on a large scale with the intention of saving its universities, Japanese students with a desire to study will do so overseas. Japanese universities will be monopolized by lazy Japanese and foreigners who are in the country for the purpose of working and not study, and Japanese higher education will fall into ruin.

***

There's something I'd like to point out here. The relationship between Japanese students and international students on university campuses is not what could be called a good one; in fact, the groups could actually be said to be estranged.

According to an acquaintance who is a university professor, the sight of Japanese and international students happily hanging out, drinking together, and debating with one another is a rare one. International students hang out with other international students. Japanese students gather among themselves. That professor's impression was that—even though current Japanese students aren't xenophobic—they're cooler toward and less interested in international students than Japanese students were in the past when international students were less common.

It must be said that for the young people who shoulder the future of Japan to maintain a respectful distance from their foreign counterparts is something that we should be concerned about for Japan in an era of immigration, when we will be establishing a society based on multiethnic coexistence.

I want Japanese students to proactively approach international students. Judging from my many conversations with international students, they want to be friends with Japanese. International students with at least one Japanese friend will come to like Japan and likely come to want to live in Japan permanently.

A UNIVERSITY REVOLUTION IS ALSO NEEDED

Both the immigration and university revolutions are aimed at the same goal: the securing and cultivation of global human resources. In that sense, the plan for 300,000 international students that was laid out by the Fukuda Yasuo administration in July 2008 became a strong driving force for the Japanese-style immigration policy that emphasizes education.

Currently, about thirty-five percent of international students remain in Japan after graduating from their university or other school. To dramatically increase the productive population through immigration policy, we need to raise that number to close to seventy percent.

Meanwhile, in recent years there has been an increasingly large number of "international student workers"—international students who have actually come to Japan mainly with the intention of engaging in part-time work. The entrance of this kind of "fake international student" into the country cannot be permitted. I want the immigration authorities to strictly and fairly deal with this issue.

If Japan is to secure global human resources, first, Japanese universities need to draw young foreigners with a vigorous desire to learn, provide them with a full education, and then send these superior human resources out into Japanese society.

Second, international students who have obtained specialized knowledge and skills at higher vocational schools should be introduced to jobs in fields yearning for immigrants such as the caregiving, agricultural, forestry, and fishing industries.

The government should work to improve the job-hunting environment for foreigners so that international students who have graduated from universities and graduate schools can participate in job hunting on an equal footing with Japanese students and find appropriate work.

At the same time, with the era of low childbirth continuing, Japanese companies seeking to survive in the global marketplace should include population changes in their calculations and make plans for proactively recruiting international students from the viewpoint of securing human resources able to deal with the globalization of the economy.

Third, the Ministry of Justice needs to lay out a policy of preferential treatment for international students. Foreigners who have secured admission to a university or higher vocational school should be immediately granted the status of residence of "Student" (with a validity equal to the length of their school term, i.e., two to four years). Foreigners who have graduated and received a job at a Japanese company should, in principle, be granted "permanent residency" five years from the point when they entered Japan.

If the above three-point reform plan on international students is implemented, Japan's higher educational institutions will become treasuries of human resources, gathering ambitious young people from around the world. They will produce immigrants who are high-level human resources. The foundation of the Japanese-style immigration policy will be strengthened and the admission of ten million immigrants into the country will be off and running.

A MONOCHROMATIC PEOPLE WILL NOT SURVIVE THE GLOBAL AGE

When the Japanese people — who are almost all of the same ethnicity — joined together and worked hard, they were able to raise Japan all the way to being one of the world's few economic powers. However, since entering the twenty-first century, the economic decline and weakening of Japan's national strength has been noticeable. And the decline in the level of governance and administration has become obvious to all.

While it's undeniable that the issue of population decline is at the root of that, it's not the only cause. Doesn't it seem that it is only the Japanese—with our uniform language and race—whose systems for politics, administration, economics, and society have broken down?

I believe that this is related to the fact that we have entered a global age but have the narrow vision of a pureblood ethnicity. We are poor at viewing things in a broad and diverse way. The population problem that Japan faces is not just that the number of Japanese is falling rapidly. There are less quantitative problems, more serious issues of character. We are slowly running out of human resources that can compete internationally in fields like administration, economics, education, academics, journalism, and most notably politics. And there's something that proves this more than anything else.

Right now, as Japan faces the unprecedented national crisis of population collapse, there is an urgent need for revolutionaries and unconventionally talented people to grapple with the fundamental reform of the Japanese state. However, that sort of unique human resources is nowhere to be found in Japan.

During the turbulent time from the mid to late 19th century—the golden age of imperialism—samurai rose up to fight against the threat of colonial control by the Western powers. In this generation, Japan again is in an age of great crisis that will determine the survival of our nation and people. So why is it that no "Seven Samurai" have appeared in the *Heisei* era to save us from this national crisis?

Observing the ecology of the Japanese elite—politicians, bureaucrats, and business leaders who have all been raised through the same education that emphasizes uniformity—I feel that an ethnicity that was already homogenous has become one where there are many small people who merely obediently do what they're told.

The world has entered an age where the nuclear powers America, Russia, and China possess large stockpiles of nuclear weapons and compete ruthlessly with each other on the global stage. To remain a largely monochromatic ethnicity stranded on an island nation means to be unable to realistically grasp the entire picture of our global society exposed to the threat of nuclear war.

In the field of biology, hybrids are considered to have superior survivability over purebloods. Breeds are improved through hybridization. Humans are the same. Doesn't an immigrant society continually receiving the blood of fresh ethnicities have a higher chance of survival than an ethnically uniform society that takes pride in its ethnic purity? A citizenry who views things from a single perspective has a narrower field of vision than one with multiple perspectives; doesn't the latter have a higher chance of survival?

With Japan's fate in the global age in the balance, the time has come to welcome the various peoples of the world as immigrants (future citizens) and make the structure of our people more ethnically diverse. This means accepting ten million immigrants as future citizens and transforming into a people with diverse appearances.

Additionally, isn't our "monocultural society," which has been composed of ninety-nine percent ethnic Japanese for generations, a monotonous, ink wash painting? It is undeniably lacking in unpredictability and appeal to an extent. If we instead accept immigrants on a scale of ten million and become an "immigration society" in which all the peoples of the world are gathered, we will develop into a "dynamic society" powered by chemical reactions arising from the interactions of each ethnicity's energy. Just as a hot pot that contains all kinds of ingredients — fish, shellfish, meat, vegetables, mushrooms, spices, and more — becomes more tasty as all the ingredients blend together, a multiethnic society that gathers people of differing languages, cultures, and ways of thinking will expand into a "a world of brilliant people" in which the distinctive qualities of each ethnicity are on display. It will also be fun to wait and see what unique geniuses will appear through mutation.

I suspect that the Japanese cuisine of an immigration society will incorporate the flavors of various ethnic cuisines and gain a deeper flavor.

IMMIGRANTS AND THE JAPANESE LANGUAGE

Educating immigrants is important for them to understand Japan well. And education in the Japanese language is particularly important. All of the institutions of the Japanese life and lifestyle are contained within our language.

We can't put off improving the system for Japanese language education. As has become clear as we've accepted nurses and caregivers through economic partnership agreements, the key to successfully accepting immigrants depends on the Japanese language ability of foreigners. Foreigners who have mastered Japanese adapt quickly to our society. For example, second-generation immigrants who have been born and raised hearing the superior vowels of Japanese can enjoy the chirping of insects just as Japanese children can.

The government should, as soon as possible, prepare for the era of large-scale immigration by implementing a system for properly teaching elementary and junior high school children from foreign countries that can't speak Japanese. If the children of foreigners living in Japan become proficient in reading and writing Japanese and study together with Japanese children, they will be able to understand their classes in school. They will be able to go on to higher education. They will be able to find jobs that they want. They will be able to make friends with Japanese. They may have foreign origins, but their bodies and spirits will be Japanese; it will be the birth of a new type of Japanese citizen.

The methods used to teach Japanese need to be fundamentally reconsidered. I want the rapid reform of Japanese language education with an eye on large-scale immigration: for example, research and development put into developing a teaching method that allows foreigners to gain conversational ability in Japanese in a short amount of time, the technical development of a method for learning kanji using computers, and research into Japanese teaching methods that take into consideration immigrants' native languages.

I also want a method of teaching Japanese to be created that makes the young people of the world feel a closeness with the language and able to enjoy mastering it. In particular, I want effort to be put into researching methods of Japanese language education for foreigners coming from countries that don't use Chinese characters.

Incidentally, foreigners reportedly learn *kanji* by branding them in their memory as "beautiful pictures." It's a rational method for memorizing the hieroglyphic *kanji*. They also learn *kanji* with many strokes by rote, writing them correctly. Why not have the government officially designate a "foreigner *jōyō kanji* list" of a thousand or so Chinese characters that it wants foreigners residing in Japan to learn to best function here? (Ordinary Japanese learn about 2,000 characters.)

I hold the hope that the young people of the world—who are passionate about Japanese culture—will completely master Japanese, including elements regarded as difficult for foreigners to learn such as kanji and classical literature. It is necessary for those involved in Japanese language education to be careful in expanding Japanese education for foreigners with interests in both Japanese and Japanese culture.

Japanese education can't be left simply to volunteers. Specialists able to quickly and accurately teach foreigners Japanese is what are needed. That is the work of professional Japanese teachers who have studied the methods of teaching Japanese. I have a proposal for the education ministry. I want it to create a licensing system for Japanese language instructors to raise the standard of Japanese language education and improve the social status of Japanese language teachers.

I also want the government to enact a "Japanese Language Education Law" to implement Japanese education for immigrants under its auspices. This law will stipulate things like the ideals of Japanese language education in an age of immigration, the basic nature of Japanese education, the system for training Japanese instructors, and requirements for establishing Japanese schools.

I have a request for all of the foreigners who wish to live in Japan permanently. I want you to not only be able to converse in Japanese but to be able to read and write kanji so that your descendants will live happily, familiar with Japan's manners and customs. Even *kanji*, something considered difficult, can be enjoyably learned using computers to engrave them into your memory as pictures. You'll be able to easily write about a thousand. I want you to have the courage to challenge yourselves with kanji.

***

Apart from the above, I also want efforts to be made in native-language education for second-generation immigrants. There needs to be a system readied for teaching the second generation of immigrants their parents' mother language so that they inherit the culture and sensibilities of the first-generation immigrants — in other words, the establishment of a "minority language education system."

To that end, I want "minority language research centers" to be established at Tokyo University of Foreign Studies and Ōsaka University (comprising, since 2007, the former Ōsaka University of Foreign Studies), two schools well known for their instruction of foreign languages, for second-generation immigrants to learn about their native languages and cultures. These research centers will teach second-generation immigrants their native languages and cultures while also studying the world's minority languages and language policies. These talented graduates will thus be truly multi-cultural and multilingual.

If the admission of ten million immigrants goes smoothly, mixing between Japanese and immigrants will become commonplace and the number of citizens able to speak multiple languages will increase. A majority of Japanese — particularly the young — feel attracted to those of different cultures and races. There will likely be many who learn minority languages or marry those of different ethnicities.

The following is the ideal Japanese society of 2050 that I picture:

> A system implementing Japanese and native language education for second-generation immigrants has been implemented and Japan has become a society where marriage between people of different countries of origin (such as between Japanese and immigrants) has become commonplace. There are more than ten million citizens who are second-generation immigrants or the children of interethnic marriages. A "multilingual society" is forming where people speak Japanese, the language of their parents' homeland, and English. Japanese people able to proficiently use multiple languages are active throughout the world.

CREATING A SUPPORT SYSTEM FOR LONG-TERM FOREIGN RESIDENTS

Looking at the current state of foreign permanent residents in Japan, there is a noticeable number who have been unable to adapt to Japanese society. Why did things turn out that way? The primary reason is the almost total lack of support provided to long-term foreign residents after they're allowed into the country, such as for Japanese language education and finding employment. "Social integration policy" — aiding the adaption of foreigners in Japan to our society—is the area of Japanese policy toward foreigners that is lagging the farthest behind.

We need to rapidly implement policies to reconcile long-term foreign residents to Japanese society if we want to solve Japan's foreigner problems and implement a system for admitting immigrants as a way of adequately coping with our shrinking population. If this problem is left unaddressed, the Japanese view of "foreigners" will only become worse as will foreigners' views of Japan. And if that happens, the path to dealing with the issue of population decline through immigration could be cut off.

Even if Japan becomes an "immigration nation" made up of people of different ethnicities, the fundamental framework of the state will still be centered on Japanese culture (represented by the Japanese language) and Japan's social, economic, and legal systems. The purpose of social integration policy is to prepare a social environment within the Japanese state's basic order in which those of foreign origin can have the feeling that "I'm glad I came to Japan. I want to quickly become a Japanese citizen."

So, what do we need to do to reach that goal? First is the creation of a foreigner education system to teach the Japanese language and basic social rules to foreigners who have entered Japan. Next is building a "society that provides foreigners with dreams," one that guarantees all people equal opportunities regardless of their nationality or ethnicity.

Support for newcomer foreigners learning Japanese will be the core of our social integration policy. Especially important is creating a robust Japanese language education program for second-generation immigrants born in Japan. If these second-generation immigrants master Japanese, their adaptation to Japanese society will proceed infinitely more smoothly as all of the Japanese way of thinking, culture, and customs are contained within the language.

Based on my experiences engaging with long-term residents of many nationalities (especially *Zainichi* Koreans) as an administrator, I believe that they have an extremely high ability to assimilate into Japanese society. In the past, I was criticized for using the term "assimilation" with regard to the *Zainichi* Korean issue, but the assimilation I'm talking about wouldn't be forced. It's "spontaneous assimilation" in which immigrants naturally come to feel that they want to be Japanese citizens. The process could be soon, or gradual. In any case, it is up to the individual.

Many of the foreigners in Japan like our natural environment rich in changes, our gentle social climate, and our well-ordered Japanese society. They unanimously say that Japanese cuisine and culture are attractive. My view is that foreign permanent residents, having (from the second generation on) studied in Japanese schools and grown up in a society without prejudice or discrimination against foreigners, will come to love the Japanese people and assimilate into Japanese society.

THE PRESSING NEED TO TRAIN IMMIGRATION COUNSELORS

If Japan changes course on immigration policy, "immigration social workers" (immigration counselors) will be essential to support the social adaptation of immigrants. They will consult with immigrants on their various mental or life-related worries, provide guidance on residency and citizenship procedures, and offer career counseling for their children.

As the door is opened to immigration, there will be a need to establish immigrant residency support centers and multiethnic coexistence centers in areas with large numbers of immigrants. The question is whether we will be able to secure enough Japanese language teachers and employees with foreign language ability and a deep knowledge of Japanese and foreign cultures to work there.

I've heard that there are currently tens of thousands of staff and volunteers at nonprofits (just counting those in involved Japanese language education) across the country who engage in support activities for foreign long-term residents. They are engaged in a diverse range of activities under various banners such as Japanese language education, refugee settlement support, protecting foreigners' rights, eliminating ethnic discrimination, multiethnic coexistence, and more.

The volunteer activists who I've met are passionately grappling with residency support, social education, and systemic reform from the perspective of minorities.

I believe the only practical method to secure immigration counselors is to train immigration counselors from among the NPO staff and volunteers currently actively engaged with various foreigner issues.

I also have another idea: making use of an immigration network in which immigrants that have been in the country look after newcomers. Local governments will cooperate with minority groups to systematically develop immigrant residency support networks. These will promote the economic independence and social advancement of immigrants.

It will be necessary for the government to appraise the work of the immigration counselors and pay them an appropriate salary. Why not designate a portion of ODA (official development assistance) funds for this? The work of supporting immigrant social adaption and Japanese language study is consistent with the purpose of ODA. Companies in need of this labor may also want to chip in somehow, in addition to the taxes they already pay.

THE YOUTH OF JAPAN SEEK TO BE GLOBAL CITIZENS

I have long asserted that "the Japanese must evolve into a hybrid ethnicity over the next hundred years." I can vividly remember how, immediately after President Barack H. Obama, whose father was an international student from Kenya, took office in January 2009, he was asked by a reporter about the breed of dog that he would keep in the White House. He answered that it would be "a mutt like me." These significant words were a revelation for me.

Japan has not experienced a large-scale landing of people from another country for more than a thousand years. During that time, the descendants of the Japanese—a people who have lived on the Japanese archipelago since the *Jōmon* and *Yayoi* periods—have lived in close proximity with only their "blood relatives." It cannot be denied that as a result the Japanese are a people particularly weak in diversity.

The twenty-first century is a global society in which global networks stretch everywhere as part of the internet. It will difficult for us to survive this tumultuous global age if we do not accept diverse human resources from across the world and look at global affairs with a broad perspective, as if looking down from an artificial satellite.

To compete with global talent in a global society, we Japanese must aim to become global citizens. The first step will be building a utopian immigration society on the Japanese archipelago that the young people of the world will be excited to move to. It will be an ideal immigration society in which the unique ideas, sharp senses, and deep thoughts distinctive to each ethnicity will compete with each other. If ten million immigrants that comprehensively contain all the peoples of the world are welcomed as members of Japanese society, Japan will transition becoming a multiethnic society composed of people of all kinds.

I perceive our unprecedented population crisis as a one-in-a-million chance to make a great leap to a society built upon multiethnic coexistence. The wise public will borrow the strength of immigrants and survive the population crisis. The Japanese and all the other ethnicities will lower their guards, become one, and take up the challenge of "multiethnic harmony." The Japanese archipelago will be rebuilt as a society based on the human community, and an immigrant utopia created that the young people of the world will dream of living in.

This society based on the human community will be one where each ethnicity will have its own presence and yet be one as Japanese citizens. It will be a society composed of Japanese citizens of various ethnic lineages such as Mongolian-Japanese, African-Japanese, European-Japanese, Arab-Japanese, and American-Japanese in addition to those who have been Japanese for countless generations. I believe that the existence of "a new type of Japanese citizen"—citizens each living with different cultural heritages—will be essential to the coming immigration society.

In order for many ethnicities to band together into one people, it will be necessary for there to be widespread belief in the cultural anthropological common-sense idea that "humanity is one. We are all humans despite any differences of race, ethnicity, and religion."

At that time, what will be sought from the Japanese people who have lived on the Japanese archipelago since the *Jōmon* and *Yayoi* periods will be to acknowledge the newcomer ethnic groups as an equal presence while still maintaining their own ethnic identity as Japanese. In other words, it will be important to both welcome newcomer immigrants as members of society and respect the inherent cultures that these minority ethnicities possess, while still protecting the spirit of harmony that the Japanese people have maintained continuously from ancient times. I envision the ideal Japanese person as being one who incorporates both an ethnic pride as well as the welcoming spirit of tolerance.

The Japan that the many peoples of the world will want to permanently live in is a society where Japanese have pride as Japanese and immigrants have pride as immigrants. The society based on the human community that I envision is a society where Japanese and immigrants peacefully coexist, respecting both the other's way of living and themselves.

TO THOSE LIVING IN A GLOBAL AGE

The diversity of humanity—that is, the fact that it is divided into various races and ethnicities—can be given as one of the reasons that humanity has been able to survive to the present day. Humanity, just one race, has spread across the Earth seeking new homes and successfully adapted to a diverse array of living environments, from the equator to the arctic, surviving. If humanity had remained just one race/ethnicity living in Africa, humanity as a species wouldn't be able to adapt to sudden changes in their living environments, like natural disasters. The species may have disappeared from the face of the Earth early on.

Today, there are said to be more than two thousand ethnic groups. The human community that arises from a diverse ethnic society will have strong vitality. Each of the many ethnicities in it will have pride in their unique culture. What will be the future of this human society rich in diversity? Thinking over the future of humanity on a scale of thousands of years from the perspective of civilization theory, the image of humanity that comes to me is not one where it follows a path of further diversification. I see humanity following a course where its diverse groups repeatedly mix, converging into a single race.

Homo sapiens feel a sense of kinship and love for those of other races and ethnicities as comrades belonging to the same species. It is possible that the humanity of a thousand years from now will have formed a society where people are attracted to those of different races and ethnicities and intermarriage among races and ethnicities is the norm. I was absorbed by that kind of fantasy fifty years ago when I was a student.

While I had no idea at the time that I was fated to find work related to immigration policy, the fantasy I embraced at that time is even now still

burned into my brain. That might be my mental scenery, why I'm attracted to the thoughts of the *Jōmon* people and a world made up of
human communities.

***

When my Japan Immigration Policy Institute held a "Multicultural
Coexistence Essay Contest" in September 2012, I submitted a piece to the
Sankei Shimbun at the time. Those words—my earnest thoughts to the
younger generation—appeared in the social pages of the September 8
issue of the *Sankei Shimbun* under the title "To Those Living in a Global
Age":

> According to the government's population statistics, the Japan of fifty
> years from now will be a society in which each member of the working
> population will have to support one elderly person. The future that
> awaits the younger generation is an extremely unfair one in which they
> will be forced to bear a heavy burden while they work and then receive
> no welfare in their old age. The only countermeasure available to Japan
> for avoiding population collapse is for young people to welcome immi-
> grants. Your future will be determined based on whether a Japan can
> be created that accepts the peoples of the world with tolerance and
> where diverse values can coexist. I want those of you who will live in a
> global age to turn your thoughts to a vision of the humanity of the
> distant future, one where there is a multiracial human community and
> where humanity—attracted to those different from themselves—con-
> verges into a single race through repeated intermarriage and mixing.
> Humanity may have divided into diverse races and ethnicities, but
> because we all have the same ancestors, we share many cultural ele-
> ments such as a sense of camaraderie and love for other cultures. Ima-
> gining the global society of a hundred years from now, we will likely
> have entered an age of large-scale population movements and become
> a society where intermarriage between different ethnic groups is re-
> garded as natural.

This commentary—which received a good amount of space on the
page—sent a shock through those who read it. According to the *Sankei
Shimbun*, which is known as a very conservative newspaper, there were
no criticisms or arguments from readers regarding my immigration policy theory and its forecast for the global society of a hundred years from
now. I received no criticisms addressed to the JIPI either. I was surprised
at this unforeseen development. Perhaps the anti-immigration faction
was overwhelmed by my vigorous article.

Looking at the current tone in the national papers, more than six years
since the *Sankei Shimbun* ran my article showing a future-oriented theory
of immigration policy, there has been a noticeable shift toward positive
coverage of immigration policy. And as the crisis of population collapse
becomes more serious, public opinion in favor of opening the country to

immigration has become the majority, especially among the younger generation.

THE JAPANESE VISION OF AN IMMIGRATION NATION IS THE FOREMOST IN THE WORLD

In order to survive the era of population decline, we Japanese will have to change the way we live. We need to be prepared to create an "immigration nation" where foreigners with diverse cultural backgrounds migrate to the Japanese archipelago and take active part in society, where we make good use of the attributes of each ethnicity. I want the Japanese to become a group who are excited about meeting people of different cultures and religions and who look different from us. While it's fine for us to live harmoniously with our fellow Japanese, I want the Japanese to become willing to actively engage with people of different ethnicities and religions, to learn from immigrants, and to earnestly feel that "I'm glad I engaged with another culture." The Japanese, who have relatively little racial, ethnic, or religious discrimination compared to Westerners, can take the lead in the world and establish relationships of coexistence with immigrants. I want us to properly meet new immigrants with the mindset of past immigrants who have been living on an island nation in the Far East since ancient times.

I, an archetypical Japanese who believes in the infinite *kami*, advocate for the universal and creative ideal of a human community based on the worldview that "humanity is one. We are all citizens of the Earth." This is where our approach differs from Western immigration policy which is rooted in white supremacist thought.

The time when Japan alone among the developed countries closed itself off from immigration and indulged in idleness has come to an end. As Japan's population crisis and the world's humanitarian crises worsen, there is a need for us Japanese to become prepared to accept immigrants on a scale that suits an economic power and to contribute to world peace and stability.

I believe that the vision of Japan as an immigration nation that lies at the base of the concept of human community has the ability to attract the young people of the world.

If—even as Western immigration nations are closing their doors to immigrants—the Japanese government issues a declaration opening the country to immigration at the opening of the 2020 Tokyo Olympics and Paralympics and says that "the Japanese, who are considerate to immigrants, will welcome ten million immigrants in the spirit of harmony," the highly skilled human resources of the world will flock to Japan. I have no doubt that once the immigration nation Japan is born, the spotlight will shine upon it as an immigration society loved by the talented young people of the world.

A FORECAST OF THE IMMIGRATION NATION OF FIFTY YEARS FROM NOW

My first prediction is that the Japan of fifty years from now, with a population of ten million immigrants, will be the second largest immigration power in the world behind the United States. A society built upon multiethnic coexistence will have been perfectly achieved with all discord between the majority Japanese and minority immigrant populations dispelled. Based on trends and current proportions, eight million immigrants will likely live in urban areas and two million in agricultural areas. There will be many villages and towns where immigrants represent a majority of the population.

My second prediction is that Japanese who come in contact with the active efforts of immigrants will also be filled with the enthusiastic energy; Japanese politics, economics, and culture will enter a new age. A "society of talent" will have been realized where geniuses of Japanese and foreign origin are active in their specialized fields.

Third, with the large-scale immigration of people of various cultures, Japanese culture will incorporate these minority cultures and take pride in its freshness and diversity. There will be remarkable advancements in sports and the arts by foreign-born immigrants who possess the sensibilities and abilities that are unique to foreigners. For example, by then, two-thirds of senior-ranked *sumo* wrestlers will have been born in foreign countries. Through their efforts, sumo will have become one of the most popular sports in the world. Foreign-born newscasters and hosts will appear on Japanese television. Japanese cuisine will skillfully incorporate foreign ingredients and preparation methods, becoming richer and a favorite of the gourmands of the world.

Fourth, with the increasing aging of society and decline in children, the social security systems (such as the pension and national health insurance systems) will have briefly been on the verge of collapse before being stabilized by the influx of ten million (mostly young) immigrants. There will be foreign-born doctors and nurses in major hospitals. Most of these nurses will be women from Southeast Asia. They will be highly appreciated in that profession due to their warm, cheerful, and protective natures.

Fifth, the society of agricultural and mountain villages is where the coexistence between Japanese and immigrants will have made the most progress. "Mother Earth" will be revived as agricultural immigrants become the driving force behind restoring abandoned fields and mountain forests; Japan's self-sufficiency ratio on food and timber will reach eighty percent.

My sixth prediction is that a "meritocratic" management policy will have taken hold in the business world that doesn't discriminate against country of origin or ethnicity. Those of foreign origin who can think globally will be chosen for management positions. The more diverse a company is in terms of its employees' countries of origin and ethnicities, the better it will be able to compete in the global marketplace. Negative growth due to the contraction of domestic demand will become normalized and businesses will shift to the foreign investment model for the economy, making effective use of their massive overseas financial assets. Companies related to robotics will grow into leading Japanese firms.

Seventh, the systems related to the education of foreigners (the system for admitting one million international students, foreigner vocational training system, and Japanese language and native language education systems) will have been completed and have the highest standards in the world. Japanese language education will be emphasized to promote multiethnic social unity. In elementary and junior high schools, a diverse array of ethnicities (including Japanese) will receive their educations in Japanese. Enlightened courses will be included in the curriculum in order to create a society built upon multiethnic coexistence. The immigration policy emphasizing education will have achieved wonderful results and immigrants who have become highly skilled human resources will be active throughout society. The young people of Japan will be heading into the world as global citizens.

Eighth, there will be an interethnic marriage boom. Marriages between Japanese and those of foreign origin will be rapidly increasing as will the number of Japanese who speak three or more languages (mainly the children produced by these marriages).

Finally, immigrants and their descendants will be grateful to the Japanese government and people who warmly welcomed them. In national elections, many of the ten million immigrants will vote for the political party that had opened the doors to immigration fifty years earlier. Many second-generation immigrants will run as candidates for the Diet. Among these will be unique, globally minded politicians.

NOTES

1. Kenneth Boulding, *The Meaning of the Twentieth Century: The Great Transition* (New York: Harper Collins, 1964).

TEN

The Return of Japanese Left Behind in North Korea

THE JAPANESE WOMEN WHO HAVE ESCAPED NORTH KOREA AND SECRETLY RETURNED HOME

The fierce global ideological conflict that followed Japan's defeat in the Second World War divided the Korean Peninsula in two, leaving the 600,000 *Zainichi* Koreans at the mercy of international conflict on the peninsula. After an armistice was reached in the Korean War, that community's sense of despair—the feeling that the discrimination they had faced since the Japanese annexation of Korea in 1910 would never end—was transformed into a great enthusiasm for the "communist paradise" of North Korea. Soon, the "North Korean Repatriation Movement" was launched.

From 1953 to 1984, 93,340 *Zainichi* Koreans moved to North Korea. This number also includes approximately 6,800 Japanese wives and children who accompanied them.

I view the North Korean returnee issue as an extension of the *Zainichi* Korean issue. And I believe that neither issue can be completely resolved until these "returnees" can freely travel back to Japan. Some of these Japanese wives and their families have actually fled from North Korea and then secretly returned to Japan via China.

More than fifteen years ago, the *Yomiuri Shimbun* broke this story with a shocking series of articles on this topic.[1] These articles (which the paper gave broad coverage to) appeared on the front page under the title "Japanese Wives Flee North Korea, Secretly Return Home." This was subtitled "Foreign ministry has issued passage papers to forty (including families) since 1994." The title of the article in the social pages was "Destitute and Without Aid from their Homeland, Many Await Salvation in China" (this

199

was subtitled "North Korean Repatriation Project—Upon Arrival, 'Oh, no'."). An interview with me was entitled "The Need for a System of Acceptance."

It was actually a submission from me that sparked this coverage. On the night that Prime Minister Koizumi Junichirō visited Pyongyang on September 17, 2002, with Abe Shinzō, then a young deputy chief cabinet secretary known for his hawkish views on North Korea, I saw the coverage saying that the prime minister had been told that eight of the Japanese who had been abducted by North Korea had died. As I watched this, I was struck by the thought that those who had repatriated to North Korea, had also—against their expectations—been subjected to the same cruel treatment as the abductees. I was overwhelmed by the whole-hearted desire to "let the public know the plight of those who had returned to North Korea." I wrote the draft of an article in a single sitting and sent it to the *Yomiuri Shimbun*. That's where everything started, as that draft would eventually be developed into a string of articles, including an interview with me.

I had wanted to properly make my views on the North Korean return-ee issue known, but I needed an opportunity. Immediately after the announcement of Prime Minister Koizumi's visit to North Korea, I received a request from the *Yomiuri* that I write a piece on "the *Zainichi* Korean issue in the wake of the visit." I knew that—with the public's heightened interest in the North Korea abductions of Japanese citizens—"now is the time."

I had the following to say in my interview with the *Yomiuri*:

> When I heard the news that eight of the abductees had died, I immediately thought of the cruel fates of the *Zainichi* Koreans who had returned to North Korea and the 6,800 Japanese who had accompanied them as their wives and children. My heart aches when I think that they must have received the same treatment as those who were abducted. Returnees were given the low social status of members of the "wavering class." They were targeted for discrimination and surveillance and, inevitably, a life suffering from hunger. I've also been told that many were sent to concentration camps and died in them. Isn't this a larger issue than the abductees? Given the circumstances the return-ees are in—starved, their human rights suppressed—there's a high likelihood that they would return to Japan if they were able to freely leave North Korea. The Japanese government and *Zainichi* Korean community need to seriously engage with this issue in preparation for the return of returnees to Japan, such as by establishing a system for accepting them.

The "abductions" aren't the only serious issue between North Korea and Japan. There are many other "Japanese" suffering in North Korea. I wanted that fact to be widely known in Japan. Isn't it the responsibility of the government to make the truth of the North Korea Repatriation Movement clear to the public? If they don't, then who will?

With the fact that both the "6,800 Japanese who went to North Korea" and the abductees were in the same wretched circumstances having thus been publicized, the issue of the returnees attracted the public interest in the same way as the abductee issue. Newspapers and television channels followed the *Yomiuri's* lead and widely reported on the North Korean returnee issue, making it widely known. And historical perception of the North Korea Repatriation Movement was utterly changed for not just the *Zainichi* Korean community but all of Japanese society.

In 1959, the North Korea Repatriation Movement was praised as a "great ethnic migration" from a capitalist country to a communist one. But the truth has become clear that it was a "grand abduction" planned by North Korea.

Since that day, I have taken responsibility for my words and worked to return these Japanese women and children to Japan. Ten years later, in January 2012, I established the "Japanese Wives Residency Support Center (*Nihonjinzuma Nado Teijū Shien Sentaa*)" within JIPI to press both the Japanese and North Korean governments on the return of Japanese remaining in North Korea. This effort may have achieved some success.

Under the Stockholm Agreement reached in May 2014, the North Korean government indicated that it would permit the return of Japanese citizens and their spouses to Japan. My persistence since the 1975 "Sakanaka Essay" (and 1977 "Sakanaka Thesis") had finally borne fruit. I await the day when the Japanese trapped in North Korea can set foot back in their homeland.

SEEKING THE IMMEDIATE PERMANENT RETURN OF THE JAPANESE WIVES

In the May 29, 2014, Stockholm Agreement, a path was opened for all Japanese in North Korea—including victims of abduction, Japanese spouses, those who had been left behind after the Second World War, and missing persons—to return to Japan. Six months prior to this, I had sent an appeal to Prime Minister Abe entitled "Seeking the Immediate Permanent Return of the Japanese Wives" on December 14, 2013. It is possible that my letter is in some way connected to this historic agreement.

The following is the appeal in its entirety:

> Prime Minister Abe Shinzō said at the May 20, 2013 meeting of the House of Councillors Audit Committee that "the abduction issue must be resolved through Japanese leadership. Unfortunately, no other country will do it for us." He was correct in his perception. The lives of Japanese must be protected by other Japanese. The Japanese govern-

ment is the only one who can rescue them. I have long held doubts about our basic diplomatic policy towards North Korea of seeking a "comprehensive solution on abductions, nuclear issues, and missiles." While the issues of North Korea's nuclear weapons and missiles are serious ones for Japan, they're also international issues that involve six countries: Japan, North Korea, South Korea, China, America, and Russia. Seeking to comprehensively resolve this international issue—one that is complicated by the interests of the involved countries and the abduction issue between only Japan and North Korea—is a non-starter. Pursuing that course means that the abduction issue will never be resolved. The six-party talks and Japan-North Korea talks should be conducted in parallel. I have argued for years that the abductee issue and that of the Japanese remaining in North Korea need a unified solution. While the course of events which led to these people being in North Korea are all different, they are all still "Japanese" which need the Japanese government to urgently rescue them. I understand that the Japan-North Korean foreign minister talks held in Ulan Bator, Mongolia on November 15-16, 2012 were constructive along those lines. If North Korea truly desires to normalize relations with Japan, it should permit the exit of all Japanese trapped in North Korea as evidence of that. The Japanese government should insist that negotiations on normalizing relations with North Korea will only then begin after that has been done. In the modern world, it is considered a universal right of all people to be able to leave a country, regardless of whether they are a citizen of that country or a foreigner. The Declaration of Human Rights and international human rights agreements also clearly state this. However, North Korea is one of the few countries in the world that does not recognize free exit. In particular, it is likely the only country that prohibits foreigners from leaving the country. If North Korea permits the exit of foreigners in accordance with international law, the Japanese abductee and Japanese wives' issues will be completely resolved. Japanese who wish to leave North Korea will leave and those who wish to stay will stay. The normalization of exit and entry to the country is essential for the normalization of relations. Normalized relations mean that the freedom of Japanese to leave North Korea will be protected. Of course, the right of *Zainichi* Koreans to freely leave Japan will also be protected. The Japanese government should make the unconditional exit of all Japanese (abductees, Japanese wives) from North Korea a precondition for negotiating the normalization of relations with North Korea. It would be unthinkable to normalize relations without guaranteeing the freedom of Japanese to exit the country. Most of the about 1,800 Japanese women who travelled to North Korea with their *Zainichi* Korean husbands did so from 1959 to 1961. These women were in their twenties and thirties at the time and would be in their seventies and eighties now. However, as some have been executed, died due to stress, committed suicide, or starved to death, there are only a few who are still alive. The roughly hundred or so Japanese wives who still live speak have voiced their keenly-felt desires: "I want to die on Japanese soil," and "I want to apologize to my parents at their graves before I die." These Japanese women, whose lives have been filled by the wholehearted desire to return to Japan for more than fifty years, believe intently that the Japanese government will save them. They increasingly die with their hopes unanswered. They have little time left. This is a matter of the protection of Japanese nationals and requires urgency. Recently, the North Korean government has communicated to the Japanese government that it would accept "the return of the Japanese wives." The Japanese should respond appropriately to this consideration on the part of the North Koreans. I believe that if the permanent return of the Japanese wives is realized, the public's view of North Korea will improve and that it will also aid in the rapid resolution of the abduction issue.

THE SAKANAKA THESIS PUT AN END TO THE NORTH KOREA REPATRIATION MOVEMENT

I devoted significant coverage to a possible end to the North Korea Repatriation Movement (*Kitachōsen Kikoku Undō*) in the chapter "The Treatment of the *Zainichi* Koreans" in *On the Future Nature of Immigration Administration* (the so-called "Sakanaka Thesis"):

> In the absence of some other special reason, the likelihood is low that *Zainichi* Koreans will return to a homeland with which they have only weak regional and blood ties and that has different social and economic systems. This point is confirmed by the fact that the number of applicants wishing to return via the so-called 'North Korea Repatriation Movement' has become extremely low recently. While 88,611 *Zainichi* Koreans returned to the Democratic People's Republic of Korea through the North Korean repatriation effort based on the 'Agreement between the Japanese Red Cross Society and the Red Cross Society of the Democratic People's Republic of Korea on the Return of Koreans in Japan' (1959) in the period from 1959 to 1967, looking at the number of returnees since this resumed in 1971, they have declined each year. 237 (including 4 accompanying Japanese) returned in 1971, 1,003 (22) in 1972, 704 (30) in 1973, 479 (11) in 1974, 379 (28) in 1975, and 256 (20) in 1976. The number who has returned in the last two to three years has fallen to be very small. It must demand a fair amount of resolve for the *Zainichi* Koreans—who have struggled over many years to establish lives for themselves in Japanese society and whose ties to their homeland have grown distant—to restart their lives from scratch in Korea. This is surely even truer for the generation who has been born in Japan, don't understand the Korean language, and have been influenced by Japanese culture. It must require serious resolve to return to the Democratic People's Republic of Korea with its socio-economic system different from that of our country. It is not easy for *Zainichi* Koreans accustomed to capitalist Japanese life to grow used to socialist Korea and it's also been reported that young men and women who return have difficulty finding marriage partners.

Since writing the "Sakanaka Essay" in 1975 and subsequent publication in 1977 as the "Sakanaka Thesis," I have not for a moment forgotten the cruel fate that awaited the *Zainichi* Koreans and their Japanese companions who travelled to North Korea as part of the North Korean Repatriation Movement. I always thought about what I could do to save these men and women who had been placed in circumstances in North Korea akin to being "caged birds."

It took a long time, but with the May 2014 Japan-North Korean governmental agreement, a path has been opened for "Japanese wives" — the most pitiful victims of the North Korean Repatriation Movement — to return to their homeland.

SUPPORT FOR THE NORTH KOREAN RETURNEES ORIGINATED WITH THE SAKANAKA ESSAY

The true nature of the North Korean Repatriation Movement is that these *Zainichi* Koreans travelling to North Korea were not "returning home." They were "emigrating." The majority of *Zainichi* Koreans consisted of a first generation from southern Korea and a second generation born in Japan. For them, communist North Korea was — even if geographically part of their homeland and somewhere with a largely common language and culture — in reality an unknown world. They were not "repatriating" in the sense of returning to a country they had formerly been in. They were effectively "emigrating" to a foreign country they knew of only through terribly distorted propaganda.

However, the fact that approximately two hundred people have since returned to Japan shows more than anything else that problems originating from this counterfeit repatriation movement (international population movement) still exist. And because the phenomenon of returnees making a U-turn for Japan continues, the issue of the returnees has developed into an ongoing humanitarian problem between Japan and North Korea. I would like to emphasize the significance of this.

Speaking as someone who has worked to pin down the essential nature of the North Korean returnee issue, I sense indications of a new international population movement in the future. I believe there is a possibility that eventually a hundred thousand or more humanitarian immigrants will return to Japan.

This time it will be a "great ethnic migration" from a dictatorship to a liberal country. As this will be people migrating from a country with wretched living conditions to one with good living conditions, it will be an "international population movement" in the true sense of the term. The time is coming when the North Korean returnee issue will be resolved in the natural form of people — having grown disillusioned with the country they emigrated to—returning to the country they used to live in and feel fondness for.

In 1975, the Ministry of Justice's Immigration Bureau solicited papers from its employees as part of its activities for its twenty-fifth anniversary. I responded, writing an essay entitled "On the Future Nature of Immigration Administration."

I added to this essay this and had it subsequently published. This new manuscript—known as the Sakanaka Thesis—became an indispensable reference when considering the *Zainichi* Korean issue.

The Sakanaka Thesis served as the starting point for my current efforts to aid returnees such as the Japanese wives. In the section entitled "The Treatment of *Zainichi* Koreans," I pointed out that "it must be acknowledged as a natural trend that the number of *Zainichi* Koreans who desire to return to their homeland is declining as time passes" regarding the North Korean returnees. I've continued to be interested in the issue ever since. And I published a timely opinion on it at a critical juncture.

For the following discussion, we need to go back to 1994, when there were discussions within the government on how to handle large-scale refugees from North Korea in the wake of a Korean contingency due to the initial nuclear standoff. I gave an interview that was published in *Shūkan Minsha* (Weekly Democratic Socialist Party), the official magazine of that now-defunct party.[2] I stated that "there is a high probability that approximately 100,000 *Zainichi* Koreans and their spouses (so 300,000 including their families), who are being oppressed in North Korea and forced to live in poverty, will flee to Japan."

On the basis of my comment, the information on the 93,000 North Korean returnees that had been piled up in a Ministry of Justice warehouse was digitized in 1994. Ever since 1996, the North Korean returnee registry that was entered into the computer at that time has been used as the only method for proving the identity of returnees during immigration procedures.

In June 2003, I had an article entitled "A Path for *Zainichi* to Become 'Korean-Japanese'," published in the monthly intellectual journal *Chūō Kōron* (Central Review). In it, I emphasized that the *Zainichi* Koreans needed to break with the Korean Peninsula in order to resolve the North Korean returnee issue, one of the most important longstanding issues between Japan and North Korea:

> The 93,000 returnees—including 6,800 Japanese—have been given the lowest status in North Korean society, subjected to discrimination and surveillance, and had to live lives of hunger. I've also been told that many were sent to concentration camps and died there. Given the actual circumstances of the returnees, with their human rights suppressed and in a state of starvation, it's highly likely that many would return to Japan with their families if they were able to leave North Korea. These returnees have been forced into a desperate state and are waiting for

help that can't come soon enough. If the *Zainichi* Koreans resolved to provide absolutely no funds to support the inhumane North Korean state, we could expect a faster resolution of the returnee issue as it would destroy North Korea's "money collection system" —holding returnees hostage and extorting money from Zainichi Koreans.[3]

Then, with my retirement from the Ministry of Justice Immigration Bureau imminent in March 2005, I released *Immigration Battle Diary*. In it, I touched upon the work that I would do after my life as a public servant came to an end:

> My life as an immigration control official was a rich one in terms of "discovering problems" and "enacting policy." It's fair to say that I was truly blessed as an official. But as I approach retirement, there is just one thing that bothers me: the issue of the "North Korean returnees" that I spoke of in my interview in the *Yomiuri Shimbun* on November 9, 2002. Unfortunately, I can still see no way to resolve this issue. It seems that it will become "homework" for me to take on after leaving my position in the government. During my life as an official I made "carrying through on what I say" my motto; this is the last that I still need to "carry through" on. This is work that I feel a sense of mission for, that I must do even as I retire from the frontline. Working together with *Zainichi* Koreans who feel the same, I am determined to stand up and aid those who have fled North Korea and returned to Japan. And I will devote the rest of my life to resolving the issue of those returnees remaining in North Korea.[4]

THE ZAINICHI KOREANS ARE BEING EXTORTED FOR RANSOM

With the threat of North Korea's nuclear and missile development increasing, I would like to leave the following record of the hidden history of the North Korean Repatriation Movement.

The reason that the North Korean authorities initially took the returnees as "hostages" was to prevent *Zainichi* Koreans from breaking away from the activities of the General Association of Korean Residents in Japan (*Chongryon*). Later, they adopted a hostage policy of using the returnees as a meal ticket through which they could extort money from their Japanese families. It's believed that Kim Il-Sung had realized the effectiveness of hostages by 1971 at the latest, as it was in that year that the leadership of *Chongryon* made children return to North Korea as "sacrifices."

By the late 1970s, the North Korean government had set its sights on valuables sent to returnees from Japan. Until that point, letters from returnees had only requested daily goods such as clothing and food. Now, at the direction of the authorities, Japanese families of returnees began receiving letters asking them to send 500,000 or 1,000,000 yen in cash. Before long, if a bribe of five million yen or so were given to the authorities, permission would be given for their returnee relative to move to Pyongyang.

And, as it became known that the treatment of the returnees depended on the size of the bribes, some families gave government leaders donations in the hundreds of millions. As they say, "money opens all doors." With the monetary amounts escalating so dramatically, the nature of the support provided to returnee relatives changed drastically. Families in Japan began to receive "ransom" demands from the North Korean government.

The more money that Koreans in Japan sent, the more that the North Korean government became fixed to its "hostage policy" of demanding money. Meanwhile, the families in Japan couldn't escape from this ridiculous money collection system. At some point the money that *Zainichi* Koreans had sent with good intentions had become a funding source supporting North Korea's nuclear and missile development. Not only that, but there were also cases where *Zainichi* Koreans—unable to disobey the North Korean government because their relatives had been taken hostage—were forced to cooperate in the abduction of Japanese citizens.

Has any government in the history of the world been more merciless in how it treats its citizenry? And yet—despite being so oppressed by their homeland—the *Zainichi* Koreans endured in silence. It's enough to make one begin to question whether there was a give-and-take relationship between the Koreans sending money and the North Korean government extorting it.

Today, as the international encirclement of North Korea has become stricter due to its nuclear tests and missile development, there are still some wealthy *Zainichi* Koreans who obediently submit to the threats of the North Korean government and send it massive amounts as ransom.

NOT ALLOWING THE ISSUE OF JAPANESE LEFT BEHIND IN NORTH KOREA TO BE BLURRED BY HISTORY

In a meeting of the House of Councillors Budget Committee on March 15, 2010, Minister for the Abduction Issue Nakai Hiroshi touched upon the issue of the return of the Japanese wives saying, "I will give my all at every opportunity to promote global awareness of this issue and get them home as quickly as possible. I have been directed by Prime Minister Hatoyama Yukio to rescue all surviving Japanese in North Korea." This was groundbreaking Diet testimony that declared that the Japanese wives would be saved.

The "surviving Japanese in North Korea" mentioned in this Diet testimony of course includes those who were abducted in addition to the Japanese women married to *Zainichi* Koreans who accompanied them to

North Korea. Furthermore, while they've been completely forgotten in Japan, those Japanese who were left behind (*zanryū hojin*) in North Korea following the Second World War (including their children, or *zanryū koji*) were also included.

The history of the North Korean returnee issue begins with a telegram on January 6, 1954, six months after the end of hostilities on the Korean peninsula, from the Japanese Red Cross Society to the Red Cross Society of the Democratic People's Republic of Korea. In it, the Japanese Red Cross informed its counterparts of the Japanese government's intentions: "If the evacuation of the Japanese still remaining in North Korea after the war is permitted, we would like to use that evacuation ship to aid the return of those Koreans in Japan who would like to do so." The Japanese government's primary interest was thus the evacuation of Japanese citizens.

But while the return of *Zainichi* Koreans to North Korea was realized via the North Korean repatriation efforts that began on December 14, 1959, only thirty-six Japanese returned from North Korea in 1956.

Afterward, the Japanese government made no efforts to rescue the Japanese remaining in North Korea, leaving many behind there. This is not the fault of North Korea. The Japanese government bears heavy responsibility for neglecting the protection of Japanese nationals. It remains unclear why no finger was lifted to help the Japanese there. Most left behind ended up dying. This is one of the greatest sins of the Japanese government in the postwar era.

Several Japanese who escaped from North Korea and made it back to Japan have said that they met and spoke to Japanese who had been left behind after the war. One Japanese wife described meeting an elderly woman who—with a look of nostalgia and a lonely voice—told her "You're Japanese, aren't you? We're never going back to Japan, are we?"

Generalizing from the accounts of escapees, many of these Japanese are grouped together deep in the mountains, where they survive primarily on potatoes.

Even without any prodding from North Korea, it would only be natural for the Japanese government to seek to allow relatives to visit their graves and have the remains of Japanese returned from a purely humanitarian standpoint. But what the government should prioritize is rescuing those Japanese who are still alive in North Korea. Abandoned by their homeland and deserted, these Japanese are forced to live lives so severe as to beggar description and dream of the day when they can return to Japan.

We can't allow the issue of the Japanese left behind in North Korea—one of the great regretful matters of postwar history—to fall into the darkness of history. Even if it is long overdue, we Japanese must save those still struggling to live in that cruel country.

In January 2012, I established the "Japanese Wives Residency Support Center" within JIPI to push the Japanese and North Korean governments to allow those Japanese in North Korea to return home at an early date. Of course, the "Japanese left behind in North Korea" (including orphans) are included in this effort.

I have a request for all conscientious Japanese. I want you to warmly welcome all "Japanese" who return from North Korea. To fulfill my responsibility for raising the issue, I will lead the way in rousing public support for welcoming the return home of Japanese from North Korea.

A WAY HOME HAS BEEN OPENED FOR THE JAPANESE REMAINING IN NORTH KOREA

Following the agreement reached between the Japanese and North Korean governments in Sweden on May 29, 2014, I was interviewed by a reporter from *Kyōdō News* regarding the issue of the return home of Japanese and their spouses in North Korea. The following are the questions and answers from that interview:

Q: The North Korean government announced on May 29, 2014 that it would undertake a "comprehensive, full-scale investigation into all issues involving Japanese, including the remains and graves of Japanese, Japanese remaining in North Korea, the spouses of Japanese, victims of abduction, and any missing persons." This Japan-North Korea agreement has expanded the scope of the investigation. What do you think of this move by North Korea?

A: The scope has been significantly expanded beyond the agreement reached in Ulan Bator, Mongolia in November 2012 by adding "missing persons," for example. It is particularly significant that the agreement explicitly states that if someone is determined to be Japanese, they will "return to Japan."

Q: What problems have there been in the Japanese government's response to the issue of Japanese remaining in North Korea?

A: The Japanese government bears a grave responsibility for abandoning the Japanese in North Korea to their fates even as they eagerly anticipate returning home. They must at least rescue all Japanese still alive in North Korea as a penance.

Q: Why haven't any Japanese in North Korea been able to return since the thirty-six in 1956?

A: Because the Japanese government forgot the nation's primary mission of protecting the lives of Japanese citizens. I am angered by the heartless apathy of the Japanese people towards saving the Japanese who weren't able to be evacuated from North Korea. Had a series of prime ministers tenaciously demanded that North Korea return these Japanese, many of them wouldn't have been driven to regrettable deaths. Many Japanese could have stepped foot on Japanese soil alive. I have to say, this was one of Japan's greatest mistakes of the postwar period.

Q: Why is it that this time the North Korean government went along with what you've been calling for?

A: I don't know the exact reason. Perhaps the North Korean government is recognizing that I've been the only expert grappling with the issues of the return of Japanese wives who went to North Korea and the legal status of *Zainichi* Koreans ever since I published my essay in 1975? I've been seeking for North Korea to return the Japanese remaining in North Korea since 2009 and immediately received a positive reaction from the North Korean government. Especially in recent years, I've been calling for a unified solution to the issues of Japanese left behind in North Korea, the Japanese wives, and the abduction victims. The North Korean government has adopted my idea and the Japanese government has finally responded.

Q: You been working on your own in support of the return of Japanese from North Korea, but what specifically have you been doing?

A: Feeling that the return of Japanese from North Korea was near, I established the "Japanese Wives Residency Support Center" within the Japan Immigration Policy Institute in January 2012. That's one example. The center supports "Japanese Wives" and "Japanese left behind in North Korea." When they manage to return to Japan, the center provides support for things like life counseling, Japanese language education, and reuniting them with their families so that they can spend their remaining years in their homeland.

Q: At present, about how many Japanese have returned from North Korea and about how many are still there?

A: Six of the Japanese wives and dozens of other Japanese (largely the children of these women) have made it back to Japan. The number of Japanese living in North Korea is unknown. Most of the surviving Japanese are estimated to be seventy or older. Limiting things to Japanese citizens, there were about 1,800 Japanese women and 5,000 children who crossed to North Korea with their *Zainichi* Korean husbands/father as part of the North Korean repatriation efforts that ran from 1959 to 1984. Other than that, there are also believed to have been a fair number of ethnic Japanese who renounced their Japanese citizenship when they left for North Korea. We must save these people as well.

Q: What should be done now? What do you want from the public?

A: Since we can expect at least several thousand Japanese to return, it's the country's responsibility to make sure that comprehensive preparations are made for accepting them. But as to how we meet our comrades returning from North Korea, that's an issue depending on the Japanese character. The people of the world will be watching. I want us to greet them with warm hearts.

WHY DID THE NORTH KOREAN GOVERNMENT HEED MY WORDS?

Amidst the very tense North Korean situation over nuclear and missile development, the North Korean government made clear in April 2017 that an organization had been formed for Japanese wives remaining in North Korea and unveiled five surviving Japanese wives to the world media. One of these, an eighty-four-year-old Japanese woman from Kumamoto Prefecture, said "I want to return to Japan." I interpreted this as a gesture making clear that the North Korean government was prepared to permit the return home of the Japanese wives and desired a dialogue with the Japanese government.

I request that the Japanese government sincerely respond to this. I want it to skillfully address the "repatriation of Japanese remaining in North Korea" issue, the tether that even now binds our two countries together. I believe that a clue for finding a resolution of the abduction issue can be found here.

With the exception of a few vocal groups, the Japanese public hasn't really been demanding the return of either the Japanese left behind in North Korea or the Japanese spouses. Nor has the government proactively worked to protect these Japanese nationals. Despite these facts, a path forward suddenly appeared with the Japan–North Korea agreement reached in May 2014.

Ever since the fall of 2009, when a change in administrations in Japan led the government to establish a new headquarters to deal with the abduction issue, I have been telling the government that it had to rescue every last Japanese left behind in North Korea after the war, every Japanese wife, and every abduction victim. I am an incendiary man who speaks the truth, but for some reason the North Korean government went along with my words and the two governments reached an unprecedented historic agreement mentioned previously.

Several years earlier, I was asked by someone influential in political circles, someone knowledgeable about the abduction issue, "why does the North Korean government listen to what you say?" I answered that "I don't know the North Korean government's intentions. This is just a guess, but perhaps they recognize my many years of accomplishments such as striving to stabilize the legal status of the *Zainichi* Koreans?"

I have reason to believe this. As we approached the fiftieth anniversary of the beginning of the North Korean repatriation effort, I participated in a Buddhist service in Niigata harbor on December 14, 2009, in which I prayed for the peace of the spirits of the victims of the repatriation movement and swore to seek the release and return of all those still confined in North Korea (The name of this ceremony was "The Day I Can't Forget: Niigata Harbor Memorial Service," sponsored by JIPI.). This event received not a word of criticism from the North Korean government. Perhaps my accomplishments in resolving the *Zainichi* Korean issues were related to this.

NOTES

1. See *Yomiuri Shimbun*, November 9, 2002.
2. "What Scale of Refugees Can We Expect if They Come?" *Shūkan Minsha*, No. 1691 (September 30, 1994), p. 162.
3. Sakanaka Hidenori, "Zainichi wa 'Chōsenkei Nihon Kokumin' e no Michi o (A Path for *Zainichi* to Become 'Korean-Japanese')," *Chūō Kōron*, Vol. 118, No. 7 (July 2003), pp. 209-210.
4. Sakanaka, *Nyūkan Senki*, p. 204.

ELEVEN

The Path Travelled by the Director of the Japan Immigration Policy Institute

"ON THE FUTURE NATURE OF IMMIGRATION ADMINISTRATION"

I have made the formulation of immigration policy my life's work ever since I proposed basic policies on immigration such as on the treatment of the *Zainichi* Koreans in my first essay, "On the Future Nature of Immigration Administration" (written in 1975, revised edition published in 1977, hereafter referred to as the "Sakanaka Thesis"). I decided to do this on the basis of intuition, without any wavering. Since then I have carried out that intention, producing a large number of writings intended to pull Japan's immigration policy forward.

After persevering alone through countless trials ever since the original Sakanaka Essay, I have been acknowledged as the leading Japanese figure in the field of immigration policy research. At some point I came to bear the heavy responsibility of trying to save Japan from demographic collapse through a revolutionary immigration policy. In recent years, I have been called "an expert on immigration policy" and "Mr. Immigration" by the global media. If my life were to be compared to a baseball career, it could be said that when it came to creating an immigration nation, I've appeared in every game and thrown all my pitches with all my might.

Let's return to 1975. The Ministry of Justice's Immigration Bureau solicited papers from its employees on the theme, "On the Future Nature of Immigration Administration." The paper I wrote in response was chosen as the best entry. I have the selection and critique of my entry by Takemura Teruo (then deputy director of the Immigration Bureau and chief judge of the entries):

Sakanaka's essay, the best of Category I, is truly wonderful in its view-points, its structure, and its use of evidence. Its contents are absolutely suitable for marking our "twenty-fifth anniversary." It has been recommended unanimously by the jury as the best entry. Placing immigration administration within the context of global historical changes, it provides an outlook of the future that aims to reconcile national interests with a clear awareness of protecting the rights of foreigners, conforms to realistic issues, and never engages in vain idealism. Its approach of advancing its arguments while returning to these points and the depth of material that provide the basis for its examination makes it forceful in its impact.

The Sakanaka Essay was born after being discovered by discerning immigration officials. However, the future that awaited it was one of being tossed about by the world's fierce waves.

While it has been regarded as a classic reference when considering the *Zainichi* Korean issue ever since it was published in 1977 at the recommendation of Takemura, a fierce argument has raged between researchers and activists for close to twenty years over how to assess it.

The thoughts that I laid out in that essay remain basically unchanged some forty years later. When I started to write it, I had no ambition to create an immigration nation. But, in the end, it became a grand work of immigration policy that foresaw what the nature of Japan and the world would be a century from now. And most of its policy proposals—such as stabilizing the legal status of *Zainichi* Koreans and joining the treaty on refugee status—were realized in the early 1980s. Now even the *Zainichi* Korean community recognizes the Sakanaka Thesis's prescience.

The task remaining to me is the construction of the world's foremost immigration nation. Considering the recent rapid increase in support for accepting immigrants among young people and the intensifying debate over immigration policy in the Diet, the possibility has arisen that this great aspiration, too, will be met.

As I enter the twilight of my life, I receive news that hints—like a dream—that all of the Sakanaka Thesis's policy proposals might be achieved. If my life of writing that began with that essay were to be summed up in one phrase, it would be that it was dedicated to "adding the finishing touches."

As I reach the conclusion of my life's work of creating an immigration nation, I frequently recall the course followed by the Sakanaka Thesis. I am satisfied with my life, one that was dedicated to immigration policy and in which—accompanied by the Sakanaka Thesis—I cleared the difficult path to an immigration nation. Now, the Sakanaka Thesis is coming to the end of its turbulent life. Or perhaps, after the death of its author, it will watch over the growth of our immigration society with an affectionate eye as a trailblazing work that led Japan to becoming an ideal immigration nation.

THE SAKANAKA ESSAY LED TO THE RESOLUTION OF THE ZAINICHI KOREAN ISSUE

The Sakanaka Essay led to the resolution of the *Zainichi* Korean issue, the greatest minority issue for Japan in the 1970s. As its author, I could possibly lead the way toward the resolution of the population issue that confronts Japan today as well. Be that as it may, I'm convinced that if the public learns from the history of the *Zainichi* Korean issue and earnestly faces the population crisis, they'll be able to create an ideal immigration nation.

Today, *Zainichi* Koreans are noticeably active in every field, including business, sports, and entertainment. Many are engaged in specialized professions like doctors, lawyers, and accountants.

It's impossible to discuss the music industry without mentioning the *Zainichi* Koreans. And *Zainichi* entrepreneurs have appeared one after another—most notably Son Masayoshi, the founder of Softbank. And it is because of those who came from the Korean Peninsula that Korean barbecue and kimchi have become favorite foods of the Japanese.

We Japanese cannot forget that the Koreans who remained in Japan following the war and their descendents have contributed to the development of Japanese society, culture, and the economy. The *Zainichi* Koreans have added color to our highly monochromatic society and brought diversity to our culture. If not for them, Japanese society would be almost entirely dominated by those with Japanese ancestry. We would be utterly uniform.

There's something else that I should add. I believe that our experience resolving this difficult minority issue—one that involved the ethnic identity of the *Zainichi* Koreans and challenged the historical perception of the Japanese public—should give the Japanese confidence that they can welcome immigrants on a large scale.

I am confident that if the ninety million Japanese make good use of their experience sincerely improving relations with the *Zainichi* Koreans and greet the ten million immigrants in sincerity, they will be able to construct friendly human relations with them.

Eight years ago, I realized that a long-desired wish of mine had been granted. Of the businessmen who donated great sums for the victims of the March 11, 2011, Great East Japan Earthquake, Japanese originating from the Korean Peninsula—most notably Son Masayoshi, the CEO of SoftBank, who contributed ten billion yen for relief funds—are an overwhelming presence. The "Korean-Japanese" people who I had once only fantasized about have swept into the forefront of Japanese society. It was a wonderful sight. I have no doubt that their noble spirits and patriotism are engraved into the hearts of the public.

I feel proud that the stabilization of their legal status and abolishment of workplace discrimination that I proposed in the Sakanaka Thesis were later enacted into law, opening the path to the resolution of the *Zainichi* Korean issue.

Thinking about the fact that 650,000 immigrants originated from the Korean Peninsula and their descendants have achieved such great work, I am filled with great expectations imagining the kind of masterpieces and great works that will result from welcoming ten million immigrants from across the world.

THE RESULTS OF MY THEORY OF *ZAINICHI* KOREAN POLICY

At the time I first wrote the Sakanaka Essay in 1975, Korean ethnic organizations in Japan like *Chongryon* and *Mindan* and many individual *Zainichi* Koreans said that they had no intention of remaining in Japan and being discriminated against forever. They would return to their homeland after the Korean Peninsula had been reunited.

By the mid-1970s, the second and third generations—who had been born in Japan, had strong ties to Japanese society, and had built lives for themselves here—had become a majority of the *Zainichi* Korean community. It was presumed that their actual intentions were to settle in Japan permanently.

Ill feeling over the historical circumstances that caused them to be in Japan remained in the *Zainichi* Korean community, however, and it was taboo to speak of permanently living in Japan. The *Zainichi* Korean issue was not discussed in a way that focused on making their residency permanent.

In "The Treatment of the *Zainichi* Koreans" that was released in 1977 in the form of the Sakanaka Thesis, I said that the *Zainichi* Koreans had settled and become deeply rooted in Japanese society and that their only way forward was to live as Koreans within Japanese society. I also summarized the current situation of the *Zainichi* Koreans and their future trends in the following way:

> While the *Zainichi* Koreans are currently "foreigners" under the law, in actual practice they are becoming something that could be termed "semi-Japanese." It seems likely that their Japanization will continue and they will become "Korean-Japanese" (citizens). The term "Korean-Japanese" here is modeled off of terms like "Japanese-American" and "Japanese-Brazilian" and means someone who—while having a Korean cultural background—lives permanently in Japan and is able to take Japanese citizenship.[1]

The reason that I emphasized that the *Zainichi* Koreans were people who "live permanently in Japan and are able to take Japanese citizenship" is because it is essential that we recognize their permanent residency if we are to improve the status of Koreans in Japanese society. This is because if there is no common understanding that the *Zainichi* Koreans are going to continue living in Japan, the *Zainichi* Korean issue will not take even a single step toward resolution.

Why does the Japanese government have to guarantee a stable residential status to foreigners who say that while they may be in Japan at present, they will return to their homeland someday? And similarly, the *Zainichi* Koreans can't step forward and demand stable legal status and improved treatment from the Japanese government while holding to the position that they were only in Japan for the time being, can they?

The mood at the time the essay was written is best symbolized by the fact that a fair number of *Zainichi* Koreans resided in Japan on the basis of the temporary legal status of "people eligible under Law 126-2-6" ("individuals who may continue to reside in Japan without a residency status until their residency status and term are determined as set out elsewhere in law").

While my argument for permanent residency for the *Zainichi* Koreans was criticized by some, by the late 1970s, the livelihood and treatment of the *Zainichi* Koreans came to be seriously discussed among researchers and activist groups (particularly ethnic organizations) in a way that presumed their permanent residency in Japan.

Taking this "Korean-Japanese" argument as my starting point, I proposed a practical policy for the treatment of the *Zainichi* Koreans that conformed to reality.

In the 1977 thesis, I wrote that "leaving 640,000 Koreans as foreigners of uncertain legal status also causes problems for the Japanese state, such as the possibility of ethnic disputes with the Japanese public or that they will become the cause of a conflict with a neighboring country." Because of these possible dangers, I argued for a *Zainichi* Korean policy that can be broadly summarized as consisting of three points: stabilizing their legal status as foreigners, encouraging naturalization, and encouraging repatriation.

My basic thinking was that "when considering the distinctive nature of the *Zainichi* Koreans' residency in Japan, we must take a multi-faceted and comprehensive view. Rather than just considering the stability of their legal status as foreigners, their residency must be examined in conjunction with other issues such as their integration into Japanese society and issue of social welfare, education, and discrimination."

The actual course followed by this policy proposal can be summarized as follows. The biggest issue when "stabilizing their legal status as foreigners" was fundamentally correcting the abnormal situation where—due to the circumstances of the Cold War—the legal status of the *Zainichi* Koreans who supported the DPRK (North Korea) had become significantly less stable than that of those who supported the ROK (South Korea). Given that the historical circumstances that had caused them to live in Japan as foreigners were identical, by all rights they should be granted the same stable legal status.

The legal mechanism used to stabilize their legal status was the partial revision of the Immigration Control Law (1981 Law No. 85) that came into force on January 1, 1982. Under this revision, all those of North Korean origin and their descendants who had the temporary legal status of "people eligible under Law 126-2-6" would be granted permanent residency, the most stable residency status, if they applied for it.

And my policy goals were completely realized with the passage of the "Special Law related to Immigration Control for those who Lost Japanese Citizenship due to Peace Treaties with Japan" (1991 Law No. 71) in 1991. All those who had lost Japanese citizenship through a peace treaty (and their descendents) were granted the legal status of "special permanent resident"—the most stable legal status for a foreigner—without regard for which Korean government they supported. Koreans with special permanent residency were granted exceptions for immigration control. They can only be deported in extremely limited circumstances and are allowed to leave Japan for up to five years of a time via a re-entry permit.

Despite this, there has been no change in my argument that "no matter how stable the legal status of the *Zainichi* Koreans has become, as long as they have the status of foreigners, their status is still fundamentally different from that of Japanese nationals" and that "fundamental doubts will continue to remain about how appropriate it really is for the *Zainichi* Koreans to live in Japanese society as foreigners and for the Japanese government to treat them as foreigners."

On the second policy point, "encouraging naturalization," I wrote that "if Japanese society guarantees equal opportunities in education and employment to *Zainichi* Koreans and provides an environment of free competition, the *Zainichi* Koreans will become hopeful towards living in Japanese society. Some of them will make progress and become highly regarded in society for their 'abilities' and 'occupations.' When that happens, the view the Japanese have towards the *Zainichi* Koreans will naturally change. A consensus will form within the *Zainichi* Korean community that actively approves of naturalization."

Looking at the progress made by the *Zainichi* Koreans over the past forty-four years, they have largely proceeded in the direction that I described in my essay. It can be said that the *Zainichi* Koreans have found it to be worth living in Japanese society where their educational and vocational choices are guaranteed and that—by making full use of their abilities—they have contributed to the development of the Japanese culture and economy.

The progress made by the *Zainichi* Koreans who have achieved great economic, cultural, and social accomplishments while an ethnic minority in Japanese society is worthy of special mention in the history of the world's minorities. Looking at marriage trends for the *Zainichi* Koreans, more are marrying Japanese every year. The rate has surpassed ninety percent in recent years.

At the same time, the Japanese view of the *Zainichi* Koreans has greatly changed from being exclusionary and somewhat negative to being tolerant and favorable. This reflects the many contributions to Japanese society that the *Zainichi* Koreans have made and the fact that they have economically prospered. As Japan thus changes to become a country where *Zainichi* Koreans can live freely, facing little discrimination, there is an increasing trend of *Zainichi* Koreans taking Japanese citizenship. Judging from this rapid increase, we can see that "a consensus has formed within the *Zainichi* Korean community that actively approves of naturalization."

On the third policy point, "encouraging repatriation," I pointed out that all *Zainichi* Koreans are freely permitted to leave Japan and return to Korea but that "in the absence of some other special reason, the likelihood is low that *Zainichi* Koreans will return to a homeland with which they have only weak regional and blood ties and that has different social and economic systems."

The number of *Zainichi* Koreans who have returned to Korea over the past forty-three years is very small. It seems unlikely that the *Zainichi* Koreans of the twenty-first century will return to the Korean Peninsula, where they have little in the way of personal or economic interests.

Still, about 93,000 *Zainichi* Koreans did return to the "earthly paradise" of North Korea from 1959 to 1984 through the North Korean repatriation movement. Naturally, they believed that they would be warmly received by the people of their homeland. The reality that awaited the returnees in North Korea greatly differed from what they had expected, however. It seems highly likely that judging from their situation—severe oppression and pitiful economic circumstances—if they were allowed to leave North Korea, many would return to Japan with their families.

THE SAME POLICY ARGUMENTS APPLY TO BOTH IMMIGRATION AND THE *ZAINICHI* KOREANS

I provided a vision of the future of the *Zainichi* Koreans in "The Treatment of the *Zainichi* Koreans," a section of *On the Future Nature of Immigration Administration*: "While the *Zainichi* Koreans are currently 'foreigners' under the law, in actual practice they are becoming something that could be termed 'semi-Japanese.' It seems likely that their Japanization will continue and they will become 'Korean-Japanese' (citizens)."[2]

I then further developed my argument for a *Zainichi* Korean policy based on the concept of "Korean-Japanese":

> Inherently, nothing can be done on the issue of naturalization if the *Zainichi* Koreans themselves don't have the desire to become Japanese citizens. It's not something for the state to force upon them. What the Japanese government can do, however, is to work to create a social

environment in which *Zainichi* Koreans naturally come to want to take Japanese citizenship. This should be done with the basic understanding that the *Zainichi* Koreans becoming Japanese citizens is in conformance with their status and future trends. In that sense what is needed more than anything else is for the *Zainichi* Koreans to be widely permitted educational opportunities and freedom of vocational choice. The government should take the lead in the creation of this "open Japanese society" by opening up employment as public servants and in public corporations to the *Zainichi* Koreans, arousing public opinion, and seeking the understanding and cooperation of private businesses. If Japanese society guarantees equal opportunities in education and employment to *Zainichi* Koreans and provides an environment of free competition, the *Zainichi* Koreans will become hopeful towards living in Japanese society. Some of them will make progress and become highly regarded in society for their "abilities" and "occupations." When that happens, the view the Japanese have towards the *Zainichi* Koreans will naturally change. A consensus will form within the *Zainichi* Korean community that actively approves of naturalization.[3]

Criticism of the Sakanaka Thesis was focused on the sections that I have quoted. They were savaged by ethnic organizations, activists, intellectuals, and the *Zainichi* Korean community. "It's a further progression of the policy of assimilation" and "it closes people off from being able to return to the Democratic People's Republic of Korea" were frequent criticisms.

Recently, I made a discovery as I reread these passages. I feel that if the word "immigrants" is substituted for "*Zainichi* Koreans" in the quoted text, it creates a theory of immigration policy that is quite applicable for the coming immigration era. The Sakanaka Thesis may have been subjected to almost twenty years of fierce criticism and ridicule, but it hasn't faded at all. It has splendidly developed into a sound argument. I guess it's only natural that the basic ideas behind the theories for immigration policy and *Zainichi* Korean policy are the same given that they were ideas born from the same mind.

Incidentally, in September 2017, I gave a lecture at the central headquarters for *Mindan*, the Korean Residents Union in Japan, where I spoke about my overall vision for the Japanese-style immigration nation concept. When I did, the Union's leadership praised it: "Your theory of immigration policy is entirely consistent with the Sakanaka Thesis. It's perfect. In particular, the human community concept is a wonderful idea that could have occurred to no one in the world other than you." Thinking back on the time when the Sakanaka Thesis was met with a great chorus of criticism and jeers, it feels like it was eons ago.

RETURNING TO THE ORIGINAL INTENTIONS BEHIND THE
SAKANAKA ESSAY

In 1975, the year that the Sakanaka Essay was written, my most important work, Saigon fell. The Vietnam War ended on April 30.

The outrageous "Mun Se-gwang incident" had occurred on the Korean Peninsula a year earlier. A twenty-two-year-old second generation *Zainichi* Korean attempted to assassinate South Korean President Park Chung-hee; while this was unsuccessful, he did kill two others, including Park's wife, Yuk Young-soo.

"The Korean Peninsula should be unified by North Korea, led by Chairman Kim Il-Sung, who will defeat Park's military regime, nothing but a puppet of America"—while the 1970 renewal of the U.S.-Japan Security Treaty was over, some remnants of the mass protests on university campuses still remained and I believe there were many commentators who held this view.

No doubt there were scholars and activists considered better suited than I to discuss the "*Zainichi* Korean issue," a social problem of which there were fierce ideological clashes between the left and right.

At the time, anti-immigration activists converged on the Ministry of Justice Immigration Bureau every day. And it was truly not easy to prepare myself to take that kind of energy head on and speak on the *Zainichi* Korean issue, especially for someone like me, a greenhorn who was in his fifth year at the ministry and just taking his first steps in the immigration control administration.

I took on the "treatment of the *Zainichi* Korean" controversy head on without the slightest idea that it would cause such an uproar.

However, couldn't it perhaps be said that I was fortunate in that I was able to see into this issue from a conceptual framework completely free of those kinds of impurities—the ideological conflict between left and right, the various political and social movements related to the *Zainichi* Koreans, the exclusionary atmosphere of the *Zainichi* Korean community where criticism of them by Japanese was not permitted, and the climate where speaking what one truly thought was considered taboo?

I've heard that various *Zainichi* Korean groups held many study sessions which made use of the Sakanaka Thesis. There seems to have been intense debates over how to regard it.

In the "*Zainichi*" world—one which had become unable to face reality and in which historical circumstances meant that statements were a thorough mix of both real beliefs and *pro forma* ones—there were lively debates but not one effective concrete policy proposal was produced. Then the Sakanaka Thesis suddenly appeared before them.

No particular ideology is needed to come to the conclusion that a system should be established in which the *Zainichi* Koreans could live happily. Leaving the legal status of the second and third generation of

Zainichi Koreans—who were born and raised in Japan—in an unstable state was clearly not the right thing to do. It was just common sense that led me to the belief that it needed to be corrected.

Reflecting back on my thoughts and actions at the time, I just spoke about what I saw, and I wrote about what I felt. I think that I just wrote down an idea that was born out of the human compassion of a "normal person." It wasn't done from the position of an administrator.

Setting aside the activists who faced administrators on the front lines and viewed them with hostility, I have no doubt that the average *Zainichi* Korean who was just living their normal life within Japanese society wanted someone, somehow, to do something to alleviate the obstacles of daily, various inconveniences and thoughtless discrimination that they faced.

While immigration administration is a job that deals with "foreigners," I believe that the good and bad of it ultimately comes down to one's view of humanity—that is, "do you view foreigners as individual human beings?" And I believe that the superiors who held my essay in high regard and I had a common understanding on how to view them. My "thoughts for the *Zainichi* Korean community" might have ended as nothing but a passing fancy if they had not been blessed by the time and people involved. Instead, I was able to rush straight ahead with them, putting them first into a proposal and then later into actual policy.

The Sakanaka Thesis—born from my youthful recklessness and blessed by too many coincidences and good fortune—could perhaps be said to have been in the right place at the right time.

So, what kind of lasting influence did the Sakanaka Thesis have on the Immigration Bureau as an administrative organization?

Naturally, I was aware that the Immigration Bureau of the time was not fertile ground for proactively accepting the Sakanaka Thesis and its revolutionary policy arguments. It was a place where there was a generally dominant attitude that we should "maintain a respectful distance" from the *Zainichi* Korean community. But at the same time, it was not an organization so passionately opposed to those arguments that its officials would rise up in fierce opposition, either.

This environment fostered an unusual situation: so long as there were no active voices of opposition, even policies not particularly welcomed by the organization as a whole could gain momentum and ultimately become government policy.

In other words, even though the policy changes advocated for in the Sakanaka Thesis were clearly considered within the Immigration Bureau to be my own personal opinions, because I had spoken up and put forward an actual policy proposal, the organization passively accepted it.

The day came unexpectedly quickly. It was the spring of 1980, five years after the Sakanaka Essay had originally been written. I received a special assignment from the Ministry of Justice leadership to "turn the policies proposed in the Sakanaka Thesis into legislation." For me this was like a dream, an unparalleled opportunity to realize a national policy of my own making. I carried out my duty, burning with a sense of purpose and thinking there could be no higher honor. Not to delve too deeply into the technical detail of revising laws, but I was able to experience the daring feat of using two laws to revise one law. I also changed the name of the "Immigration Control Order."

And many of the policies proposed in the Sakanaka Thesis came into being in the "Law Partially Amending the Immigration Control Order" (Law No. 85) and the "Law Adjusting the Immigration Control Order and other Related Legislation for Joining the Convention on the Status of Refugees" (Law No. 86) that were unanimously passed in the 94th regular session of the Diet in 1981. A notable accomplishment of these laws was the establishment of the "special permanent residency system" which guaranteed *Zainichi* Koreans a stable legal status. These two laws went into force a year later in 1982. I remember that university professors knowledgeable about the *Zainichi* Korean issue named this new immigration system the "1982 System."

The above was a review of the time when I guided the difficult *Zainichi* Korean issue to a solution through the Sakanaka Thesis. The policies proposed in that essay were enacted as law with an unbelievable rapidity. It could be called "Sakanaka magic."

***

But let's move from the *Shōwa* era, the heyday of the Sakanaka Thesis, to the new imperial era, *Reiwa*, when immigration policy has suddenly emerged as a political issue. The question is—what kind of approach should I take to realize the "immigration nation concept" which has reached a crucial stage? I believe that the Sakanaka Thesis's method used for resolving a difficult problem—raising ambitious but reality-based ideals and then waiting for the time to be ripe—has many points that can be referenced when creating an immigration nation.

There's something I want to emphasize here. It is the view of the author of the Sakanaka Thesis—the document that played a primary role in the resolution of the *Zainichi* Korean issue—that if we use the history of the smooth resolution to the *Zainichi* Korean issue—which involved the historical circumstances which led these Koreans to be present in Japan (Japan's colonial control of the Korean Peninsula) and complicated ethnic sentiment—as a guide, the creation of the world's foremost immigration nation by we Japanese is not a dream.

The following is my ideal scenario for applying the method used to resolve the *Zainichi* Korean issue as an analogy for the construction of an immigration nation:

> Voices of support for immigration suddenly rise from among the public—from young people, in particular—and the immigration nation

concept that politicians had not been particularly interested in gains momentum as a way to save Japan from its the deepening population crisis and return it to life. It ultimately becomes government policy. The immigration nation vision was initially nothing more than the personal view of Sakanaka Hidenori. But because it sets out an effective plan for rebuilding Japan that anticipates the next hundred years, it comes to be considered the most powerful countermeasure to the population crisis within the government. It is perceived as a new national vision in which to entrust Japan's future. The Immigration Law and other related legislation passes with bipartisan support from Diet members. An immigration nation is born that is a model for the world.

THE SAKANAKA ESSAY DETERMINED MY ENTIRE LIFE

In 1971, the world was still locked in a time of fierce ideological conflict. I first became involved in immigration administration a year after I entered the Ministry of Justice. That April, I began hands-on training at what was then the Ministry of Justice Ōsaka Immigration Control Office at the age of twenty-five.

At the time, nearly all "immigration control administration" performed by the Immigration Bureau was focused on the *Zainichi* Koreans. My time as an inspector in Ōsaka led me to draw one conclusion regarding the essential nature of the *Zainichi* Korean issue.

It was a question of how to resolve the contradiction of the *Zainichi* Koreans, a group that had the legal status of living in Japan as foreigners even though they were—in actual substance—extremely close to being Japanese. And I came to deeply want to bring about the day when the *Zainichi* Koreans' "legal status" matched their "substance" (i.e., they were made Japanese citizens and were no longer subject to Japanese immigration control) as soon as possible.

But at that time, the *Zainichi* Koreans who were subjected to discrimination, their ethnic organizations, and the immigration administration did not merely turn a deaf ear to that idea, but also they viewed it as dangerous and severely criticized it. And yet, as if by a trick of fate, I would get the opportunity a few years later to realize my desire. That was in 1975.

A paper that I wrote in response to a call by the Ministry of Justice Immigration Bureau was chosen as the best entry. And at that moment, the path I would walk for the rest of my life was decided. As was perhaps apt, it was the Sakanaka Thesis that decided the course of my life.

The first paper, "On the Future Nature of Immigration Administration," I ever wrote at the Ministry of Justice was chosen as the best policy paper would become a tremendous opportunity for me. I would go on to write numerous policy papers on minority issues, most notably on the *Zainichi* Korean issue. And even after retiring as a public servant, I continued to think about the state of the country and to earnestly write papers related to a national commitment to immigration, though I now did so from the position of director of the JIPI. As a result of being captivated by immigration policy and continuing along that path, I became a dangerous thinker called an "immigration revolutionary" by foreign journalists.

The works in which I describe my entire vision for an immigration nation and my plan for a new state in detail are immortal. However, the limitations of the era cannot be escaped. In the near future, heroes with the mindsets of global citizens will build off of my concepts and produce masterpieces of immigration nation theory that are more feasible.

THE ESSAY THAT PREDICTED THE INEVITABILITY OF IMMIGRATION POLICY

Where did the idea come from that the era of population decline could be dealt with by transforming Japan into an immigration nation? The answer goes all the way back to the Sakanaka Thesis. That paper serves as the starting point for my immigration nation concept.

When I wrote it in 1975, I thought—based on factors like Japan's population trends—that the country's basic immigration control policy of not permitting "immigration" should, in general, be continued into the foreseeable future. This is why: "Given that our country is already extremely densely populated and that our population will continue to grow naturally into the near future due to a clear trend of births outpacing deaths, Japan's immigration control policies must continue to follow the basic policy of not worsening a population problem that will become increasingly serious."

Let's move to 2005, thirty years after the original essay was written. As a result of that year's national census, it became clear that Japan had reached a historic turning point. The population—which had supported the Japanese economy and society for the roughly hundred and fifty years since the beginning of the Meiji period—had entered a period of decline. The government's future population statistics show that the population will have fallen to two-thirds of its current size fifty years from now and that it will have declined to under fifty million a hundred years from now.

When Japan reached its historic turning point and went from population growth to decline in 2005, I changed my thinking and began supporting opening Japan to immigration. The great premise underlying the policy of not permitting immigration has come undone. Because I've had a strong interest in the relationship between population and immigration policy ever since the time of the Sakanaka Thesis, the idea of becoming an immigration nation naturally came to me as soon as it became clear that

Japan had entered a long-term period of population decline. This was the "twenty million immigrants over fifty years concept" that I presented in chapter 9 ("A Utopia in 2050") of *Immigration Battle Diary*.

The following is a summary of the introductory section of the chapter "International Population Movements" in the Sakanaka Thesis. While it is an immature argument as I was young when I wrote it, this passage served as the starting point for my theory of immigration policy. Forty-four years ago, I alluded to the inevitability of Japan becoming a society with few children and many elderly people and to the unavoidability of Japan adopting immigration policy.

> Today humanity is divided into many ethnicities and nationalities spread across the world, but all of these ethnicities and nationalities were formed by migrants seeking lands with more suitable living conditions (and their descendants). And in the future as well, humans will no doubt continue to actively move not only within but across national borders to earn a living or seek a comfortable life for themselves. Regarding international population movements (immigration), as long as there are unbalanced population distributions and economic development on the planet, population movements from countries with dense populations and a labor surplus to those with small populations and labor shortages. The movement of people from poor countries to richer ones is inevitable so long as there is an uneven distribution of wealth on the planet. Looking at the current state of the world, there is a striking contrast between the population explosion and stalling social and economic development in the developing world and the population revolution and active economic development of the developed countries. There is a vicious cycle of population increase and poverty in the developing countries. Meanwhile, rich societies have been formed in the developed countries and both the birth and death rates have fallen. They are becoming societies with fewer children and more elderly people. A new problem of labor shortage is rearing its head in basic industries such as the manufacturing industry, the heavy and chemical industries, and the service sector.

THE IMMIGRATION BATTLE DIARY ERA

When I retired from the Ministry of Justice Immigration Bureau in late March 2005, I wrote something with the desire to leaving it behind for others. This was *Immigration Battle Diary*. The following is an excerpt from its Introduction. I am now "Mr. Immigration," but I rushed through the period shown in the book as an "uncompromising bureaucrat." I hope that it serves as a clue for understanding what I am currently struggling with and what I am trying to do.

> With the extreme shortage of children, Japan will shortly enter a period of rapid population decline almost unparalleled in world history. We

are projected to fall below one hundred million people by 2050, and by 2100 we will be sixty-four million people, half of our current population. What will become of Japan's future? To deal with a society undergoing rapid population decline, we must seek a great national turning point comparable to the Meiji Restoration. And just as there was a fierce debate from the end of the Edo period to the Meiji period that divided national opinion in two over whether to "expel the barbarians" or "open the country," we should now have active popular debate that leads to a great national reform. In this book I put forward two scenarios for dealing with population decline, distinguished by how they view "accepting foreigners." One is a path towards "Small Japan," a society that shrinks in total conformity with the natural decline in population. The other is a path towards a "Big Japan," one that admits foreigners to make up for the natural decline in population and maintains its status of an economic power. "Small Japan" will severely restrict immigrants from entering Japan with the goal of becoming a "comfortable Japan" suitable for the reduced population. "Big Japan" will admit many foreigners to deal with natural population decline with the goal of becoming an "active Japan" with continued economic growth. What will Japan look like in 2050? Will it follow the path of "Small Japan" and have formed a "mature society" with a population of one hundred million people with Japanese forming an absolute majority? Or will it follow the path of "Big Japan" and have formed a "fully active society" with a population of one hundred twenty million people including twenty million people of foreign origin? The time has come for the public to decide its approach to this most important task, a true long-term national policy for Japan. It is ultimately the people who will decide what position should be adopted on the question of admitting foreigners. For that reason, I anticipate public debate. Regardless of which scenario is chosen, we who live in a society with a declining population will face grueling tests. In particular, our future will be determined by what kind of relationship we build with immigrants. What can we do to coexist with immigrants? The answer is to incorporate the "world" into Japan. This means tolerating the presence of other ethnicities. Do we Japanese have the readiness and pride needed to create that kind of future society? When thinking about this, our minds should immediately race to the history of our relations with the Zainichi Koreans, a group who up until this point have confronted the contradictions of this country as "foreigners." Can we create a "Japan who provides dreams to foreigners?" I believe that the answer relies upon whether or not we who have been in Japan since ancient times can think of ourselves as "*Zainichi*" Japanese, that is, if we can assume the position of just one of the ethnicities composing this country and create an "open and fair society" that the people of the world will want to live in and become citizens of.[4]

WITH THE ELITE AT THE TOKYO REGIONAL IMMIGRATION BUREAU

On April 1, 2003, the Shinjuku Office of the Tokyo Regional Immigration Bureau, a long-held dream of immigration personnel, was launched. The immigration inspectors and control officers who were gathered at the office boldly launched an all-out attack on nests of illegal immigrants with a strong sense of mission.

Sixteen years have passed since then. The Tokyo neighborhood of Kabukichō—known as Japan's den of crime—has greatly changed. Even the foreign gangsters who infested the place and acted as if they owned it have been forced to lie low. The ringleader of a powerful smuggling organization in Shinjuku was arrested. The numerous foreign prostitutes who lured customers from dimly lit corners are gone. The salons that illegal Koreans and Chinese used to have there have also disappeared from Kabukichō.

So, why did I establish this office in Shinjuku/Kabukichō, adopt a resolute stance on foreigner crime, and attempt to drive a stake into the foreign crime organizations? To jump straight to the conclusion, it was because I believed that the kind of relationships we built with foreigners would determine what our future in the rapidly approaching time of population decline looked like. At the very least, Japan's future will be controlled by the relations between Japanese and foreigners.

I believed it was necessary to thoroughly eliminate the root causes of ill will between these two groups in order to create a society where Japanese people didn't have an excessive adversion toward foreigners and our country could become a "society built upon coexistence with foreigners." In other words, I believed it necessary to thoroughly crack down on foreigner crime so that the Japanese view of foreigners wasn't worsened and so Japan's doors could be properly opened wide for accepting the kind of foreigners who we did want in the country.

It was with these thoughts that I hoped that the Shinjuku Office would play the role of laying the environmental groundwork for the coming "Japan open to immigration." It was done in preparation for the future society built upon multiethnic coexistence.

RESOLVING THE FALSE CHINESE REFUGEE INCIDENT

During the thirty-five years prior to my retirement from the Ministry of Justice Immigration Bureau in March 2005, I remained in the field of immigration control administration.

The first twenty years or so were largely involved with the *Zainichi* Korean issue. During the last seventeen years or so, however, I turned all my energy to enforcing immigration controls on Chinese intending to enter or work in Japan illegally. In particular, I was in charge of the administrative work to resolve the Chinese precollege student problem known as the "Shanghai Incident" that occurred in November 1988 and the "False Chinese Refugee Incident" of the following year.

During the Shanghai Incident, 38,000 Chinese swarmed the Japanese consulate in Shanghai seeking to be issued student visas. While they applied to enter Japan with the stated purpose of studying at Japanese language schools, their true intention was to work. The Immigration Bureau was surprised by this incident. It was a major incident that let the world know how tremendous the Chinese "fever for migrating to work" was.

I was deeply involved in this incident as the Immigration Bureau's deputy director and decided "We need to punish all of the Japanese language schools who are involved in this nonsense!" As a result, a majority of the 38,000 visa applications were rejected.

This decision not only led to howls of protest from those involved in the Japanese language schools, but we were also criticized by ambassadors in the foreign ministry and by Sinophilic politicians who said that we "should at least approve 20,000 for the sake of Sino-Japanese goodwill."

The Chinese government also applied strong pressure for the "acceptance of students for Sino-Japanese friendship." But I countered with the question, "how are unprepared Japanese language schools supposed to possibly accept 38,000 students?" I refused these demands, saying "That's not Sino-Japanese friendship. It would cause problems for future Sino-Japanese relations."

Unfortunately, at the time of the Shanghai Incident, 28,000 Chinese precollege students had already entered Japan; roughly half of these would remain in the country illegally. Some of them would later become "snakeheads" (smuggling brokers) or gangsters heavily involved in foreigner-connected crime.

Then there was the False Chinese Refugee Incident the following year. In this incident, 2,800 Chinese posing as Vietnamese refugees entered Japanese territorial waters. I also held the leadership position during this incident and came up with the policy to resolve it.

Not doubting that they were Vietnamese refugees, the Immigration Bureau initially gave these people—who were arriving at various places in Kyūshū on refugee ships—permission to land and placed them in locations like Catholic churches.

However, by chance a Chinese woman studying at a Japanese language school in Yokohama came forward saying "I want to find my husband who drifted ashore on a refugee ship." When she was allowed to meet her husband (who was being kept at a Catholic church in Nagasaki), he was obviously Chinese. That led to it being discovered that the boat people who had entered Japan were all Chinese disguised as Vietnamese refugees. And the boat people who came afterward were also found to all be Chinese. The Immigration Bureau is a small organization, but we dealt with this incident through an organization-wide effort. We were unlucky to lose two employees to overwork, but we completed the deportation procedures for all 2,800 Chinese and returned them to China.

I have no doubt that the practical experience of protecting the national border and resolving these two incidents almost perfectly are deeply engraved into the hearts of the employees of the Ministry of Justice Immigration Bureau. I believe it became a large source of self-confidence and an asset for the immigration control staff.

And our accomplishments managing through this crisis were well-received within the government. This became an opportunity for the immigration organization to expand significantly.

The incident of Chinese people thronging the Japanese archipelago in the guise of Vietnamese refugees and the efforts of the Immigration Bureau were reported on every day as a top news story by the national media. The Immigration Bureau had previously been only a small, nameless government body in the eyes of the public, but it now became widely known. Afterward, the immigration control system, including its organization and personnel, would be strengthened and expanded at a rapid pace. For example, while there were just over 1,800 immigration officials in 1989, that number had grown to roughly 4,600 by late 2017.

I am convinced that if large-scale illegal immigration from China occurs in the future, the elite officials at immigration control who experienced and grew through these harrowing experiences will be able to handle it appropriately.

My personal doctrine while in the Immigration Bureau was to thoroughly crack down on foreigner crime so that the Japanese view of foreigners wouldn't worsen, and our doors could be properly opened wide for the foreigners who we do want to come to Japan. Even after having retired from the Ministry of Justice, my basic thoughts haven't changed.

HUMAN TRAFFICKING: THE FINAL BATTLE AGAINST THE "PHILIPPINE PUBS"

The following events happened in 2004. At the time, roughly 130,000 dancers and singers entered Japan as "entertainers" per year (80,000 of whom were Filipinos). These women performed at about 10,000 bars, clubs, and pubs in Japan and there were a thousand or so production companies that the promoters who brought them into the country worked for.

As can be understood from these numbers, this was big business and the organized criminal organizations behind it made massive illicit profits from their illegal acts. This was the lawless zone I was fighting in.

As director of the Tokyo Regional Immigration Bureau, I established an investigative team within the bureau in July 2004 to follow up on foreign women who had entered the country on an "Entertainer" visa. This was part of an effort to stop the international human trafficking of women, which had been correctly criticized by the United States in its Department of State annual *Country Reports on Human Rights Practices*. Privately, I had decided that the time had come to win the fight that had been raging against the "Philippine pubs" for ten years.

This specialized team was composed of immigration inspectors and immigration control officers who were knowledgeable on the "entertainer" issue. The team tracked those who had entered Japan as "entertainers" and exhaustively investigated each of the pubs, clubs, snack bars, and bars they were "performing" at.

The team conducted on-site investigations of one hundred twenty businesses in 2004. Of those businesses where it was clear that women were engaged in activities not allowed by their visas, immigration control officers obtained search warrants for seventeen particularly vile ones and exposed their crimes, such as coerced prostitution.

As a result of this investigation into immigration violations, we were also able to confirm that the businesses that we had targeted held absolutely no performances that could be called shows, the purported reasons for the visa in the first place. The women had been employed as "hostesses" (bargirls) from the beginning and acts close to (or actually) prostitution were occurring in these businesses on a daily basis.

As part of the investigation, I personally visited many of the locations and supervised immigration officials in the performance of their duties first-hand. I'll give an example.

We assembled at ten p.m. before heading to the business. Our team consisted of twenty immigration control officers from the Tokyo bureau, supported by fifteen police officers we had requested from the Metropolitan Police.

The mood at the business changed drastically as our officers rushed in. Noisy footsteps and brief shouting were heard here and there, and then the loud music playing in the business was cut off and replaced by a tense silence.

The foreign hostesses huddled together in small groups on sofas here and there and were absolutely still. In such an atmosphere, the voices of the officers carried clearly.

While you might think that the young Filipino women who were arrested would be despondent at having been caught by Immigration, that wasn't actually the case. In fact, most of the women were relieved. Indeed, an overwhelming majority of our investigations into businesses were prompted by receiving an "SOS" from a Filipino woman working there asking to be saved from the forced servitude.

Entering the waiting room in the back of the business, my eyes immediately jumped to something that showed that the women there had certainly not been enjoying their time in the hostess industry. It was a log that listed and numbered their work by type and included the entries for "escorts" and "dates." I could immediately tell from the log that they had been made to compete against each other in their earnings.

The women who were being deported in accordance with the Immigration Control Law were not merely putting on a brave face. I saw many who were happy to be returning home, at having been freed from the unbearable forced "escorting" and "dates" that they hated.

As they went through the deportation process, I felt relieved as I looked on their expression and saw that they were happy at the prospect of soon returning home and being able to see their families.

The Tokyo Regional Immigration Bureau's organization-wide effort grappling with the trafficking of foreigners problem yielded results. And in response the government followed up on it.

The criminal code was revised during the 2005 regular session of the Diet to include "human trafficking" as an offense and the Immigration Control Law was amended through the "Law to Partially Revise the Criminal Code and Other Laws" to protect victims of human trafficking.

This finally brought about an end to the all-out war between the Immigration Bureau and the "entertainment" promotion industry. As someone who had been on the front lines and taken that industry straight on, it was an emotional moment for me. Taking that as my parting gift, I retired from the Ministry of Justice Immigration Bureau in March 2005.

Had the dishonor of the international community's labeling of Japan as "a paradise for human trafficking" remained in place, as the former director of the Tokyo Regional Immigration Bureau, I would likely be condemned by the world as unqualified to speak about building an immigration nation. And naturally, I would not be called "Japan's Mr. Immigration" by the global media.

A LIFE DEVOTED TO IMMIGRATION CONTROL

It was the spring of 1995. As director of the Residency Section at the Ministry of Justice Immigration Bureau, I took a scalpel to the issue of entertainment visas, something that had been considered untouchable due to the influence of organized crime on Japanese politics. I took charge and implemented a national fact-finding survey from May 1995 to March 1996 of the bars, cabarets, and other businesses where those who had entered as entertainers were "performing."

That survey found that illegal acts (such as hostess activities and prostitution) were occurring in 412 (ninety-three percent) of the 444 businesses surveyed. Based on this survey, the regulations for entering Japan on an entertainer visa were tightened.

This enforcement measure triggered a fierce backlash by the production companies who invited these entertainers and from the managers of businesses that used them as hostesses.

This led to politicians pressuring me to stop. "What on Earth are you doing?! It's stubborn officials like you that cause problems for the business community. You should be transferred." I didn't budge in the face of these attempts by powerful politicians with influence over immigration control (including the then-chairman of the House of Representatives Judicial Affairs Committee Katō Takuji) to steamroll me. I pushed forward, using the law as my shield.

The result of my dogged persistence was being labeled a "stubborn official" by politicians beholden to the hostess bar industry or other organized crime. In the April 1997 personnel changes, I was appointed director of the Sendai Regional Immigration Bureau. I would never work in the Ministry of Justice's home office again.

I retired from the Ministry of Justice in March 2005 after serving as director of the Fukuoka, Nagoya, and Tokyo regional immigration bureaus. Not bad for someone who had made powerful enemies.

What did I do during my eight years serving as a regional director? I continued to put my energy into writing and grappling with the entertainment visa problem. As a result, I published the following five books (titles rendered in English):

1. *A Clause-by-Clause Explanation of the Immigration Control and Refugee Recognition Act (Revised Edition)*, (Tōkyō: Nihon Kajo Shuppan, 1997), (co-author)
2. *The Development of Policy for Zainichi (South and North) Koreans*, (Tōkyō: Nihon Kajo Shuppan, 1999)
3. *A Clause-by-Clause Explanation of the Immigration Control and Refugee Recognition Act (Fully Revised Edition)*, (Tōkyō: Nihon Kajo Shuppan, 2000), (co-author)
4. *A Framework for Japanese Immigration Policy*, (Tōkyō: Nihon Kajo Shuppan, 2001)
5. *Immigration Battle Diary*, (Tōkyō: Kōdansha, 2005)

The first and third books are major works that were written to provide a definitive commentary on the Immigration Control Law. They are still being well used in the legal world as authoritative guides to the law, have been written by the leading researcher of it. The second book is a compilation of my writings on *Zainichi* Korean policy theory. With the writing of this book, my efforts on my first life's work—the *Zainichi* Korean issue—came to a close for the time being and I prepared myself for seriously taking on my second life's work—immigration policy. Afterward, I turned my efforts to theoretical research on immigration policy. While I didn't use the word "immigrant" in the title, the fourth book is a compilation of my writings related to immigration policy. It could be considered an introduction to my theory for that policy.

I also focused on another area of study. From the fall of 1997, I devoted myself to contemplating what the immigration policy of a society with a declining population should look like, as that was what Japan would face within a decade. Chapters 9 ("A Utopia in 2050") and 10 ("Small Japan and Big Japan") of *Immigration Battle Diary* were the results of that research.

While I presented a Utopian tale in the introductory section of chapter 9, my true intention at the time was that it would serve as a "declaration of an immigration nation" that would push a Japan headed toward rapid population decline to change and become an immigration nation:

> And just as there was a fierce debate from the end of the *Edo* era to the *Meiji* era that divided national opinion in two over whether to "expel the barbarians" or "open the country," we should now have active popular debate that leads to a great national reform like the Meiji Restoration. In this book I present two scenarios for dealing with population decline—"Small Japan" and "Big Japan"—that are distinguished by how they view "immigration." I want to provide you with a vision of Japan in the year 2050, one based on the premise that Japan greatly changes course, admits twenty million immigrants, and wholeheartedly pushes forward towards the ideal of "a society based on multiethnic coexistence." You may read it either as a prologue intended to raise certain issues or as mere a Utopian tale.[5]

Chapter 10 of *Immigration Battle Diary*—"Small Japan and Big Japan"—was written with the hope that it would raise the problem of the century and cause people to deeply consider what immigration policy should be like in an era of population decline. It was an utter failure. It was likely far too early for a debate over immigration policy. Fourteen years ago, this piece drew the attention of almost none of the public. And there was no response from the world of politics, business, academia, or the bureaucracy, either. The era of immigration policy's winter continued.

However, writing this essay caused me to develop an argument linking the population decline issue with immigration policy and establish the theoretical groundwork for the Sakanaka Theory of Immigration Policy. My thirty-five years working in the Immigration Bureau came to an end in March 2005, the time that this book was published. Writing it hardened my determination to continue my research into immigration policy even after retirement. Ignored by the world, a fire had sparked to life in my spirit and I resolved to take the lead in challenging Japan's rejection of immigration.

Looking back now, my time in professional exile was extremely fruitful. It was those eight years spent biding my time that led to completion of the world's leading theory of immigration policy. Driven by my sense of justice, I was frequently demoted for stubbornness (i.e., not looking the other way). I believe it was my life of constant struggle in the Immigration Bureau that gave me my undauntable disposition. Even being demoted can have its upsides.

***

There's something I'd like to say here about my relationship with government leaders. As mentioned above, I had to go through the hardship of being demoted due to pressure applied by politicians who were in bed with corrupt businesses. However, the government has—from beginning to end—remained silent on the theory of an immigration revolution that this dangerous thinker has been calling for. A free man (or woman) who has nothing to fear or lose can speak openly and directly to the government leadership about what kind of immigration policy should be adopted. He or she needn't hold back and can be indifferent to the scheming of politicians and movements within the political world.

Japan is rare in that it is a country where the views of a private citizen belonging to a small organization can be put forward to the government. I feel that the government has watched over the growth of my immigration policy theory with warmth and appreciation. In order to meet those expectations, I have worked hard to draw up an ideal immigration nation that can stand up to any in the world. I have held to the logic and ethics of an immigration nation. I have persisted in my principles and ideas. I have devised a systematic, universal immigration nation concept. I have formulated a vision of the immigration nation that global authorities on immigration policy research have praised for its creativity.

I believe that it is fortunate that the important job of drawing up the blueprints for an immigration nation was left to my hands with the tacit approval of the government, if for no other reason than because it meant that immigration policy was able to be formulated without becoming a pawn in political fighting. Working as if possessed by God, I was able to rapidly complete the vision of an immigration nation that will become a model for the world.

"SMALL JAPAN" AND "BIG JAPAN"

Around the time that I was transferred to become director of the Ministry of Justice's Sendai Regional Immigration Bureau in 1997, I came to believe that it was necessary to seriously contemplate what the immigration policy of a society with a declining population should look like as that was what Japan would face within a decade. This is because population trends, the nature of a state, and that state's policies for foreigners are all closely linked. At that time, whenever a meeting was held at the justice ministry, I stated that Japan had two choices for how to live in an era of population decline: "the path to a beautiful decline" in which foreigners were not admitted even as the population fell and "the path to maintaining a diverse, vigorous society" in which the decline in population was ameliorated by admitting foreigners. This idea was logically expanded upon in an article published in the February 2004 issue of *Chūō Kōron*.

This article—entitled "Our Policy on Admitting Foreigners is a Long-Term Plan: Should We Aim for 'Small Japan' or 'Big Japan'?"—was the starting point for my immigration policy theory.[6] These were emergency proposals regarding how a society with a declining population should approach admitting foreigners. I put them forward because Japan was shortly to become such a society.

After presenting two scenarios—a "Small Japan" that shrinks in total conformity with the natural decline in population and a "Big Japan" that takes in foreigners to make up for this decline and to maintain its status as an economic power—I discussed what kind of foreigner policy would be suitable for each.

In the portion of the article where I touched upon the immigration policy for a "Small Japan," I stated that "it is advisable to consider the foreigners that we admit as an urgent countermeasure to the rapid decline in the population as people who we want to become members of Japanese society (Japanese nationals); in other words, as 'immigrants.' Rather than by treating them as migrant laborers, we can secure capable human resources resolved to live out the rest of their lives in Japan by guaranteeing them the legal status and treatment appropriate to future Japanese citizens." I already believed in 2004 that the foreigners that Japan admitted as its population declined should not be foreign workers but rather "immigrants"—potential future Japanese citizens.

The main focus of the article was on presenting a theoretical model for Japan's future course and policy toward foreigners in an era of population decline, and to spark a national debate. However, this article only caught the attention of a few foreign journalists; it did not go so far as to affect Japanese public opinion.

When I retired as an official in March 2005, I believed it necessary to follow-up on the issues that I had raised in my article. That August, I established the "Foreigners Policy Institute," a non-governmental organization. At the same time, I led a study group called the "Foreigners Policy Study Group" that held monthly discussions on the immigration policy of a society undergoing population decline with experts such as researchers, administrators, and journalists. And I developed my theory for an immigration policy based around the keywords "immigrants" and "multiethnic coexistence."

It took a long time, but debate over whether or not to adopt an "immigration policy" finally began in the Diet in October 2018. The word "immigrant" has come into usage in the mass media and the world of academia. A common understanding that "immigration will save us from the population crisis" has been reached.

MY DECLARATION OF AN IMMIGRATION NATION

The government's population estimates that projected that the population would fall to ninety million people over the next fifty years filled me with a sense of crisis. From January 2007, I began unveiling my theory for a practical immigration policy in many media outlets, primarily national papers. As a result, the phrase "ten million immigrants will save Japan" has spread ahead of the age of population decline.

First, in the Japanese language weekly *Ekonomisuto* (January 30, 2007 issue) I raised the possibility of accepting nurses and caregivers from the Philippines based on an economic partnership agreement.[7] In this article, I criticized the fact that while the current system for accepting these nurses and caregivers gave the appearance of opening the door to foreigners, in actual practice, the national examination requirements meant that there was a high probability that many would be excluded. I proposed a "foreigner policy that cultivates human resources and encourages permanent residency" as an alternative system — that is, a policy of accepting foreign nurses and caregivers as permanent residents and educating them in Japanese vocational schools.

I also proposed a "human resource cultivating program for admitting foreigners" in the "Hatsugenseki" column of the January 28, 2007 issue of the *Mainichi Shimbun*.[8] This program would educate and train the children of Brazilian permanent residents, cultivate them into becoming skilled technicians, and accept them as members of Japanese society.

Next, an interview article, titled "Japan as an 'Immigration Nation'? Adopting a Policy of 'Cultivating Human Resources'," ran in the February 9, 2007, *Asahi Shimbun's* "Three People, Three Arguments" column.[9] In the article I said the following: "let's say the population declines by forty million over the next fifty years. If we work hard, we can admit ten million immigrants during that same period and transition to being a population of one hundred million people." I was worried that this bold statement would lead to a torrent of criticism, but according to the *Asahi Shimbun* there were no hostile opinions or protests. What does that mean? At the time, I interpreted this reaction as meaning that the proposal had been completely ignored as "nothing more than a pipe dream of Sakanaka Hidenori's."

Then in the *Yomiuri Shimbun's* March 14 "Ronten" column, I proposed creating a "foreigner vocational training system" suitable for an era of population decline and having this take the place of the problematic Technical Internship Program that was introduced during the time that

Japanese had a rising population.[10] This system would have "promoting of permanent residency" and "securing domestic human resources" as its objectives. This proposal evoked a response: Justice Minister Nagase Jien announced two months later that the Technical Internship Program would be abolished.

The July 3, 2007 issue of the *Nihon Keizai Shimbun* included a special feature: "The Foreigner Training System at a Crossroads (II)."[11] Included in this was an interview with me under the title "Accepting Working Immigrants." During this interview, I mentioned accepting immigrants for the agricultural, forestry, and fishing industries because they are suffering a remarkable labor shortage:

> We should accept these foreign workers properly, not as interns but as immigrants. This would be good news for those industries experiencing serious labor shortages due to the decline in population. It's also easier for businesses to invest in the education of foreign workers when they have permanent residency. I want to propose a model for accepting immigrants that cultivates human resources. Both the public and private sectors should prepare vocational training schools for foreigners; after they've arrived in Japan, they should study the Japanese language and specialized skills for one or two years and then be introduced to private companies on the condition they will be employed as full-time workers. If stable employment is guaranteed, then there's little risk of increased crime. These domestically cultivated foreigners should predominantly be placed in sectors like the agricultural, forestry, and fishing industries that are suffering remarkable labor shortages because young Japanese people keep a respectful distance from them. This will not seriously impact Japanese employment and it will shore up our declining domestic industries.[12]

In October, in a book I co-authored entitled *Immigration Nation Japan: Ten Million Immigrants Will Save Japan*,[13] I proposed a foreigner policy of accepting ten million immigrants over the next fifty years and declared that "it is the beginning of our actions to become 'Immigration Nation Japan'." I also answered questions like "Why immigrants?", "Is Japanese society capable of accepting ten million immigrants?", "Can the Japanese coexist with foreigners and those of other ethnicities?", and "What kind of framework would be needed to successfully accept ten million immigrants?"

Around this time, I contributed to the 2008 edition of *Bungei Shunjū*'s annual publication, *Nihon no Ronten* (Japan's Issues), drawing a picture of what Japan's future as an immigration nation would look like.[14] In the article, I encouraged Japanese to stir themselves, saying that "becoming a society with a rapidly falling population is a once-a-millennium opportunity to create a new Japan; the Japanese should acknowledge this crisis and consider coexisting with foreigners."

Entering 2008, the weekly *Ekonomisuto* (January 15 issue) put together a special feature entitled "Opening the Country to Labor: Accepting Immigrants will Save Japan." I presented a practical policy for admitting ten million immigrants in a three-page article.[15] The central part of this policy was preparing a system for accepting immigrants that emphasizes granting them permanent residency and cultivating human resources. I also said that the Japanese needed to be prepared for a "social revolution" if they admitted immigrants: "To drive this human resource cultivating immigration policy forward, universities and vocational schools should be opened up to the young people of Asia. Having admitted these foreigners as immigrants—that is, future Japanese citizens—Japanese will need to be prepared to renounce their various vested rights and undergo a 'social revolution'."

I also spoke about "accepting immigrants" on television. On April 20 of that year, I appeared with former Liberal Democratic Party Secretary-General Nakagawa Hidenao on *TV Asahi*'s "Sunday Project" where I unveiled my groundbreaking policy proposal that Japan "needs to accept ten million immigrants over the next fifty years."

A BRIEF OVERVIEW OF THE HISTORY OF JAPAN'S IMMIGRATION POLICY

Before the Second World War, our country adopted a policy of sending large numbers of emigrants overseas due to domestic conditions such as an overcrowded population and the impoverishment of agricultural villages and labor surplus caused by rapid modernization. At the same time, it severely restricted the entry of foreign workers into Japan who intended to settle permanently (or were likely to do so).

This policy of, in principle, not permitting the entry of foreigners who intended to permanently settle (immigrants) or work in Japan was also confirmed for many years after the war.

The "Immigration Control and Refugee Recognition Act" (Cabinet Order No. 319 of 1951; hereafter, the "Immigration Control Law") stipulated that the "Permanent Resident" status of residency could be granted during landing procedures. However, the Immigration Bureau did not authorize for this status of residency to be granted at time of entry.

Regarding foreign workers, when the "Basic Plan for Employment Measures" was adopted in 1967, it was agreed at a cabinet meeting that the plan presumed that "the admission of foreign workers will not be undertaken" would be a basic employment policy for the country. This policy would remain in place until 1990.

I will attempt a rough sketch of the history immigration policy below by following the changes in the categories of the status of residence stipulated by the Immigration Control Law.

The Immigration Control Law determines the status of residence of foreigners permitted to enter Japan based on the type of activities that they will perform after entering Japan. The categories of status of residence make Japan's policies toward foreigners public in the sense that they make clear what activities by foreigners are specified by law as beneficial to Japanese society and say that foreigners who are engaged in applicable activities can be permitted to enter the country.

Accordingly, by tracing revisions to the statuses of residence, the general course of Japan's immigration control policy (its policy towards admitting foreigners) from the past to the present can be made clear.

Fortunately, I was in charge of the partial changes to the statuses of residency in the 1982 revision of the Immigration Control Law and the complete overhaul of the status of residence system in the 1990 revision of the Immigration Control Law.

In particular, I believe that the new status of residence system of 1990 established a highly transparent system for admitting foreigners such as by publicizing the landing permission standards related to the statuses of residence and establishing an immigration system with the highest standards in the contemporary world in terms of the range of foreigners who are permitted entry and in their entry and status procedures.

Statuses of Residence at the Time of the Enactment of the Immigration Control Law in 1951

The Immigration Control Law was issued as a Cabinet Order "related to orders issued in accordance with the acceptance of the Potsdam Declaration" on November 1, 1951, during the Allied Occupation of Japan. It took force as law on April 28, 1952, through the stipulations of the "Law on Various Foreign Ministry Orders Based on Matters Related to Orders Issued in Accordance with the Acceptance of the Potsdam Declaration" and remains in force to this day.

Because experts on American immigration law who had been invited by the Supreme Commander for the Allied Powers (GHQ) were deeply involved in writing the Immigration Control Law, it was strongly influenced by the American "Immigration and Nationality Act of 1952."

The following points are notable, for example:

1. The Minister of Justice is the highest official on immigration control (the Attorney General had this authority in the United States at the time).
2. The basic system for managing the entrance and residence of foreigners was the same as that used in the United States.
3. The majority of grounds for refusing entry and deporting foreigners were the same.

4. The advance procedures prior to administrative punishment being carried out such as the adoption of a three-instance system for landing and deportation procedures are stipulated in detail.

The various statuses of residency that laid out which foreigners could enter Japan also reflected the intentions of the American government. It has been conjectured that this was partially done to create the statuses of residence that would be necessary for Americans to succeed or remain in Japan, as it was known that authority over immigration control would soon be returned to the hands of the Japanese government and that Americans would become subject to these immigration controls once the American-led Occupation came to an end.

For example, statuses of residence were established that Americans would be the largest beneficiaries given the contemporary state of international society. These included the "Trader/Business Manager/Investor," "Missionary," and "Provider of Advanced Technology" statuses of residency, all of which were given the maximum length of stay of three years (with the possibility of renewal).

Meanwhile, there was no "Child of Japanese National" status of residence created. And there were no procedures for foreigners born in Japan or those who had become foreigners and lost their Japanese citizenship to gain a relevant status of residence. It is believed that this is because America practices *jus solis* and doesn't recognize the revocation of citizenship.

The statuses of residence thus had the nature of being a parting gift from General MacArthur. But as they accepted a wide range of foreigners and were able to adequately deal with the increased international movement of peoples, this system for admitting foreigners could be considered to have been, by the standards of the international community in the early 1950s, revolutionary.

The "Trader/Business Manager/Investor" status of residence allowed foreign traders and executives into Japan, guaranteeing freedom of investment and business activities. The "Missionary" status of residence allowed priests and missionaries dispatched by foreign religious organizations into Japan and guaranteed freedom of religion and missionary work. The "Journalist" status of residence allowed newspaper reporters and photographers dispatched by foreign journalistic organizations into Japan, guaranteeing the freedom of the press. And the "Provider of Advanced Technology" and "Highly Skilled Worker" categories of the status of residence allowed skilled foreign human resources that could aid in the reconstruction of Japanese industry into the country. There was also a status of residence for "those specially authorized to reside by the minister of justice" prepared that made it possible to admit foreigners flexibly in response to changes in the economic and social situation.

Had the Japanese government independently devised a system for the entry of foreigners into Japan in 1951, it is unlikely that it would have created one so open to admission of foreigners.

Additionally, a status of residence for "those who wish to reside permanently in Japan" was created, leaving open the possibility of allowing foreign "permanent residents" (immigrants) to obtain residency in Japan during landing procedures. This was another regulation that owed its existence to the influence of America, a country open to immigration. However, because Japan is not a country that easily admitted immigrants, there was never a case where this procedure was applied, and a foreigner permitted to land and granted the "permanent resident" status of residence.

This stipulation was removed in the 1990 revision of the Immigration Control Law as not being in line with the conditions in Japan and its management.

Statuses of Residence in the 1990s

At the time of the 1990 revisions, the statuses of residence had become unable to adequately manage the demands of an era where the number of foreigners entering the country and the form their residency took had greatly changed from the time of their enactment. This is because they had only received minor adjustments in 1982 since the creation of the Immigration Control Law in 1951.

With Japanese society's rapid globalization, the number of foreigners entering the country was increasing and their activities had become more diverse. When admitting foreigners who intended to perform activities that did not have a clearly applicable status of residence, officials had no choice but to grant the general status of residence of "those specially authorized to reside by the minister of justice."

This framework—granting a status of residence to foreigners with specialized knowledge and skills on the basis of the justice minister's free discretion—made it unclear whether a given foreigner would be admitted to Japan or not, something that no doubt could cause anxiety. And the number of these foreigners was expected to continue to increase.

In addition to the above serious issues affecting the status of residence system—the mainstay of the Immigration Control Law—the law also came under pressure to respond to the foreign worker issue. There was increasing public demand for more specialist foreign workers to be allowed into the country.

Thus, in the 1990 revision of the Immigration Control Law, a fundamental revision of the types of statuses of residence and the range of activities applicable to those statuses was undertaken to establish a new status of residence system able to handle the increasingly active international flow of people. What activities foreigners residing under one of these statuses could perform was made clearer.

New statuses of residence were created, such as "Legal/Accounting services," "Medical Services," "Researcher," "Instructor," "Specialist in Humanities/International Services," "Intra-company Transferee," and "Cultural Activities." These were mainly types of activities for which "those specially authorized to reside by the minister of justice" status had previously been flexibly used to allow foreigners into Japan. Existing statuses of residence such as "Journalist," "Business Manager," "Engineer," "Student," "Entertainer," and "Skilled Laborer" had their permissible range of activities widened with the intention of expanding the range of foreigners admitted.

"Spouse or Child of Japanese National" and "Long-Term Resident" ("those who are authorized to reside in Japan with designation of period of stay by the Minister of Justice in consideration of special circumstances") were also newly established as statuses of residence in the law.

As a result, the descendants of Japanese nationals such as the Japanese-Brazilians became able to obtain theses statuses and set foot on Japan, the land of their parents or grandparents.

The 1990 Revision of the Immigration Control Law Was a Milestone for the Immigration Nation

In fact, it is because of the categories of status of residence laid out in the Immigration Control Law that the Japanese-Brazilians are able to obtain statuses like "Spouse or Child of Japanese National," "Long-Term Resident," and "Permanent Resident" that most foreigners usually can't.

As mentioned earlier, the Immigration Control Law was created in 1951. This system where the immigration control of foreigners was based upon a basic law drafted shortly after the Second World War ended continued until the late 1980s.

At that time, Japan was in the midst of the high point of its bubble economy. The domestic and international situations surrounding Japan had greatly changed; in particular, immigration officials were being overwhelmed by the flow of people pressing in from overseas. Pressure from the booming business community to let foreign workers in increased by the day. Naturally, it was apparent to all that the various problems being faced could not be dealt with legally unless something changed.

In April 1988, I became deputy director of the Ministry of Justice Immigration Bureau. I was suddenly told by my superior that "the Immigration Control Law's statuses of residence don't suit the times." I was given the special mission of "creating the draft for a total revision of the statuses of residence to deal with the foreign worker problem."

At the time, Japan was suffering from a serious labor shortage and the business community was demanding that the Immigration Bureau admit foreign workers.

In response, a consensus was reached within the Ministry of Justice over adopting a basic policy of "opening the door to foreigners with specialized knowledge and skills but not manual laborers."

They were being pushed to rapidly respond to the various changes in conditions. I was told "anyway, do it quickly" and given two weeks by my superior.

No matter how pressing the issue, however, there was no way that I could have readily accepted the assignment if it had meant starting completely from scratch.

But I actually had a "preconceived scheme" for a draft on revising the statuses of residence. I had a "tentative plan for revising the status of residence system" that I had been diligently working on since 1974. Using that as a reference, I was able to draw up the outline for a plan for a total revision of the status of residence system—the backbone of the Japanese immigration control system—in a short time frame.

Thinking back now, the 1990 revision of the Immigration Control Law brought about a historical turning point for the immigration control administration. Up until that point, the immigration control administration had strictly limited the entry of foreigners into the country who intended to work or settle there long term. The total revision of the statuses of residence system in the 1990 revision of the Immigration Control Law established a new status of residence for long-term residency and greatly expanded the statuses of residence that permitted foreigners to work. While the complete revision of the status of residence system based on the 1990 revision of the Immigration Control Law did not use the term "immigrant," my belief is that it can be viewed as essentially a milestone along the path to an immigration nation.

A QUIXOTIC DREAMER?

Looking back on the long journey toward an immigration nation, I released more than a thousand pieces on immigration policy but the days of being unrewarded for the effort stretched on. I have strong feelings about having been able to make it this far, healthy in both mind and body and able to write prolifically the whole while. I give my thanks to my late mother who gave me such a durable, healthy body.

When I released the "Sakanaka Thesis" in 1977, I was flooded with criticism. Likely it was making it through that that gave me the spiritual strength to take on the immigration issue—considered the strongest taboo in Japan—alone.

After I retired as a public servant in 2005 and began my life as a private citizen, I told my wife and son that I would "devote myself to researching immigration policy as a volunteer."

My family, who had always warmly watched over my work, told me, "Father, when you were at the Immigration Bureau, you were always doing the impossible. From here on it's okay for you to use your retirement pay as you want." Having watched me from up close, it may have seemed to them like I was chasing an unfinished dream.

That was the romantic element in the heart of the realist who had been known as a coolheaded bureaucrat while working. I think that perhaps, in general, the people who come up with unprecedented plans have both the elements of realists and idealists in them; perhaps the blood of a quixotic dreamer flows within me.

The majority of my works—papers related to the fundamentals of state policy—were produced in a chemical reaction between my romantic and realist elements. It was with my romantic eye that I drew up a utopian plan that looked a hundred years into the future. And with my realist eye, I looked at reality square on and put forward a broad solution to the most important task facing Japan. Compared to those written by scholars, it could perhaps be said that my papers have a strong tendency to grasp the essence of an issue through a long-term and idealistic stance, based on practical experience on the front lines.

I'm an obstinate person who won't compromise on my principles. I'm a strange person whose only thoughts are of formulating immigration policy. I drew up a long-term plan for an immigration nation with the romantic goal of creating Japan's future. I also received a Heaven-sent opportunity to perform the rare feat of releasing a paper that—like a come-from-behind home run—changes the course of the game.

Especially over these last six years, I've written daily on immigration policy and posted my painstaking efforts on the JIPI homepage. A total of one thousand of my short essays have circulated around the internet. As these essays have piled up, one after another, they've grown into a great power propelling immigration policy forward and overturned the deep-rooted negative feelings that the Japanese people have toward immigration. The Sakanaka theory of immigration policy has widely affected the younger generation and become more likely to influence our times.

My vision for an immigration nation might have ended without ever seeing the light of day. Instead, it has moved the hearts of the youth of Japan. Today, we've entered a new phase where sixty percent of those aged eighteen to twenty-nine approve of immigration policy.[16]

My reading of the trends of the times are that any government leadership which publicly states that it "will not adopt immigration policy" will be unable to stand against the voices calling for immigration that will come surging up from among the younger generation. It is thus just a question of time before the country is opened to immigration. The young people who will have to live desperate lives in an unprecedented era of low childbirth wait anxiously for the turn toward an immigration nation to be made, but it is an inevitability of history. An immigration nation will be born in Japan in accordance with the trends of the world.

The prime minister who makes the decision to make a national commitment to immigration and thereby changes the hearts of the young from despair to hope will be forever carved into the annals of Japanese history as a great statesman.

THE FUTURE OF JAPAN HAS BEEN ENTRUSTED TO AN AUTHORITY ON IMMIGRATION POLICY

Although I've released many papers and books, I am ultimately an amateur writer. I haven't studied writing or anything. I only learned how to use a computer in the past decade. Driven by the need to formulate immigration policy, I've always been careful to clearly express the ideas that come to me and insisted upon writing policy proposals that get to the essence of a problem in a way grounded in logic and conforming to rules and principles. It's possible that, having devoted the past forty-four years to writing papers on immigration policy, I've learned how to put forward a persuasive policy proposal to an extent. I've mastered the "Sakanaka style" of writing a paper: taking a taboo issue head-on and pushing for the fundamental revision of a basic national policy. This approach is why I'm feared as a "revolutionary."

I wrote various things in my spare time while working at the Immigration Bureau and released collections of essays such as *On the Future Administrative Management of Immigration* (1975), *The Development of Policy for Zainichi [South and North] Koreans* (1999), *A Framework for Japanese Immigration Policy* (2001), and *Immigration Battle Diary* (2005).

While I grappled with national issues in these books, the responsibility for the wording is never heavier than when laying out the vision for an immigration nation that will reshape the nation from the ground up. Failure is absolutely not an option when something touches directly upon national survival. And I couldn't hope to gain the understanding of the public if I didn't lay out a problem accurately and put forward a solution that gets to the core of the issue. It will be up to history to judge whether my policy proposals have been correct. Accordingly, being the formulator of a grand design for a new nation requires a preeminent imagination and an insight into the future. The dedication to absolutely carry through on the policies that you've laid down on paper is also demanded.

Because my views match those of the public, I have been recognized as someone who would be difficult to replace. This is likely an acknowledgment of my many years of accomplishments in the field of immigration policy research. During those years, I felt deeply responsible—as the pioneer who blazes a trail toward an immigration nation—for guiding national public opinion toward welcoming immigrants.

Recently I have begun to frequently think about how difficult it will be to overturn the "Japanese myth"—the idea that that Japanese have been able to manage our state, society, and economy without major mistakes for over a millennium all on their own. This will be difficult work and has the potential to damage the self-confidence and pride of the Japanese. With only limited time remaining in my life, it would perhaps be best for me to be pragmatic and withdraw, leaving this as something that will naturally be resolved with time if we open Japan to immigration.

To go further, my mission does not end with the completion of my theory for the immigration nation. The work of laying the foundation for the world's premier immigration nation still remains. If this great long-term national undertaking is accomplished in full, my concept of the immigration nation will enjoy perfect success. I no longer have the strength to fully carry out these lifelong great works, however. I want to leave that to the hands of the brilliant talents of the next generation. In truth, I believe that no one in this world has had a life where every little thing has gone their way.

I've held a philosophy of life since my twenties that no one in human society has absolutely everything go their way. And even though I've now reached an age where I leave things to Heaven's will, I believe that my own life is one of making gradual progress as I persevere through difficulties and troubles.

I actually find a life that leaves behind much still to be done attractive. It shows more than anything else that that person embraced big dreams. As a public servant, I lived by the motto "follow through on what you say." But the creation of a global human community—what could be called an eternal task for humanity—is something fated to end as an incomplete symphony no matter how I struggle.

Having embarked on an immigration revolution—a task that any number of lifetimes would be insufficient to complete—I believed that I had no choice but to release timely papers that provoked discussion and brought public opinion to my side. And over the long years of doing so, I mastered the art of writing controversial policy papers. A writer with too much time on my hands, I spend most of each day writing papers. Once I've finished writing a book, I feel content, thinking I've completed my final work. But this time of satisfaction doesn't last. With nothing else to do but write papers, I immediately begin writing another book. That cycle has continued over the fourteen years since I retired from the Ministry of Justice.

But I feel that I've aged and my mind has dulled. Fresh ideas have stopped coming to me. I've exhausted topics to write about. Recently,

I've noticed passages that I've written that are stereotypical and lack novelty. I'm earnestly trying through various methods to press in on the essence of these issues and use clear, detailed logic, but even so, I seem to have reached my limit.

I've come to feel that my life as a writer is approaching its end. Given that my books are essentially policy papers, they don't sell at all and publishers give me the cold shoulder. Or perhaps they are just hesitant at releasing the works of an immigration revolutionary. But then an idea suddenly occurred to me and during the period from 2016 to 2018 I released works privately published by JIPI almost every month.

But the end has come for this final effort as well. Having become unable to write anything other than rehashes of my earlier works, the desire to write a new book has faded. I wrote almost compulsively prior to this point because I had so much to write about. Now, I'm completely exhausted.

What lies ahead for the director of an immigration policy institute who has become unable to write? Writing policy papers had been my life up until this point. What should I aim for from here on when I don't know any other way to live?

Ah. Let's use this as an opportunity to break with a grinding life of pursuing policy goals. I should consider it fortunate that I have no choice but to stop writing, withdraw from the world of immigration policy, and enjoy the rest of my life in comfortable retirement. Even so, as it means putting down the pen after forty-four years of papers, I will likely become overcome with loneliness. My task from now on is to persevere against that and see how long I can live.

After constantly writing papers on immigration policy and carving a path leading to an immigration nation, I've arrived at a place where I can just about see the glorious sight of that new nation. I have no regrets about living a life where I poured my soul into one paper after another.

If a life can be compared to a paper, mine can be said to have been one organized around the pursuit of the true nature of the immigration nation. I mastered immigration policy studies through self-study. I dedicated myself to the kind of immigration policy research that I wanted to and completed my interpretation of the ideal immigration nation.

I could perhaps be said to have been privileged to spend the course of my life in the creation of an immigration nation.

FOURTEEN YEARS AS DIRECTOR OF THE JAPAN IMMIGRATION POLICY INSTITUTE

I established the "Foreigners Policy Institute" in August 2005 as a private research organization with the goal of making immigration policy proposals for an era of population decline. With Japan entering such an era, I had come to believe that the admission of immigrants had become an urgent national issue. I expanded that organization's framework in April 2009, creating the Japan Immigration Policy Institute.

The JIPI was formed as an organization with the goal of creating a society based on multiethnic coexistence and preventing and eradicating unjust discrimination and prejudice toward immigrants here in Japan.

I am well aware that taking on a long-term national plan requires superhuman abilities a hundred times greater than my own. I clung to the shadow of a hope that—by working as hard as several people—I might perhaps be able to achieve this great historical undertaking. Fortunately, because the field of immigration policy is something that I am unrivaled in, I was able to do everything by myself just as I wanted to. It was like drawing a picture of my own choosing on a blank sheet of paper.

It was a proudly independent life. I set out alone to undertake this great national matter—one that the fate of the Japanese people rests upon—and pursue the ideal relationship between Japan and the world. My family tells me that I only chase impossible dreams. It's possible that I'm the biggest dreamer in Japan. Fantasizing about a bright future may be an odd hobby to have, but doesn't it aid in the creation of a Japanese society that will stir the hearts of everyone? I'm a serious person whose thoughts can only focus on immigration policy, but even now I'm absorbed in these fantasies.

***

We seem to have gotten off track. Let's return to the topic at hand. Looking back on the fourteen years that I've spent as director of the JIPI, there were times when I worried about whether I would be able to fulfill my responsibility of creating this new future and others when I wanted to quit. The books I published on my vision for an immigration nation continued to be completely ignored by both the public and intellectuals. But at the same time, there were also times when I thought better of this and realized that I had to champion a national commitment to immigration at all costs in order to save my homeland from the threat of demographic collapse.

Then, in the spring of 2013, my mental attitude changed. I don't really know why I became so positive. Perhaps it was that my true character as one who loved the sacrificial spirit of the warriors of old—"nothing ventured, nothing gained"—emerged. My doubts disappeared. Having been fated to perform the historic task of reshaping the nation, I approached the creation of a conception of the immigration nation—one that would become a model for the world—with unwavering determination.

In accordance with my fate of having been granted the sacred calling to be the creator of an immigration nation, I'm currently putting all my strength into creating the design for an immigration nation that gathers the essence of Japan's spiritual culture while also envisioning what the world of a century from now will look like. I feel that I've developed a writing style over the years that gets directly to the heart of issues and has increased my intellectual productivity.

Recently, the JIPI has suddenly been drawing both domestic and international attention. There might be those who think that it is a large institute. In truth, it is an institute in name only; it is small and without any researchers or staff. It could be said to the one-man operation of Sakanaka Hidenori. Without the ability to develop an organization, I had come to the conclusion that I could only fight on with my lone pen. That was ultimately a good thing. I wrote constantly, driven by frantic thoughts about the need to protect my isolated stronghold of the JIPI. This is why my brain has remained active and I've been able to perform my writing activities in good health to the age of seventy-three.

The following are the books related to immigration policy that I've published over these past fourteen years. I am personally amazed that I've written eighteen books. These are all serious works, the products of ideas and national policies extracted from my own brain. They have absolutely no thinking borrowed from the West. I worked hard to ensure that they were rich in both quality and contents. Although the overall structure of the immigration nation concept has not changed, new innovative policy proposals have been added over time such as the theories of the human community and the Japanese Revolution. My awareness of the issues has also expanded to encompass the current state of world immigration policy. I believe that my thoughts have become more insightful and that my persuasiveness has increased.

These combined works, the ones published since retirement, form the central theoretical system for the Japanese-style immigration nation. I hope that my collected writings on immigration policy will see good use as a textbook that leads Japan to become an ideal immigration society.

1. *My Mission is Aiding Those who Escape North Korea and Return to Japan*, Dappoku Kikokusha Shien Kikō, 2005.
2. *Immigration Nation Japan: Ten Million Immigrants Will Save Us* (co-author), Nihon Kajo, 2007.
3. *The Japanese-style Immigration Nation Concept*, JIPI, June 2009 (expanded edition September 2009).
4. *Towards a Japanese-style Immigration Nation*, JIPI, 2009.
5. *The History and Tasks of the North Korean Returnee Issue* (co-author), Shinkansha, 2009.
6. *The Japanese-style Immigration Nation Ideal*, JIPI, 2010.
7. *The Path to a Japanese-style Immigration Nation*, Tōshindō, 2011 (expanded edition 2013, new edition 2014).
8. *Population Collapse and the Immigration Revolution*, Nihon Kajo, 2012.
9. *Japan as a Nation for Immigrants*, JIPI, 2015.
10. *The Creation of a Japanese-style Immigration Nation*, Tōshindō, 2016.

11. *The Japanese-style Immigration Nation will Change the World*, JIPI, 2016 (private printing).
12. *I want to Establish the Framework for an Immigration Nation Prior to the Tokyo Olympics*, JIPI, 2016 (private printing).
13. *The Prospects for Japanese Immigration Policy*, JIPI, 2017 (private printing).
14. *Collection of the Sakanaka Theory for Immigration Policy*, JIPI, 2017 (private printing).
15. *My Mission is to Record the History of the Immigration Nation*, JIPI, 2017 (private printing).
16. *The Global Expansion of the Japanese-style Immigration Nation*, JIPI, 2018.
17. *Japan's Immigration Nation Vision*, JIPI, 2018.
18. *Japan's Immigration Nation Vision (New Edition)*, JIPI, 2018.

Perhaps in the near future I will become the man of the hour. I might become the father of the immigration nation. And yet, I somehow can't just be happy about that. It's an unknown world for me. I've grown inured to any disparagement and can take being completely ignored in stride. But it feels unendurable for the assessment of me as a person to completely change.

I've already received plenty of honor as well as infamy. I don't need any more of either. If anything, I would say I'm attracted to the secluded life of a hermit.

If I were to frankly state my feelings right now, I would say they are to calmly accept that the new era has arrived and that I want to finish my life as the director of a private immigration policy institute in accordance with my nature, helping others, especially the next generation, understand this great nation's true potential as a society open to immigrants.

THE TIME THAT WILL DETERMINE HISTORY HAS ARRIVED

A proposal for a national policy that determines the future of Japan must be put together with a broad, long-term perspective and be based on firmly rooted, persuasive reasoning. It will be history that decides whether the proposal was to the benefit of the nation and its people. And the next generation will hold us accountable for the outcome.

Shrewd politicians and intellectuals know this and will absolutely avoid any issues that they foresee as having a difficult, complicated journey, such as one that involves the ethnic sentiments of some conservative Japanese people who oppose the creation of an immigration nation.

Ultimately, unwilling to take action, they have entrusted the work of saving Japan from its national crisis to me, the man esteemed as "Japan's Mr. Immigration" by the intellectuals of the world.

The basic theory for the Japanese-style immigration nation—one that stands at the forefront of global immigration policy—was completed in June 2018, just in time to step forward for the critical fight. With the publication of *Japan's Immigration Nation Vision (New Edition)*, my days of being absorbed in research came to an end. Having waited until the time was ripe and for the prevailing winds of public opinion to shift in favor of immigration, I will now put all my strength into the work of moving the bureaucracy and political leadership.

I will advance forward, proud that my many policy proposals were sound. I am confident in the prospects for the immigration nation; even the most stubborn politician cannot oppose a policy proposal steeped in reason.

In my judgment, we've entered an era where the domestic and international circumstances for immigration policy are in tumult and the time has finally come to change Japanese history. I am fully aware of the weight of the responsibility I bear. As the one who espoused the vision of a Japanese-style immigration nation, it is my role to pull the public—those who will participate in the reshaping of the nation—forward. But while I'm an expert on immigration policy, can I see through missions—like the preparation of legislation for immigration—that cannot be taken on by just one man? Can I remain true to my original intentions while being subjected to criticism from all sides? Do I still have the force of will needed to withstand these trials? These are never-ending causes of worry for me.

I pose questions to myself every day even though I bear an important mission that will determine the fate of the Japanese nation: What should I do from here? How should I live?

No one understands more than I that I am not the caliber of person for such historic work. I'm neither a hero nor a man of power. I'm the director of a research institute where I'm currently the sole researcher. I'm nothing more than a petty researcher whose main occupation is writing papers related to immigration policy.

Since retiring as a public servant, I've gained a peaceful character. There's no sign of the defiant bureaucrat of years past. I have neither the authority to drive immigration policy forward, nor the power to break through difficult obstacles. I have changed completely from my time as a bureaucrat, when I was widely known for my magnificent performance, and become a powerless private citizen. Can I meet the expectations of the public? Can my pen move the hearts of the politicians who are passive on immigration policy? These are the kind of worries that have troubled me for these last several years.

I feel intimidated when I talk about my inner feelings, but I want to become worthy of being the parent of my vision of Japan as an immigration nation. My ideal person is a far-sighted warrior who transcends the hatreds and jealousies of the world.

This is the mental state that master swordsmen like Miyamoto Musashi achieved in their final years. They no longer drew their swords and fought. They could make their presence felt by just standing still. My understanding is that this would take my becoming a person with the requisite dignity for the creator of the immigration nation; being recognized as a global authority on immigration policy research; and becoming the face of a Japan that is widely recognized throughout the world as an immigration nation.

If I earnestly take on minority issues, polish my character, and remain the JIPI director for the rest of my life, my desire to be recognized as that kind of person might be granted after my death. The accomplishments of my final years as JIPI director will be passed on forever.

Ever since the Sakanaka Essay of 1975, I have had the unfortunate fate of being driven by policy goals that I myself set. Because I set extremely high ideals as my policy goals, achieving them has been extremely difficult. Recently, I met an *Asahi Shimbun* reporter for the first time in sixteen years. He gave me the kind words that "you have seen a hundred years into the future as you laid down your immigration policy. Your era will come soon. Please be careful of your health in preparation for that."

While I treat my life with care, I do not tenaciously cling to it. I have poured all of my life into a national task that no other Japanese would take on. I continually ran toward the immigration society without wavering, against the headwind. I performed the role of the mainstay leading Japan to an immigration nation. I poured all my strength into the writing of policy papers to pry open the thick gates closing the country off from immigration, something which demanded strong willpower.

As my lone struggle stretches on without end, I feel that the day is near when I reach my limit and can no longer desperately rush headfirst toward my goal. But a reckless life lacking in planning is the path I've chosen. It's an unfortunate temperament to have. But changing the way I'm used to conducting my life is difficult once I've reached this age, so I feel comfortable just leaving myself to my natural way of doing things.

When I was thirty, I found something that I would devote my life to: the formulation of immigration policy. Since then, I have regularly released proposals on that subject. But recently new ideas have stopped coming to me. I must have drained the source of my creativity. I keep in mind that an old man whose mind has dulled must not cause difficulties for his nation or people. I'm painfully aware that the time has come to seriously consider stopping.

It will be the young—with the education and sensibilities of global citizens—that will create the wonderful future of immigration nation Japan. I strongly admonish myself that I must not become something that blocks the way as they make their way in the world.

I wrote policy papers single-mindedly in the belief that if I logically explained the necessity of the change to an immigration nation, made sound, sincere arguments, and maintained a just life, Japan's future would, without question, open up. The path I walked was one with many ups and downs. I believe that it is because of my grand goal of creating an immigration nation that would become a global model that I was able to make it as far as I have.

Finally, I would like to beg your indulgence to allow me to voice one of the dreams of this rare dreamer. I would like to spend the final moments of my life as a natural person, released from my goals. I want to return to nature as a "selfless person" in accordance with the motto I've had since my youth. If it could be permitted to me, I want to experience a secluded life basking in the sun and fantasizing about my unfinished dreams.

PREPARED FOR AN IMMIGRATION SOCIETY

Should Japan follow the course of using ten million immigrants to survive its population crisis, it will first need to fundamentally revise its present system for admitting foreigners and change the Japanese people's view of them before attempting to implement that policy. It must seek to be reborn as a "Japan that provides foreigners with dreams"—a place where capable foreigners will want to live permanently—and to become a society that recognizes the value of diversity, an immigration society in which the Japanese and various ethnic groups can coexist. I champion a "meritocratic immigration society" in which people who work hard are judged fairly and can obtain appropriate social status. One which guarantees equality of opportunity for all, without regard for their nationality or ethnic origin.

If the Japanese people and society don't undergo that kind of dramatic change, Japan will be unable to secure an honorable place for itself in the global struggle for human resources. We will be unable to expect foreigners with high aspirations and abilities to gather in Japan from the various countries of the world. And if immigrants do enter Japan in great numbers without the view of them changing, it's likely that ethnic conflict will arise between the Japanese people and other groups.

Looking over current Japanese society as a whole, it can be considered neither a society that brings out and makes active use of the talents of its foreigners nor one where Japanese and foreigners socialize closely with one another. There are only a few foreigners in Japan who are really able to contribute their all to Japanese society and have high social status. These precious individuals and human resources are not fully tapped, in other words.

Unfortunately, Japanese sometimes view foreigners with an unforgiving eye and the image they have of them are not necessarily a favorable one. With the current level of understanding that Japanese have of foreigners and Japanese society's attitude about admitting foreigners, I'm concerned that—should immigrants be admitted on a large scale—there will be incessant turmoil between Japanese and immigrants over things like competition in the labor market and cultural friction. An anti-immigrant movement could arise from among the populace. I don't know to what extent the Japanese will be able to put up with the presence of foreigners in large numbers.

Recently, debate over immigration policy has increased in the Diet and the prime minister used the phrase "the realization of a pluralistic society" there. I consider this to have been a historic moment in Japanese history. However, it hardly needs to be said that "words are easy, actions are hard."

Ethnicities are formed on a timeframe of thousands of years. We should be prepared for the fact that coexistence among different ethnic groups is not something that can be achieved through only ordinary effort.

In particular, the history of the Japanese is largely one where we formed a society that only consisted of those easy for us to get along with and then lived in peace on the Japanese archipelago for more than a thousand years. We are not mentally prepared for having close relationships with other ethnic groups. It would be hard to say that we really understand how to interact with those from other countries. I cannot say that we adequately know how to associate with foreigners or live in the same neighborhood with people with differently shaped faces and colored skin or who have different values and ways of thinking.

But even if all that is true, if the Japanese decide to borrow the strength of immigrants to maintain Japan's economic stability and social order in the twenty-first century era of rapid population decline, they will need to be prepared to deal with all other ethnicities—various Asian peoples, whites, blacks, and others—as the equal of themselves (while still acknowledging their own ethnic identity). We Japanese must also adopt the stance of engaging other ethnicities with ethnic self-awareness and pride if we are to coexist with immigrants.

Next, based on the healthy view of foreigners fostered through the above, it will be essential to undertake wide-reaching systemic reform. At that time, a popular movement will need to be developed at the household, school, workplace, regional society, and national levels that support creating a society where Japanese and immigrants can live together in mutual understanding, one where immigrants are approached with a considerate spirit.

There will need to be major reform of the fundamental way that government bodies such as the newly created Immigration and Residency Management Agency view and treat immigrants. This is because if the traditional thinking that foreigners are mainly to be regarded as targets of management and regulation is left in place, a "society in which Japanese and immigrants can coexist" will not be achieved. We must promote administration that advances coexistence and co-prosperity between Japanese and immigrants and acknowledges that immigrants are appropriately viewed as future citizens and have almost the same rights as Japanese.

While the immigration inspection that takes place at airports when foreigners attempt to enter Japan is also important, it is necessary to place the focus on long-term residency support such as livelihood guidance and Japanese language education so that those foreigners allowed into the country can better adapt to Japanese society. And in order for the country to responsibly deal with the treatment of immigrants and policy toward them, an "Agency for Immigration Policy"—a national administrative body that oversees the implementation of measures to promote the social adaptation of immigrants and to formulate plans for the comprehensive treatment of immigrants—should be rapidly created.

Another important task still remains: dealing with "ethnic problems." When those of different ethnicities live together in large numbers, it is unavoidable that ethnic problems will arise due to small or large ethnic or cultural differences. Considering the religious and ethnic issues that lie behind the regional conflicts and civil wars that even now occur throughout the world, I believe that ethnic issues could become a dangerous problem in Japan (though probably not religious ones). In that case, it will be necessary to take on the difficult task of answering the question of how to integrate various ethnic organizations into the single nation-state of Japan to prevent inter-ethnic discord and conflict.

There are two basic approaches for unifying the diverse ethnic groups who will be living on the Japanese archipelago into one Japanese citizenry: "unity through assimilation" which emphasizes education in the Japanese language, which is full of the Japanese spirit of tolerance, and "unity without assimilation" which is based in multiculturalism. So, which will be adopted? What should be the unifying principle that binds together different ethnicities as Japanese citizens? And are we Japanese, with our limited experience of fierce disputes with those of other ethnicities and cultures, even capable of uniting various ethnicities into one people? What principle will the "ideal immigration society" be built upon for an era when it is commonplace to encounter those of different ethnicities in your neighborhood or workplace? I want all sectors of society to seriously debate the answers to these questions.

As for the role of government in a multiethnic society, one of its most important jobs will be achieving multiethnic national unity, not from a position of "Japanese first" but rather taking a "neutral" position equidistant to each ethnicity and striving to maintain peaceful, friendly relations between them and aiming to coordinate their interests.

SEEKING THE PINNACLE OF THE IMMIGRATION NATION

The 1960s, the time when I was a student, were the heyday of Japan's student movement. But I was just a normal, apolitical young man who desired a stable life. And so, I chose to work as a civil servant from April 1970.

Anything can happen in life. The life as a public official that awaited me was one of grappling with the issue of ethnic discrimination, something that no one else wanted to touch. Working at the Ministry of Justice Immigration Bureau (which has jurisdiction over managing the entry of foreigners into Japan), my administrative areas were the "*Zainichi* Koreans," "refugees," and "immigration." I was placed in charge of issues that minorities in Japanese society are directly faced with.

I wrote many papers on improving the treatment of ethnic minorities, most notably the *Zainichi* Koreans. In the final years of my time as an administrator, I stepped into an untrodden world and devoted myself to creating the theory for an immigration nation that would overturn the common sense of the world. The result of my steadily accumulating accomplishments in theoretical research into immigration policy was an even greater leap forward.

After retiring as a public servant in 2005, I set out to work to save Japan from the life-or-death national crisis it faced—the collapse of the demographic order—through immigration policy. Having walked only the path of immigration policy, that was truly my life's mission. I tackled it as a volunteer with high ambitions. And that was the correct decision. I was able to openly make great efforts without any restrictions being placed on me.

Drawing up a grand long-term national plan for immigration is the most difficult thing regardless of the field of specialization or job position, polishing a concept from a long-term, global perspective and setting forth a persuasive theory for it. For that reason, the politicians who had no doubts about continuing the policy of closing Japan off from immigration, the politicians who had absolutely no appetite for fighting to improve minority issues, do not have the backbone for dealing with issues that are obviously going to be difficult such as the creation of an immigration nation. And thus, by process of elimination, the end result has been that a former national public official who is well-versed on minority issues and has made formulating immigration policy his life's work has been placed in the leading position for the revitalization of Japan. This is because no other Japanese emerged to engage in the desperate fight over the immigration issue that is considered the greatest and strongest taboo in Japan.

***

I've been put in the position of being a revolutionary who seeks to fundamentally reform the shape of the nation. And there can be no doubt that I possess great luck. I believe that it was the work of destiny that caused me to encounter the work of saving Japan from its desperate crisis. Having reached an age where I can calmly look back on the path that I have taken, however, the thought that I owe being who I am today to the fact that I had the ambition to create an immigration nation unparalleled in the world and break a taboo that had lasted for more than 1200 years and had the adventurous spirit to take on a task so dangerous that it might turn the entire public against me gives me strength.

Thinking logically, the present me, the "leader of the immigration revolution," is the result of continually writing papers on immigration policy in simple-minded honesty for the forty-four years since the 1975 Sakanaka Essay. It seems rational to say that it's all been my own doing, the result of implementing the theory that I myself had laid out.

It's been an extremely reckless life, one comparable to attacking an impregnable fortress by myself, and difficulties have descended upon me like a great tsunami. I've seen hell in this world. And in truth, there were times when I lost all faith in others and thought about how much easier I would feel were I to die. But having now reached an age where I am cognizant of my own death, there are times when I am reinvigorated by Heaven and think deeply about the fact that I have reached the summit of immigration nation theory, something that I devoted all my knowledge and strength to, and that I may possibly witness the historical moment when Japan opens itself to immigration. This puts my heart at ease.

While the journey here was filled with many troubles, I've been allowed in my old age to experience a brief time of supreme bliss of having "known the will of Heaven and engaged in my Heavenly calling." I held fast to my initial belief that "where there's a will, there's a way" and that I had to consider the position of minority groups when drawing up immigration policy. Now I quietly await the day when my life will come to an end with an awareness that there is no winning or losing in life.

I must beg the forgiveness of future generations, for my life will end with much work left untouched. I was only able to raise these problems. I will tamely accept the criticism that I was an irresponsible man who bit off more than he could chew. If I could be permitted a defense, however, the concept of the human community—humanity's eternal task—will shine brighter in the near future.

Looking over my career, I can summarize it as follows: I was overwhelmed with national tasks to fulfill, subjected to concentrated criticism and ridicule, and left behind a mountain of things still to be done. Despite this, I feel absolutely no dissatisfaction about a life in which I was allowed to absorb myself in researching immigration policy and to do what I wished to my heart's content.

Even now, having reached the age to do a full accounting of my life, the only thing that comes to me is the vague answer that while there are tough things in life, there are happy things as well. It might be difficult to discuss a life-voyage rich in storms in a fully consistent way. The only thing I can say is that it was a life in which, aiming to reach the global pinnacle of the immigration nation, I set foot on unexplored ground and walked forward step by step.

NOTES

1. Sakanaka Hidenori, *Kongo no Shutsunyūkoku Kanri Gyōsei no Arikata ni Tsuite* (On the Future Nature of Immigration Administration), (Tōkyō: Ōeisha, 1977), p. 125.

2. Sakanaka, *Kongo no Shutsunyūkoku Kanri Gyōsei no Arikata ni Tsuite*, p. 125.

3. Sakanaka, *Kongo no Shutsunyūkoku Kanri Gyōsei no Arikata ni Tsuite*, pp. 131-132.

4. Sakanaka, *Nyūkan Senki*, pp. 4-6.

5. Sakanaka, *Nyūkan Senki*, p. 207.

6. Sakanaka Hidenori, "Gaikokujin Ukeire Seisaku wa Hyakunen no Kei de Aru (Our Policy on Admitting Foreigners is a Long-Term Plan: Should We Aim for 'Small Japan' or 'Big Japan'?)," *Chūō Kōron*, Vol. 119, No. 2 (January 2004), pp. 222-232.

7. Sakanaka Hidenori, "Gaikokujin Kangoshi, Kaigoshi no Ukeire Jōken wa Kibishisugiru (The Conditions for Accepting Foreign Nurses and Caregivers Are Too Strict)," *Ekonomisuto*, Vol. 78, No. 5 (January 30, 2015), pp. 70-71.

8. Sakanaka Hidenori, "'Toyota Shokugyō o Kunrenkō Sōsetsu o (Establish a 'Toyota Vocational Training School")," *Mainichi Shimbun*, January 28, 2007.

9. "'Imin Kokka' Nippon? 'Jinzai Ikuseigata' no Seisaku o Tore (Japan as an 'Immigration Nation'? Adopting a Policy of 'Cultivating Human Resources')," *Asahi Shimbun*, February 9, 2007.

10. Sakanaka Hidenori, "Gaikokujin Jisshūsei: Seishain de Koyō Teijū Sokushin (Foreign Student Vocational Training Students: Hire Them as Permanent Employees and Promote Their Settling in Japan)," *Yomiuri Shimbun*, March 14, 2007.

11. Sakanaka Hidenori, "Rōdō Imin no Ukeire o (Accepting Working Immigrants)," *Nihon Keizai Shimbun*, July 3, 2007.

12. Sakanaka, "Rōdō Imin no Ukeire o."

13. Sakanaka Hidenori, *Imin Kokka Nippon: Issenmannin no Imin ga Nihon o Sukū* (Immigration Nation Japan: Ten Million Immigrants Will Save Japan), (Tōkyō: Nihon Kajo Shuppan, 2007).

14. Sakanaka Hidenori, "Mayakashi no Gaikokujin Seisaku wa Genkai: Imin Issenmannin ga Jinkōgen no Nihon o Sukū (The Limits of Fake Foreigner Policy. Ten Million Immigrants Will Save Japan From Population Decline)," *Nihon no Ronten* (Tōkyō: Bungei Shunjū, 2007).

15. Sakanaka Hidenori, "'Ikuseigata' Imin Seisaku ni Kaji o Kire (Changing Course to a 'Cultivating' Immigration Policy)," *Ekonomisuto*, Vol. 86, No. 3 (January 15, 2015), pp. 22-24.

16. "Wakanensō no 6 Wari ga Sansei (60% of the Younger Cohort Approves)," *Nihon Keizai Shimbun*, March 21, 2017.

Conclusion

About ten years ago, a Western intellectual posed the following question to me in response to my proposals: "Can the Japanese in fact accept ten million immigrants over the next fifty years, despite the country having been closed off to immigration for more than a thousand years?"

In 2016, the global mood concerning immigration policy underwent a complete change. So did the global positioning of the vision of Japan as an immigration nation. Right now, as racial discrimination, anti-immigration sentiment, and Islamophobic activities grow stronger in America, France, and elsewhere, I am pushing the Japanese government to admit ten million immigrants based on a unique immigration policy for Japan. I am also emphasizing the legitimacy and global significance of the vision of Japan as an immigration nation to the world's intellectuals.

With Britain, France, and Germany losing the surplus strength to admit further immigrants and a wall being erected along the U.S.-Mexico border, there is a unique opportunity for Japan to contribute to the world through immigration policy. Now that a pall has fallen over the Western spirit of liberty, equality, and fraternity that has reigned over the world since the French Revolution of 1789, let us warmly greet immigrants with the Japanese spirit of hospitality, have the grit to lead the world in immigration policy, and contribute to the creation of a new world civilization. With the authority of the Western nations plummeting due to the immigration issue, Japan should seize the chance to go on the offensive as an immigration nation and make its presence felt by the peoples of the world.

I retired as a national public official in 2005. Setting as my goal "using a revolutionary immigration policy to allow Japan to survive the national emergency that will accompany demographic collapse," I aspired to construct the world's foremost theory for an immigration nation. My sense of purpose, way of thinking, and sense of scale were all different from that of Western immigration policy experts—who are mainly practitioners. There was also a major disparity in the degree of passion for immigration policy. A patriot at heart, I took on the challenge of formulating immigration policy prepared to engage in a mortal struggle for the survival of the nation of Japan.

Fourteen years have passed since then. And as a result of my combined efforts, I've reached the point where I can introduce the human community concept—the pinnacle of immigration policy theory—to the intellectuals of the world.

I'm not just advocating a vision of the immigration nation that is unique in the world. I'm proposing that Japan make establishing the world's first society based on the human community a national goal. We Japanese will aim to build a society in which those of different races, ethnicities, and religions live together as fellow humans. It's a grand plan for reshaping the country into a society based on the human community over the next hundred years.

My ambitious dream that societies based on the human community will be formed within the countries of the world is boundless. I can see an age when this revolutionary immigration concept containing the essence of Japanese spiritual culture moves the hearts of the peoples of the world, leading to societies based on it forming on a global scale, and creating a framework for world peace. Japan's immigration policy will have become a model for the world and sparked a fundamental reform of world immigration policy. It also fundamentally challenges the current global state where xenophobic anti-immigrant movements remarkably counter to the spirit of humanitarianism are spreading in the West.

If the Japanese government takes the first step forward and aims to reach the summit of the world via this original vision for an immigration nation, the basic ideals and norms of the Japanese-style immigration nation will become a model for the entire world. Most of all it will deeply influence the immigration policies of the existing immigration nations where racial discrimination sentiment and xenophobic thought is inexorably present among the public.

A new imperial era began on May 1, 2019. With the change in era, the mood of society will also change. Anxiety will continue to spread as we fail to escape the quagmire of rapid population loss. The youth of Japan will yearn for a society with a brighter future.

I can feel the first movements of the youthful energy that will create a new future and have an urgent request for the prime minister. I want you to give the young people of Japan—with their hearts rich in consideration for the people of other countries—hope for the future. I want you to make becoming "the country most open to immigrants in the world" a national goal to symbolize the new era. The younger generation will welcome immigrants with the Japanese spirit of kindness. The ultimate goal will be the creation of an immigration society that becomes an example for the world.

***

In this book, I've spoken exhaustively about the life I spent leading Japan's immigration policy for forty-five years. What did I seek? What did I do? What do I leave behind as tasks unfulfilled? I've given an account of these things, holding nothing back. As such, I have no anxiety about the future.

Having grappled with the work of creating a new future for Japan, I have the responsibility to convince the Japanese people who will live together with immigrants in an era of large-scale immigration. As the one who has drawn up Japan's immigration policy, I have the responsibility to leave behind a description of the fundamental ideals and theory for the immigration nation that will become the cornerstone of later generations. My mission is to record an account of the journey that led to the establishment of the immigration nation so it may serve as a page of Japanese history.

In this book, *Japan as an Immigration Nation*, I've laid out the blueprint of the Japanese-style immigration nation and a vision of the future of human society. Carved into this work is my life experience of walking together with immigration. I have completed this book with the desire that it be a compilation of my research on immigration policy. My greatest joy would be for this book—the last collection of my essays on immigration policy—to withstand the sands of history and be read and passed on as the bible of immigration nation theory not just among the people of Japan but of all the countries of the world.

I hope that the concept of the human community—the crystallization internationally of the Japanese spirit of harmony—shall serve as a guidepost for the global citizens living in the 22nd century golden age of immigration as they rise up and champion eternal world peace.

Contributor Biographies

Hidenori Sakanaka was born in May 1945 in Cheongju on the Korean Peninsula. His family returned to Kyoto Prefecture after the war in October. He earned his Master's Degree in 1970 from Keiō University Graduate School of Law, upon which he entered the Ministry of Justice. After working in a number of different positions throughout the country, he served as the director of the Tokyo Regional Immigration Bureau. He retired in March 2005 and established the Foreigners Policy Institute (now the Japan Immigration Policy Institute, http://jipi.or.jp/) in August 2005. He is the author of almost two dozen books about immigration policy, including *Immigration Battle Diary* (Kōdansha, 2005, in Japanese) and regularly appears in the international media.

TRANSLATORS' BIOGRAPHIES

Robert D. Eldridge, Ph.D., was a tenured associate professor at the Graduate School of International Public Policy, Osaka University, from 2001-2009 prior to joining the U.S. Department of Defense from 2009-2015. In 2012, he received the Prime Minister Nakasone Yasuhiro Award for academic and public service contributions. He is a visiting researcher at several universities and think tanks in Japan, including Hōsei University and Okinawa International University, and is regularly interviewed in print media and on TV. He is the translator of Watanabe Tsuneo's classic *Japan's Backroom Politics: Factions in a Multiparty Age* (Lanham: Lexington, Books, 2013), and author, editor, or contributor to another eighty volumes including his latest (in Japanese), *The Impact of Population Decline on the Japan Self-Defense Forces* (Fusōsha, 2019).

Graham B. Leonard earned his Ph.D. in International Public Policy from Osaka University in 2011 and is a U.S.-based independent translator and researcher specializing in Japan and its foreign relations. He has assisted in several book translations to date, including Watanabe Akio's *The Prime Ministers of Postwar Japan, 1945-1995* (Lexington Books, 2016) and Sase Masamori's *Changing Security Policies in Postwar Japan: The Political Biogra-*

phy of Japanese Defense Minister Sakata Michita (Lexington, 2017), both done with Eldridge. He was a Monbugakusho Scholar from 2007-2011 in Japan, and annually visits Japan for research and further studies.

Index

www.ingramcontent.com/pod-product-compliance
Lightning Source LLC
Chambersburg PA
CBHW031351290326
41932CB00044B/974

9 781793 614957